The Seen and The Unseen

Abortion and the Supreme Court

Taylor Carmichael

Introduction

I have Professor Ann Althouse to thank for the title of this book. And also for any insights I have into the minds of pro-choice people. I have never met her, but I like to visit her blog, *Althouse*.

The unseen, of course, are the unborn. That word, "unborn," comprises an incredible variety of human organisms, from a microscopic zygote all the way to a baby on the verge of birth. In *Roe v. Wade*, the Supreme Court ruled that the unborn are not people.[1] The Court said this so it could find a right to abort a pregnancy. And by defining the unborn this way, the Court made a sharp legal divide between the babies we see, and the babies we do not.

A law professor, John Hart Ely, wrote one of the sharpest criticisms of *Roe v. Wade*, and yet he himself is pro-choice.[2] Why is he pro-choice? "The mother, unlike the unborn child, has begun to imagine a future for herself…" And that strikes him as "morally quite significant." But Ely is honest enough to express doubts about abortion. "I hope this reaction reflects more than the psychological phenomenon that keeps bombardiers sane--the fact that it is somehow easier to 'terminate' those you cannot see."

It is, if you think about it, quite arbitrary to deny humanity to people just because you can't see them. And yet we do this all the time. If a friend or neighbor dies, we feel it more than if 200 people die in a landslide in Peru. Unless we're from Peru, and then we do feel it. I suspect this is why it was quite easy for the Supreme Court to discount the humanity of the unborn. We can't see them.

---

[1] *Roe v. Wade*, 410 U.S. 113 (1973).
[2] John Hart Ely, "The Wages of Crying Wolf: A Comment on *Roe v. Wade*," *Yale Law Journal* 82 (1973).

It has been one of the tactics of the pro-life movement to try to get people to see the life inside the womb. One way pro-lifers do this is by publishing images of aborted babies on-line. These photographs are quite awful. And yet these photographs represent an abortion. If the photographs upset you, then abortion upsets you.

When we go off to war, we have a whole ideology that goes along with us. Sometimes the media will play along, and censor images of war, to help the war effort. Other times the media will publish a photograph of a little Vietnamese girl scalded by napalm.[3]

That's why we publish photographs of atrocities. We want to remind people of humanity. We want to remind people of what they do not see (and perhaps do not want to see).

We are not there, inside the uterus, when the abortion happens. We do not feel the knife. Of course one might argue (and people do argue!) that the unborn can't feel the knife, either. At least, we hope she can't feel the knife.[4] So that becomes part of our debate. Are the unborn human, like us? Should we treat them like us? Should we love them? Should we recognize them?

A pregnant woman often feels the unborn moving inside her. You can't get more intimate than a baby kicking inside the womb of his mother. We are not talking about atrocities on the other side of the world. An abortion is as close as you can get.

Roe v. Wade was written by nine men, none of whom could get pregnant. And all of these judges are quite a distance from the abortion clinic. They like their distance, the Supreme Court, and

---

[3] Photograph of Phan Thi Kim Phuc, published in *The New York Times* (June 9, 1972).

[4] *See* www.doctorsonfetalpain.com ("an unborn child is capable of experiencing pain by 20 weeks").

they are unhappy every January 22nd, when the mobs show up to remind them about humanity.

For some reason, it appears that religious people tend to be the pro-lifers, and secular people tend to be pro-choice. (Nat Hentoff is a notable exception).[5] Perhaps this is because religious people are comfortable with the idea of the unseen.[6] Secular people want to focus on women. We can see women. They are here, now, in front of us. And the people we see are more important than the people we do not.

This book starts off by ignoring the unseen. Our subject is the Supreme Court. Who do they see and who do they not see?

Clearly **Roe v. Wade** does not see the unborn. But one of the arguments in this book is that they did not really see Jane Roe, either. It was not until **Planned Parenthood v. Casey** that the Supreme Court really started seeing the women involved.[7] And the Supreme Court has yet to see the babies.

Taylor Carmichael
August, 2014

---

[5] *See* Mark Judge, "Blackballing Nat Hentoff," **Real Clear Religion** (June 3, 2012).
[6] Many Christians repeat the Nicene Creed: "We believe in one God, the father almighty, maker of heaven and earth, of all that is seen and unseen."
[7] 505 U.S. 833 (1992).

Chapter 1

On July 7, 2009, the *New York Times* published a sit-down interview with Justice Ruth Bader Ginsburg.[8] It was a cordial, polite, friendly interview, with lots of softball questions in regard to what Ginsburg had to say about feminism, its successes and the Supreme Court. And yet, despite the easy questions and the sympathetic reporter, Justice Ginsburg would say something about *Roe v. Wade* that shocked a lot of people.

"Frankly I had thought at the time *Roe* was decided, there was concern about population growth and particularly growth in populations that we don't want to have too many of. So that *Roe* was going to be then set up for Medicaid funding for abortion. Which some people felt would risk coercing women into having abortions when they didn't really want them. But when the Court decided *McRae*, the case came out the other way. And then I realized that my perception of it had been altogether wrong."

Unfortunately the reporter, Emily Bazelon, did not ask the obvious follow-up question. Who are the populations that we don't want to have too many of? Was Ginsburg actually criticizing *Roe*? Did she see it as some sort of secret government plan to abort the handicapped, the poor, or racial minorities?

After all, there is an ugly history of eugenics in our country. And the Supreme Court has often found itself on the wrong side of this history.

For instance, in 1927 the Supreme Court issued *Buck v. Bell*, a case upholding the constitutionality of a state plan to force

---

[8] *See* Emily Bazelon, "The Place of Women on the Court," *The New York Times* (July 7, 2009).

innocent people to be sterilized against their will.[9] Justice Oliver Wendell Holmes was the author of the opinion, and he was quite blunt in his support for eugenics.

> Carrie Buck is a feeble minded white woman who was committed to the State Colony...She is the daughter of a feeble minded mother in the same institution, and the mother of an illegitimate feeble minded child. She was eighteen years old at the time of the trial of her case in the Circuit Court, in the latter part of 1924. An Act of Virginia, approved March 20, 1924, recites that the health of the patient and the welfare of society may be promoted in certain cases by the sterilization of mental defectives...It is better for all the world if, instead of waiting to execute degenerate offspring for crime or to let them starve for their imbecility, society can prevent those who are manifestly unfit from continuing their kind. The principle that sustains compulsory vaccination is broad enough to cover cutting the Fallopian tubes. Three generations of imbeciles is enough.

The American Eugenics Society, established in 1922, was founded and supported by a number of famous Americans, including John D. Rockefeller, J.P. Morgan and Margaret Sanger. The mission of the American Eugenics Society was to control reproduction and keep the wrong people from having children. Early leaders of Planned Parenthood, like Margaret Sanger and Alan Guttmacher, were actually eugenicists. As the editors of **American Medicine** wrote in 1919: "More children from the fit, less from the unfit--that is the chief issue in birth control."[10] In

---

[9] **Buck v. Bell**, 274 U.S. 200 (1927).
[10] Reprinted in **Birth Control Review** (May, 1919).

her book, ***Women and the New Race***, Margaret Sanger writes, "The most merciful thing that a large family does to one of its infant members is to kill it."[11]

Alan Guttmacher, an early President of Planned Parenthood, would also serve as a vice-president of the American Eugenics Society in the 1950's. In 1969, he said, "I would like to give our voluntary means of population control full opportunity in the next 10 to 12 years. Then, if these don't succeed, we may have to go into some kind of coercion, not worldwide, but possibly in such places as India, Pakistan, and Indonesia…"[12]

When ***Roe v. Wade*** was decided in 1973, authorities in the USA were still mandating the sterilization of innocent people. For instance, in North Carolina social workers could petition the Eugenics Board of North Carolina to have people on welfare sterilized, often against their will, or by fraudulently telling them that the procedure was reversible.[13] Started in 1933, the E.B.N.C. was finally disbanded in 1977, and the eugenics law was repealed in 2003. In 2013, North Carolina ordered that reparations be paid to the victims.

On March 08, 2012, ***CNN*** ran a special on "Eugenics in America."[14] According to the ***CNN*** report, in the 20th century more than half the states had eugenics programs. "Tens of thousands of American citizens were sterilized without their

---

[11] Margaret Sanger, ***Women and the New Race*** (1920). The next year she wrote, "As an advocate of birth control I wish…to point out that the unbalance between the birth rate of the 'unfit' and the 'fit' (is) admittedly the greatest present menace to civilization…" Sanger, "The Eugenic Value of Birth Control Propaganda," (October, 1921). ***See also*** "We've Been Guttmacher'd," www.toomanyaborted.com.
[12] Alan Guttmacher, ***The American Journal of Nursing*** (June, 1969).
[13] Julie Rose, "A Brutal Chapter in North Carolina's Eugenics Past," recounted in ***All Things Considered***, www.NPR.org (December 28, 2011).
[14] Anderson Cooper, ***Anderson Cooper 360*** (March 8, 2012).

consent. California performed so many sterilizations…Nazi Germany used its program as a model."

Indeed, according to **The Guardian**, California was sterilizing prisoners as recently as 2010.[15] The state paid $147,460 to perform tubal ligations on prisoners. The obstetrician at one prison defended the practice. "Over a 10-year period, that isn't a huge amount of money compared to what you save in welfare paying for these unwanted children."

One prisoner, who was in the middle of a C-section to give birth to her child, was surprised to hear her obstetrician talking about a tubal ligation.

> He said, "So we're going to be doing this tubal ligation, right?'" I'm like, "Tubal ligation? What are you talking about? I don't want any procedure. I just want to have my baby." I went into a straight panic.

In the context of this history, Ginsburg's comment about **Roe v. Wade** was striking, to put it mildly. Apparently her first understanding of **Roe** was that it is not a feminist opinion at all, but rather an attempt at population control by the unelected branch of our government. This is not a nice way to talk about **Roe v. Wade**!

While Ginsburg's aside was ignored by the **New York Times** reporter, and most of the mainstream media, the rightwing blogosphere blew up over her comment. Over 9000 blogs immediately grasped the significance of her remark, and ran stories about what the Supreme Court Justice had said. Damian Thompson, a blogger for the **Daily Telegraph** in the U.K., wrote,

---

[15] Corey Johnson, "California Was Sterilizing Its Prisoners As Late As 2010," **The Guardian** (November 8, 2013).

"What the hell did Ruth Bader Ginsburg mean when she linked abortion and eugenics?"

Writing on the *National Review* website, Jonah Goldberg adds this criticism. "Left unclear is whether Ginsburg endorses the eugenic motivation she ascribed to the passage of *Roe v. Wade* or whether she was merely objectively describing it. One senses that if Antonin Scalia had offered such a comment, a *Times* interviewer would have sought more clarity, particularly on the racial characteristics of these supposedly unwanted populations."[16]

Apparently this criticism hit the mark. Bazelon published an article about the controversy on the *Slate* website, blaming herself for Justice Ginsburg's comment. "I didn't ask the follow up question that would have given Ginsburg the chance to clarify what she meant--to explain who was concerned about population growth at the time, and in what context. Because I didn't do that, some conservatives pounced." [17]

It's very nice for Emily Bazelon to apologize for Justice Ginsburg's remark. One might say that it's too nice. When a Supreme Court Justice makes a remark about a secret plan to abort unwanted populations, it's not actually the job of the *New York Times* reporter to help dig the powerful official out of her hole.

Bazelon writes, "To imagine that Justice Ginsburg would endorse eugenics as a motivation for supporting legal abortion, you have to be out to get her. I say that because this notion is so entirely at odds with her life's work advocating for equal rights for women,

---

[16] Jonah Goldberg, "Ruth Bader Ginsburg and a Question of Eugenics," *National Review* (July 15, 2009).
[17] Emily Bazelon, "Talking To Ruth Bader Ginsburg," *Slate* (October 19, 2012).

especially poor women. That's why it didn't occur to me at the time."[18]

Note the difference in attitude between the powerful official and the reporter. Ginsburg is assuming the worst in other powerful officials. Meanwhile, Bazelon refuses to assume the worst in powerful officials, going so far as to ignore what they actually say.

We might ask, how does Justice Ginsburg know the secret motivation of the Supreme Court who wrote *Roe v. Wade*? How does she know that *Roe* was motivated by population control? Perhaps her *New York Times* interview is an admission that this is how she thinks about abortion. Ruth Bader Ginsburg thought it was a mechanism for population control. And then she discovered she was wrong.

In other words, if Blackmun and Marshall and Brennan had won the day in the welfare rights cases, Ginsburg would say that her perception was right. *Roe v. Wade* was about population control. Justice Ginsburg, one of our feminist pioneers for abortion rights, is saying that the authors of *Roe* secretly wanted to control the reproduction of women, not protect it.

Michael Kinsley once defined a gaffe this way: "A gaffe is when a politician tells the truth--some obvious truth he isn't supposed to say." Of course people make mistakes, too, and say the wrong thing. We all do this, all the time. Nonetheless, it's quite important to challenge the people in power when they say something outrageous. When Justice Ginsburg suggests that the *Roe* Court was concerned about "growth in populations that we don't want to have too many of," we need to ask questions. Not only should we ask who are the populations that are to be curtailed, but also who is the "we" that wants them gone?

---

[18] *Id.*

In 1992, Ron Weddington, one of the attorneys who drafted the brief for abortion rights in *Roe v. Wade*, wrote a private letter to President-elect Bill Clinton arguing explicitly for the state to use abortion as population control.[19]

> (Y)ou can start immediately to eliminate the barely educated, unhealthy and poor segment of our country. No, I'm not advocating some sort of mass extinction of these unfortunate people. Crime, drugs and disease are already doing that. The problem is that their numbers are not only replaced but increased by the birth of millions of babies to people who can't afford to have babies.
>
> In 1989, 27 percent of all births were to unmarried mothers, a huge percentage of whom were teenagers. If current trends continue, soon a majority of the babies born will be born into poverty and one half of the country cannot support the other half, no matter how good our intentions. I am not proposing that you send federal agents armed with Depo-Provera dart guns to the ghetto. You should use persuasion rather than coercion. You and Hillary are a perfect example. Could either of you have gone to law school and achieved anything close to what you have if you had three or four more children before you were 20? No! You waited until you were established and in your 30's to have one child. That is what sensible people do. For every Jesse Jackson who has fought his way out of the poverty of a large

---

[19] Letter reprinted in *The Clinton RU-486 Files*, at judicialwatch.org.

family there are millions mired in poverty, drugs and crime.

It's time to officially recognize that people are going to have sex and what we need to do as a nation is prevent as much disease and as many poor babies as possible. Condoms alone won't do it. Depo-Provera, Norplant and the new birth control injection being developed in India are not a complete answer, although the savings that could be effected by widespread government distribution and encouragement of birth control would amount to billions of dollars.

No, government is also going to have to provide vasectomies, tubal ligations and abortions...RU-486 and conventional abortions. Even if we make birth control as ubiquitous as sneakers and junk food, there will still be unplanned pregnancies. There have been about 30 million abortions in this country since *Roe v. Wade*. Think of all the poverty, crime and misery...and then add 30 million unwanted babies to the scenario.

Needless to say, Ron's wife Sarah said nothing like this in her oral argument in *Roe v. Wade*. When they are in a public forum before the Supreme Court, the attorneys talk about individual rights and a woman's right to choose. Abortion is framed in libertarian terms, as a right or freedom that might emancipate a woman from the burden of having an unwanted child. But twenty years later, in a private correspondence with Bill Clinton, Weddington is suggesting a far darker agenda. Apparently his idea in litigating *Roe v. Wade* was to improve our society by mass elimination of unwanted children.

This is not to say that this was the idea motivating the Supreme Court in **Roe v. Wade**. It's entirely possible--in fact it's highly likely--that the Court was motivated by multiple ideas. Perhaps the Justices were moved by the horrible damages a pregnant woman could inflict on herself with an illegal abortion. The author of **Roe**, Justice Harry Blackmun, who had worked as counsel at the Mayo clinic, might have been motivated by some of his medical experiences. And when Justice Lewis Powell was in private practice, he defended a young man who had accidentally killed his girlfriend while trying to perform an illegal abortion on her.[20]

Indeed, **Roe v. Wade** itself suggests that there are all sorts of reasons for supporting abortion rights. In the opening paragraphs of his opinion, Justice Blackmun writes, "We forthwith acknowledge our awareness of the sensitive and emotional nature of the abortion controversy, of the vigorous opposing views, even among physicians, and of the deep and seemingly absolute convictions that the subject inspires. One's philosophy, one's experiences, one's exposure to the raw edges of human existence, one's religious training, one's attitudes toward life and family and their values, and the moral standards one establishes and seeks to observe, are all likely to influence and to color one's thinking and conclusions about abortion."[21]

And then, almost as an afterthought, Justice Blackmun adds: "In addition, population growth, pollution, poverty, and racial overtones tend to complicate and not to simplify the problem."

The feminist argument for abortion is quite clear. "It's my body. It's my choice. I don't want to be pregnant. I don't want this baby to exist." Yet Blackmun is introducing other ideas. He's

---

[20] **See** Linda Greenhouse, "The Legacy of Lewis Powell, Jr.," **The New York Times** (December 4, 2002). Powell convinced the prosecutor not to file any charges.
[21] **Supra** note 1.

ruminating about overpopulation, pollution, poverty, and race. Apparently these are all possible motivations for a new right to abortion. And the Supreme Court is aware of these motivations, and aware of how some of them might look.

It's interesting that the Supreme Court is talking about race in *Roe v. Wade*. Why? After all, white moms will be aborting white children, black moms will be aborting black children, and interracial moms will be aborting interracial children. If we are focused on the autonomy of a pregnant woman, race would seem to be a largely irrelevant concern. Unless we suppose that a woman might abort her own child out of racial self-hatred.

But the mention of race makes sense if we see a larger agenda here. If one of the motivations of *Roe v. Wade* is getting rid of unwanted babies from unwanted people, then obviously racial fears are important. If the Supreme Court is actively trying to reduce the number of people in our society, or limit reproduction, then the possibility of hostility to certain classes of people is an important concern.

One of the interesting aspects about *Roe v. Wade* is that when you read it, the opinion itself does not seem particularly feminist. Justice Ginsburg remarked on this in her *New York Times* interview. "Unfortunately there is something of that in *Roe*. It's the woman in consultation with her doctor. So the view you get is the tall doctor and the little woman who needs him."[22]

Apparently the Supreme Court was not motivated by feminism, or a desire to protect the autonomy of women. So what was the motivation for finding a new right to abort pregnancies?

---

[22] *Supra* note 8.

Linda Greenhouse, in her biography of Harry Blackmun, argues that his concern was medical autonomy.[23] He wanted to protect the authority of doctors to do what they deem best for the patient. Indeed, some people thought that *Roe v. Wade* opened the door to many quality-of-life arguments. Do doctors have a right to assist in suicide, or to engage in euthanasia or mercy killings? What about the removal of organs from a patient who has just died?

The problem with medical autonomy arguments--or any autonomy arguments--is that they tend to run up against the autonomy of other people. If the doctor's autonomy is paramount in *Roe v. Wade*, what does that say about other people's autonomy? What about the mother, for instance?

Consider this passage from *Roe*: "Maternity, or additional offspring, may force upon the woman a distressful life and future. Psychological harm may be imminent. Mental and physical health may be taxed by child care. There is also the distress, for all concerned, associated with the unwanted child, and there is the problem of bringing a child into a family already unable, psychologically and otherwise, to care for it. In other cases, as in this one, the additional difficulties and continuing stigma of unwed motherhood may be involved. All these factors the woman and her responsible physician necessarily will consider in consultation."[24]

Here the Supreme Court is trying to expand our ideas of what a doctor might do. Of course pregnant mothers go to doctors all the time. But now the Court is talking broadly, making quality-of-life arguments, and calling these conclusions a medical decision. "Maternity, or additional offspring, may force upon the woman a distressful life and future." That may be true, but is that a medical problem?

---

[23] Linda Greenhouse, *Becoming Justice Blackmun* (2006).
[24] *Supra* note 1.

Blackmun is expanding healthcare to include things that most people would not consider an illness or disease. "Mental and physical health may be taxed by child care." The Supreme Court is imagining tired and exhausted mothers who are ill because their children have made them ill. And the doctor can resolve the problem--can cure these future illnesses--by aborting the pregnancy.

That's a remarkable argument, offering abortion as a cure for future "illnesses" that are highly speculative in nature. What if children are a joy? How is the doctor supposed to diagnose future events that have not happened yet? On what possible basis would a doctor conclude that a woman might be an ill mother? Isn't that incredibly presumptuous?

This passage suggests that the doctor will be making judgments that he may or may not be sharing with his patient. Blackmun identifies "the problem of bringing a child into a family already unable, psychologically and otherwise, to care for it." Of course doctors ask intrusive questions all the time. But now the Supreme Court is suggesting a regime where doctors are asking about our fitness as a parent. Are you ready to be a mother? Where is the father? Can you support this child? Are you emotionally stable? *Roe v. Wade* suggests that these judgments are to be made by the doctor, in consultation with his patient.

One interpretation of *Roe v Wade* is that the Supreme Court is expanding the role of the doctor in American society. The doctor is now almost a state agent, working for our larger society and judging the fitness of an individual woman to be a parent.

Obviously there was no plan for forced abortions. This isn't China. But it's entirely possible that the Supreme Court was thinking that doctors might start prescribing abortions to their patients. And the hope was that the doctor, as an authority figure, would convince these future unhappy mothers to abort their pregnancies.

In particular the Supreme Court seems to be focused on single moms and poor people. For instance, *Roe* identifies "the stigma of unwed motherhood" as a medical condition that a physician might treat. And the treatment is an abortion. Similarly *Roe* identifies families who are "unable, psychologically or otherwise" to care for children. The implication is that doctors might start diagnosing unfit mothers, particularly poor ones, and prescribing abortion as a remedy.

As Justice Ginsburg suggested, some people actually thought the Supreme Court was going to mandate that our Constitution requires free abortions for people on welfare.

This would be quite a surprising development to many other Americans. It is not a small thing for the unelected branch of the federal government to start dictating tax-and-spend policies to the American people. After all, taxation without representation incited Americans to armed revolution in 1776. Finding a constitutional right to socialized welfare would be a new controversy on top of an already controversial abortion opinion. This is perhaps why the Supreme Court blinked at the idea that free abortions ought to be mandated by unelected rulers.

Justice Blackmun was highly upset at the Supreme Court's failure to require citizens to pay for free abortions for other people. As he writes in his dissent in *Beal v. Doe*: "For the individual woman concerned, indigent and financially helpless, as the Court's opinions in the three cases concede her to be, the result is punitive and tragic. Implicit in the Court's holdings is the condescension that she may go elsewhere for her abortion. I find that disingenuous and alarming, almost reminiscent of 'Let them eat cake.'"[25]

Justice Blackmun is attacking the majority for being cold and callous. He introduces the French Revolution, and compares the other Justices to Marie Antoinette. Apparently Justice Blackmun is suggesting they are detached royalists who have little regard for the poor.[26]

Meanwhile, Justice Blackmun portrays himself as deeply concerned about the financially helpless. His opinion is an urgent call to help those in poverty. And so he is quite willing to rewrite our Constitution and start mandating free medical procedures.

Yet Justice Blackmun also seems to have a superior attitude in regard to the poor. His opinion goes on to reduce a pregnant woman and her unborn child to a cost/benefit analysis on a balance sheet.

"To be sure, welfare funds are limited, and welfare must be spread perhaps as best meets the community's concept of its needs. But the cost of a nontherapeutic abortion is far less than the cost of maternity care and delivery, and holds no comparison whatsoever with the welfare costs that will burden the State for the new indigents and their support in the long, long years ahead."[27]

Here Justice Blackmun is talking about money. Abortion is cheaper for the state than the care and support of a baby. Thus,

---

[25] *Beal v. Doe*, 432 U.S. 438 (1977) (Blackmun, J., dissenting).

[26] Marie Antoinette was decapitated by the state in 1793.

[27] *Supra* note 25. Warren Buffett, perhaps doing a similar cost-benefit analysis, is paying the poor to abort their children. *See* Betsy Woodruff, "Warren Buffett Gives Millions To Pay For Abortions," *National Review* (March 5, 2014). He's also spent a vast amount of money in abortion advocacy. *See* Dan Gainor, "Warren Buffett Has Given $1.2 Billion To Abortion Groups," *Fox News* (May 13, 2014).

Blackmun argues, it would be cheaper for the state to pay for an abortion than to help the mother with childcare.

That's hardly a nice argument, or one that's looking out for the poor. Indeed, Blackmun appears to be talking about abortion as a mechanism for the reduction of the number of poor people in our society.

Justice Blackmun continues, "There is another world out there, the existence of which the Court, I suspect, either chooses to ignore or fears to recognize. And so the cancer of poverty will continue to grow."[28]

Blackmun's metaphor is highly unfortunate, perhaps even malign. After all, **Beal v. Doe** is an abortion opinion. A pregnant mother has an unborn child growing inside her uterus. And Justice Blackmun is worried that without free abortions, "the cancer of poverty will continue to grow."

Justice Blackmun is imagining poverty as a cancer that is attacking our society. Our society, in this metaphor, is implicitly one large human organism. Poverty is a cancer, attacking us and putting us in jeopardy. And the only solution for a cancer, of course, is to kill it. We have to kill the cancer or we will die. It is a life or death situation. We need to get rid of our cancer.

And yet "poverty" is simply a word we use to describe poor people. So what is Blackmun saying about poor people? Is he imagining them as a cancer, as a threat to our society? Is abortion his solution? Do we need to abort the cancer before she grows?

Presumably Justice Blackmun does not actually think "cancer" when he sees a poor pregnant woman. Hopefully he does not think that society needs to abort her pregnancy in order to remove

---

[28] **Supra** note 25.

this cancer from our society. Justice Blackmun has negative thoughts about poverty, but not about poor people. He would like to help the poor, not terminate their children.

And yet, in the context of the case he is deciding, his method for helping the poor is to provide free abortions.

Notice that Justice Blackmun does not advocate that our Constitution be interpreted to require free food or free shelter, or other forms of free medical care. If you're really poor, homeless and destitute, exactly what kind of welfare do you need? The dissenters in *Beal v. Doe* are arguing that society must pay for free abortions. And they are casting themselves as nice, liberal people. Yet the only gift they have for the poor is a free abortion?

Perhaps, as a *New York Times* reporter might argue, this is just right-wing spin. Only somebody who was out to get Justice Blackmun would see any secret hostility to the poor in his opinion. He just wants to expand access to abortion. And since abortion is expensive surgery, Blackmun wants to provide free abortions to the poor. And in the context of trying to make economic arguments to cold-hearted capitalists, Blackmun uses an unfortunate cancer metaphor to describe a poor pregnant woman and her place in our larger society.

One might add, too, that Ron Weddington would likely deny any hostility to poor people. He thinks the poor are unfortunate and he feels sorry for them. He wants to eliminate poverty. He does not actually want to eliminate poor people.

But of course the problem with advocating abortion for the greater good of society is that you are now trying to manipulate a poor pregnant woman into making her own child disappear. You might convince yourself this abortion is for the mother's own benefit. But it is also quite a selfish argument. Blackmun and

Weddington are appealing to society's greed. If we get rid of these poor people, it will benefit the rest of us. Unborn infants are a "cancer" attacking our society; they are future criminals and future welfare recipients.

Justice Ginsburg was given the opportunity to clarify her comment at a talk she gave at Yale in 2012.[29] Ginsburg admitted that she had been quoted accurately, but said that her quote was vastly misinterpreted. "I was surprised that the court went as far as it did in *Roe v. Wade*, and I did think that with the Medicaid reimbursement cases down the road that perhaps the court was thinking that it did want more women to have access to reproductive choice. At the time, there was a concern about too many people inhabiting our planet. There was an organization called Zero Population Growth. In the press, there were articles about the danger of crowding our planet. So there was at the time of *Roe v. Wade* considerable concern about overpopulation."

Ginsburg is attempting to rehabilitate her comment. She walks back the uglier aspects of it. She denies that there are any specific people that "we" are trying to remove from civilization. Now Ginsburg is talking in more generalized terms. In 1973 there was a lot of fear about overpopulation, and *Roe v. Wade* was just trying to reduce the number of people in our society.

She denies that *Roe v. Wade* had anything to do with eugenics. On the other hand, she continues to assert her idea that *Roe* is motivated by a desire for population control.

What's remarkable about this is that Justice Ginsburg had three years to think about what she wanted to say. She was confronted and criticized about this idea that *Roe* was designed to remove unwanted people from our society. And in response Ginsburg

---

[29] *Supra* note 17.

clarifies her comment. And yet her clarification is still highly problematic.

After all, *Roe v. Wade*, and abortion rights in general, are always framed in libertarian terms. It's always said to be an individual woman's right to choose. Yet Ginsburg is characterizing the unelected men who wrote the opinion as secretly motivated by a desire for population control. They wanted to limit the number of people in our society. This is not a libertarian argument at all, but rather a form of socialist control by the state.

Indeed, this idea about abortion is not actually pro-choice at all, but rather may be characterized as pro-abortion. Instead of seeing abortion as part of a woman's right to choose, it is a policy argument that abortion is a positive benefit for our wider society. We can stop overpopulation and reduce the number of people walking around.

Ginsburg denies that she sees in *Roe v. Wade* any specific plan to eliminate the handicapped, or the poor, or racial minorities. But she acknowledges a desire on the part of the Supreme Court to control citizens and limit reproduction.

A pro-abortion argument introduces another point of view into our fight over abortion. Instead of two arguments, we now have three: pro-life, pro-choice, and pro-abortion. On the one side, we have pro-life people who see a baby, and want to protect her right to life. And we have pro-choice people, who want to protect a woman's autonomy and her right to choose an abortion or to have a baby. And now we are introducing another point of view, people who are pro-abortion. These are people who also do not see a baby. But unlike pro-choice people, they are not worried about individual autonomy. Instead they want to use abortion to solve problems like crime, overpopulation, or welfare.

Yet nobody in our society admits to being pro-abortion. Instead there are only two sides: pro-life or pro-choice. Whenever a pro-lifer suggests that her opponent is pro-abortion, they immediately deny it and say they are pro-choice.[30] For some reason, the pro-abortion argument is deemed immoral and wrong. People who want to make the argument feel they cannot. They repress it and deny it. Apparently it's a secret argument that cannot withstand open and frank discussion.

Right before Justice Ginsburg shocks us with her comment, she says "frankly," as if she is about to tell us a secret. "Frankly I had thought at the time *Roe* was decided, there was concern about population growth…"[31] Ron Weddington, who is a secret advocate for population control, also writes this: "It's what we all know is true, but we only whisper it."[32]

Why is that? Why are some people so secretive about their support of abortion? Why do they feel they must hide their support within the larger rubric of "choice"? After all, isn't abortion a right thing to do? The Supreme Court says it is. It's a legal right that people have. And what's wrong with trying to reduce crime or the number of people on welfare? What's wrong with worrying about overpopulation? Why is it bad to suggest a woman should have an abortion?

Yet this argument is deeply offensive, to both pro-life and pro-choice people. Of course pro-lifers are offended by it. They deem many abortions to be homicides. The idea of actively trying to increase abortions, or manipulate women into having abortions, is horrific to them.

---

[30] Even the term "pro-choice" has fallen out of favor. *See* Jackie Calmes, "Advocates Shun 'Pro-Choice' To Expand Message," *The New York Times* (July 28, 2014). The new euphemism for abortion is "women's health."
[31] *Supra* note 8.
[32] *Supra* note 19.

But pro-choice people hate this argument too. They respect a woman's autonomy, and her right to control her body. A truly pro-choice person is sympathetic to the pro-life side, and will hear arguments about the baby and her development. But she will also be thinking about her own life, and if she is ready to make the commitment to being a mother. Does she want to give the baby up for adoption? What about the father? Am I going to be doing this by myself?

The pro-choice side is focused intensely on the woman and her situation. She really doesn't want to hear arguments about the statistical probabilities that her child is going to grow up to be a criminal or a welfare recipient. How do you know that?

We might see Justice Ginsburg's comment as a criticism of *Roe v. Wade* specifically, not abortion rights itself. She is criticizing the *Roe* Court for having a domineering attitude towards women. Justice Blackmun seems to be defining the doctor as an authority figure who will prescribe abortions to poor, helpless women. And this same domineering attitude is present in Justice Blackmun's *Beal* dissent. The poor woman needs a free abortion. And you better give it to her, or the cancer of poverty will continue to grow.

Obviously this pro-abortion reading is a highly unpopular vision of what the Supreme Court is trying to do. Justice Ginsburg's criticism is perhaps muted because she does not want to give any ammunition to the pro-life cause. If *Roe v. Wade* is actually pro-abortion, many women will feel manipulated and used. They might be hostile to domineering authorities, particularly if those authorities are reckless and careless.

For instance, *Roe v. Wade* proclaims that a first trimester abortion is to be "an abortion free of interference by the state."[33] That is

---

[33] *Supra* note 1.

incredibly libertarian rhetoric. Freedom, yes! But if it turns out that *Roe v. Wade* actually wants doctors to induce unfit mothers to abort unwanted children, then there is a dark underside to this call to freedom. After all, unlicensed and unregulated surgical procedures are rather dangerous.

According to the *Roe v. Wade* opinion, there is to be no oversight on the abortion industry in the first trimester, even to protect the health of women.[34]

This disregard for the health of women makes no sense if you are trying to protect a woman's autonomy and her reproductive freedom. After all, abortion is the intentional causing of a miscarriage. Obviously such a procedure might damage a woman's ability to reproduce and have children in the future. But that would be a feature, not a bug, if you were actively trying to curtail reproduction, if you were really worried about overpopulation, or pollution, or poverty, or race. And Justice Blackmun has already identified these ideas as perhaps implicated in his own opinion.

---

[34] *Id.* This part of the opinion was overruled in 1992, in *Planned Parenthood v. Casey*, *supra* note 7.

Chapter 2

When the Supreme Court talks about abortion now, it always frames the issue as a woman's right to choose. It's a woman's autonomy. She's in control. It's her choice.

Yet this feminist rhetoric misses some very important issues in regard to abortion. For instance, is a woman who undergoes a surgery actually in charge of her surgery? Yes, she decides to have the surgery. But once that decision is made, isn't she out of control? The patient might be unconscious, for instance, while the doctor is cutting into her with a knife.

So this autonomy rhetoric might disguise the fact that a woman who is receiving an abortion is actually quite vulnerable. She is at the mercy of the person doing the surgery. And there is a power imbalance between the doctor and her patient. The doctor has a lot of knowledge of health risks; the patient often does not.

Recall one of Justice Ginsburg's criticisms of *Roe*, that it is unduly focused on the doctor. "Unfortunately there is something of that in *Roe*. It's the woman in consultation with her doctor. So the view you get is the tall doctor and the little woman who needs him."[35]

But doesn't she? Who is going to be performing the abortion? Surely Ginsburg isn't hoping the pregnant woman will abort herself?

Yes, pro-lifers are motivated by a desire to protect the unborn child. But maybe pro-lifers are also trying to protect a pregnant woman from an assault on her body. Is there consent, and is it

---

[35] *Supra* note 8.

informed consent? And while consent is usually a defense to an assault charge, it's entirely possible that a society might think of some assaults as so grave that we don't care about consent. Many people object to suicide, for instance, regardless of consent.

Notably, the Hippocratic Oath forbids doctors from performing abortions or assisting in suicide. It doesn't matter if there is consent. Doctors are not supposed to do surgeries on healthy people.

One way to read the statute at issue in *Roe v. Wade* was that abortion was defined as a crime of violence committed against a woman. You would be punished for up to five years if you did the abortion with her consent, and up to ten years if you did the abortion without it.[36] Under the statute, consent is not a defense. You are intentionally causing a healthy pregnant mother to have a miscarriage. If an abortion goes wrong, it risks serious harm to a woman's ability to reproduce and have children in the future.

Obviously, if you kill a pregnant woman, or inflict bodily damage on her against her will, the state will be bringing additional criminal charges. But abortion itself was deemed risky and unhealthy by the state of Texas.

This is one of the arguments confronting the Supreme Court in *Roe v. Wade*. Texas is arguing an elective abortion, a forced miscarriage of a healthy pregnancy, is inherently dangerous to a pregnant woman. Can a state outlaw or regulate abortion in order to protect a woman's health, her well-being, and her reproductive freedom?

One possible response is that a woman's autonomy includes a right to risk her own health. So if a woman wants to run the risk of infertility, or future breast cancer, or future tubal pregnancies,

---

[36] ***Supra*** note 1. The Texas statute is cited in the opinion's first footnote.

or future miscarriages, or future premature births, or Asherman's syndrome, that's up to her. It's not up to society to protect a woman from her medical choices.

That's a standard libertarian argument, and **Roe v. Wade** is not afraid to wave that flag. But there's a problem here. Most pregnant women are not doctors. They might not necessarily know all the risks of having an abortion. Especially if a doctor is inducing a miscarriage, young women might be fooled into thinking this is a healthy thing to do. Young girls in particular are vulnerable, and are relying upon medical authorities to tell the truth, and not to have a secret agenda.

Justice Ginsburg's comment on **Roe** ("there was concern about population growth") should disturb pro-choice people. What if the Supreme Court's opinion in **Roe** was pro-abortion, and not pro-choice? That would mean the opinion was not about women's autonomy at all. And it might mean that the Supreme Court committed a fraud on the American public. If the true agenda of the **Roe** Court is population control, then the health and safety of American women are secondary.

One of the startling things about **Roe v. Wade** is that there is so little discussion about medical risks to women in the opinion. There is one medical finding in the opinion ("Mortality rates for women undergoing early abortions, where the procedure is legal, appear to be as low or lower than the rates for normal childbirth"), and that's it.[37] Texas deems abortion a risky and dangerous assault on a pregnant woman, and the Supreme Court responds with one or two sentences about how the surgery is safe.

Why is this discussion so skimpy? One reason is that it's quite dangerous for the Supreme Court to start engaging in social science. It's not their job, they don't know how to do it, and

---

[37] *Id.*

medical experts often change their minds. In other words, we find out that we were wrong. We're not omniscient, we're not God, we don't know everything.

Of course the Supreme Court is not supposed to be imposing medical solutions on the American people in the first place. You're not supposed to be making a medical finding that abortion is safe, and then prescribing abortion to the American people because our country needs abortion. It's not your job to do that. You're not doctors, you're not social scientists, you're in over your head.

Where does the Supreme Court get its information about the safety of abortion? The non-doctors on the judiciary are relying on a medical brief filed in 1971 by the American College of Obstetrics and Gynecology. In it, the ACOG argues, "The medical procedure of induced abortion is potentially 23.3 times as safe as the process of going through ordinary childbirth." [38]

This is a rather surprising thing to say. A miscarriage is safer than a pregnancy?

After all, childbirth is a natural, healthy event that billions and billions of women have undergone since the dawn of humanity. And while there are certain dangers in a pregnancy, there are even more dangers to a woman in a miscarriage. Indeed, many of the dangers in a pregnancy revolve around a miscarriage. A miscarriage signals that something is wrong with the pregnancy. And when something is wrong with the pregnancy, the danger to the mother increases.

And yet in 1973, the ACOG is flipping this understanding on its head. Now the ACOG is arguing that an elective abortion--

---

[38] The brief was filed in *Roe*'s companion case, ***Doe v. Bolton***, 410 U.S. 179 (1973).

forcing a miscarriage on a healthy pregnant woman--is safer and healthier than a pregnancy itself. The implication is that pregnancy is a dangerous medical condition, and abortion is the cure.

Of course an abortion might be a cure for a pregnancy that has gone wrong. In an ectopic pregnancy, for instance, you would schedule an abortion to save the mother's life. But here the ACOG brief is saying that we need elective abortions. And so a healthy pregnancy is said to be dangerous to women. And abortion is said to be safer, much safer, potentially 23 times safer than a pregnancy.

Why would the ACOG say such a thing, unless it's true? The ACOG represents medical authorities. Shouldn't we trust what they say?

Actually, this ACOG document is a legal brief drafted by lawyers.[39] Maybe we shouldn't trust lawyers! Note that the attorney has added the weasel word "potentially," which covers a whole graveyard of mistakes. But aside from that, maybe we should stop and think about what the ACOG President is doing by signing this brief. Is he speaking for the health and safety of women? Or is he representing the goals and desires of obstetricians?

Perhaps, in 1971, a fair number of obstetricians are doing illegal abortions on the side.[40] And the ACOG represents those

---

[39] The "medical brief" was actually drafted by the James Madison Constitutional Law Institute. Clyde Randall, the President of the ACOG, signed onto it. The brief was not approved by the board of directors or by ACOG's membership. *See* Nancy Aries, "The American College of Obstetricians and Gynecologists and the Evolution of Abortion Policy, 1951-1973: the Politics of Science," American Journal of Public Health (November 2013). *See also* Clarke Forsythe, *Abuse of Discretion* (2013).

[40] *See* Carole Joffe, *Doctors of Conscience: The Struggle to Provide Abortion Before and After Roe v. Wade* (1996).

obstetricians, along with all other obstetricians. So the ACOG wants to legalize abortion so these doctors can avoid going to jail.

Or perhaps the ACOG is trying to open up a new area of medical practice for its doctors. After all, abortion would become a billion dollar industry.[41] Some doctors would become very rich from the practice.

This is not to accuse the ACOG of lying in its brief. But this secret motivation (like the idea that the Supreme Court was motivated by a desire to stop population growth) might influence what is said, what is argued.

Yes, it's entirely possible the ACOG is giving objective medical advice and has no secret agenda. But we should be aware of the other, darker possibility. Maybe the ACOG's assertions about the safety of a controversial medical procedure should not be trusted. Would we trust a doctor who wanted to do a surgery on us that is illegal? For that matter, would we trust a doctor if we know he is violating his Hippocratic Oath? (The Oath forbids abortion).

This argument from the ACOG, that abortion is much safer than pregnancy, takes us into some radical places. If miscarriages are safer than pregnancies, then we should be avoiding pregnancies. Indeed, if a woman gets pregnant, we should hope for a miscarriage. Doctors should be inducing miscarriages. Pregnancy is a dangerous medical condition, and abortion is the cure.

One of the foremost authorities on abortion practice in our country is Dr. Warren Hern. He is the author of ***Abortion Practice***, an abortion textbook widely used in medical

---

[41] IBISWorld, a firm that produces financial research for over 1000 industries, estimates the "Family Planning & Abortion Clinic" market in the United States to be $2 billion dollars. www.ibisworld.com. *See also* "Planned Parenthood's Unseemly Empire," *The Weekly Standard* (October 22, 2007).

schools. And he's a doctor who takes the ACOG argument to its radical conclusion. Unless "pregnancy is desired," Dr. Hern writes, "abortion is the indicated treatment of choice."[42] Dr. Hern compares pregnancy to smallpox and insists, "all abortions are therapeutic."[43]

Clearly, Dr. Hern is unabashedly pro-abortion. We should not be surprised at this. He's an abortion doctor, whose medical practice consists entirely of aborting pregnancies. Of course he's pro-abortion. But we still might be surprised at just how pro-abortion Dr. Hern is. In his view, pregnancy itself is not just a medical condition. It's a risky, unhealthy condition. And so he declares that abortion is what a doctor should prescribe to any woman who is pregnant.

Dr. Hern is a smart, educated man. The Supreme Court cites his textbook in the *Carhart* opinions. And yet Dr. Hern also has an ideological worldview that seems to depart from reality. For instance, Dr. Hern writes, "The relationship between the gravid female and the fetoplacental unit can be understood best as one of host and parasite."[44] That is an odd attitude for an obstetrician to have, to put it mildly. A baby is a parasite?

It doesn't sound like medical science so much as propaganda that is designed to dehumanize an unborn child. Surely Dr. Hern realizes that he's left science behind? A parasite is a different species from the host. We are no longer describing scientific reality when we define an unborn infant as a parasite.

---

[42] Warren Hern, *Abortion Practice* (1990).

[43] *Id.*

[44] *Id.* Apparently Dr. Hern is not fond of the rest of the humanity, either. He says that human beings "have become a pathological process--a malignancy--in the planetary ecosystem." Quoted by Vincent Carroll, "Warren Hern and the Malignancy of Mankind," *The Denver Post* (March 17, 2012). *See also* Warren Hern, "Has the Human Species Become a Cancer on the Planet," www.drhern.com.

One can understand why Dr. Hern feels the need to dehumanize the unborn infant in order to kill her. Yet there's an obvious danger that this mentality is at war with the practice of medicine. For instance, what if the mother is doubtful? What if she wants objective information about the baby in her womb? Is the doctor supposed to tell her that it's a parasite?

And why does Dr. Hern want medical students to think this way?

He wants to move doctors off the idea that pregnancy is normal and healthy, to the idea that pregnancy is always dangerous, and abortion is always the cure. This is the worldview that is in the ACOG brief. Pregnancy is a danger to women. Even healthy pregnancies are dangerous. So doctors should be biased in favor of abortion, and prescribe abortions to their patients.

What if this argument is wrong? What if pregnancy is healthy and normal? From a medical standpoint, this would mean inducing a miscarriage is an unnecessary and unsafe surgery. The doctor is not treating an illness. Indeed, the doctor is using his medical skills to force a healthy pregnancy to do an unhealthy thing--miscarry. This is perhaps why the Hippocratic Oath forbids abortion practice.

One of the symbols of the abortion movement is the coat-hanger, which represents a botched and illegal abortion. Perhaps that is the argument the ACOG should be making. "Some women are desperate for abortions, and if doctors are not allowed to do this surgery, these women will inflict horrible damages on themselves."

Maybe the ACOG did not think that argument was persuasive. After all, this is **Roe v. Wade.** You have to convince the Supreme Court that our Constitution requires abortion. So the ACOG goes far beyond the rational claim that a doctor-induced miscarriage is safer for a woman than a self-induced miscarriage, to make the far more outlandish claim that an intentional miscarriage is 23.3 times safer than ordinary childbirth.

Of course this amicus brief is not actually lying. It's relying on a statistical analysis of death certificates kept by our federal government.

The Centers for Disease Control tries to keep track of women who die from both legal and illegal abortions. In the year prior to *Roe v. Wade*, the CDC reports 65 fatalities from abortion in the United States.[45] That's a record of all known abortion-related fatalities, including illegal surgeries performed by non-doctors. For every 100,000 abortions, 4.1 women died in 1972.

That's quite low, right? Should we then conclude that an abortion from a non-doctor is safer than childbirth? Because the reported fatality rate for childbirth is higher than that. In 2009 the CDC reports a pregnancy-related fatality rate of 17.8 per 100,000 pregnancies.[46]

What's going on? Why is the CDC reporting more deaths from pregnancy than from all abortions, including illegal abortions by non-doctors?

It suggests a problem with the data. Even if we assume good faith and honesty on the part of doctors, and health officials, and unelected bureaucrats, we might still have a difficulty in keeping track of women who die from abortions. What if the CDC numbers are under-counting abortion fatalities? Is that possible? The low number of reported illegal abortion fatalities should clue us in that these CDC numbers might be off.

---

[45] *See* The Centers for Disease Control, *Abortion Surveillance*, www.cdc.gov (2008) (table 25).
[46] *See* The Centers for Disease Control, *Pregnancy Mortality Surveillance System* (chart).

In the USA, doctors fill out death certificates. They report to state health officials. These states are invited to turn over their health information to the CDC. Individual doctors are filling out these death certificates, and are making judgment calls. When a doctor fills out a death certificate, she is giving her best guess as to the cause of death.

Perhaps surprisingly, doctors are rarely trained on how to fill out a death certificate. As Dr. Randy Hanzlick puts it, "For many physicians, the first time they see it is when they are doing their internship or residency and one of their patients dies. The nurse hands them a death certificate and says, 'Fill this out.'"[47]

If an abortion is listed on the death certificate as part of the cause of death, then an abortion-related fatality is reported to state health officials, who in turn might report that information to the CDC. If abortion is not listed on the death certificate, then an abortion-related fatality is missed.

It's easy to guess why an illegal abortion would not make it into the CDC numbers. A woman taken into the emergency room might not want to admit to a crime, or implicate whoever performed the abortion on her. If she's conscious she will be discussing her symptoms, her pregnancy and her miscarriage, but perhaps remain silent on the abortion. The doctor may or may not guess the cause, but says nothing out of sympathy for her privacy, or because he feels a death certificate is no place for a criminal accusation. So the medical conditions that caused the fatality are reported, but not the suspected surgery itself.

Many similar issues arise from a botched legal abortion that ends up in the emergency room. While the woman is not a criminal

---

[47] *See* Carolyne Krupa, "Death Certificates Present Final Medical Complication," *American Medical News* (January 21, 2013).

accomplice, an aborting woman may feel a sense of shame or secrecy about her abortion, and not want to discuss the cause of her distress in the emergency room.

Pregnancy is a medical condition, and thus is likely to always make it into a death certificate. Will a surgical procedure make it into the death certificate? Only if the doctor is certain that the surgery caused the death. If the doctor knows about the surgery he might mention it, but if he has no specific knowledge he's not going to give a hypothesis.

Note also that when a death certificate blames a woman's death on "abortion," that death certificate is naming a human agent as responsible for the death--namely, the physician. A doctor filling out the death certificate might be outraged at a botched abortion, and might very well write "abortion" as a cause of death. But a more prudent physician might be worried about being sued for slander, or causing problems for another doctor. So instead he might write "embolism" or "hemorrhage" as the cause of death. And if the word "abortion" is not used in a death certificate, than the death of a pregnant woman is not reported as an abortion-related death.

After all, it's safe to blame a pregnancy for a death. A pregnancy is not going to sue you. But when you say that an abortion causes a woman to die, you are saying a doctor has killed his patient. You are suggesting malpractice, and you are giving ammunition to a lawyer who might be suing the doctor. Doctors who hate lawyers and lawsuits might shy away from blunt honesty in a death certificate.

This problem, by the way, is not limited to abortion. Many health officials will acknowledge the difficulty of keeping track of fatalities caused by physician error.[48] There is a natural and human tendency not to want to blame doctors for causing a death. Thus it can be hard to keep track of deaths caused by surgeons, as opposed to deaths caused by the underlying medical condition.

What this means is that a lot of pregnancy-related deaths may in fact be abortion-related deaths. We know that every abortion involves a pregnancy. So it's entirely possible that an abortion death gets reported to state health officials as due to the pregnancy.

Why not? She didn't die in a car wreck. She's pregnant, and she died from issues related to her pregnancy. If that's the case, then the pregnancy death totals are skewed by accidental deaths that happen when physicians (or non-physicians) induce a miscarriage.

Tabulating our abortion-related deaths is even more difficult because abortion is highly politicized. You can imagine a pro-life doctor blaming a pregnancy death on the abortion doctor, when it might be that the doctor's not to blame at all. And you can imagine a pro-choice doctor covering up an abortion death to protect a woman's privacy.

Our concern for privacy is yet another problem with our ability to get accurate information. Abortion is shrouded in secrecy. People do not want to talk about their abortions or admit to having abortions. Our desire for privacy makes obtaining accurate social science in regard to abortion highly difficult. Add to this our strong emotional feelings over the subject, and the possibilities for bias, and we should be suspicious of any abortion

---

[48] *See* Institute of Medicine, "To Err is Human," www.iom.edu (November 1999): "At least 44,000 people, and perhaps as many as 98,000 people, die in hospitals each year as a result of medical errors..."

social science that purports to resolve the issue one way or
another.

For instance, while many medical studies have found a causal link
between abortion and breast cancer, health officials have balked
at listing abortion as a potential risk. The American Cancer
Society website writes this: "Even though abortion is now legal,
it is still a very personal, private matter that many women do not
like to talk about. (M)any women might not report having an
abortion if asked for a study."[49]

While women with breast cancer will admit to their abortions,
women without breast cancer are less likely to. This secrecy
around abortion plagues all abortion social science. We lie about
our abortions, we don't admit to having abortions, and we don't
want to talk about our abortions. This can make it quite difficult
to get accurate health information about the medical risks caused
by an abortion.

Does an abortion increase a woman's risk of breast cancer?[50]
Numerous studies are finding a small but significant rate of
increase, which makes abortion a possible risk factor for cancer.[51]
In particular, an abortion before the birth of your first child is said
to be carcinogenic.[52]

---

[49] American Cancer Society, "Is Abortion Linked To Breast Cancer?"
www.cancer.org.
[50] When you become pregnant, your body is flooded with estrogen. Many of
these cells migrate to your breasts, so they will produce milk for your baby.
When you abort a healthy pregnancy, these cells stay immature. The medical
theory is that these immature cells will become carcinogenic over time. *See*
Joel Brind, "Abortion, Breast Cancer and Ideology," *First Things* (May,
1997).
[51] *Id.*
[52] A study in Bangladesh found that induced abortion increased a woman's
risk of breast cancer by almost 2000%. Suraiya Jabeen, et al, "Breast Cancer
and Some Epidemiological Factors: A Hospital Based Study," *Journal of
Dhaka Medical College* (2013).

Other studies are not showing an increase of risk. One huge study in Denmark found no correlation between abortion and breast cancer.[53] The leading advocate for recognizing an abortion-breast cancer connection, Dr. Joel Brind, disputes the study because the doctors altered the data for a "cohort effect."[54] If we look at the unaltered data, the Denmark study actually indicates a 44 percent increase in breast cancer among aborting women.

Cancer organizations in our country do not warn women that abortion is a possible risk for breast cancer. What they do say is that the link is unproven. Of course abortion politics may be corrupting some of this science, too. And it's indisputably hard for social scientists to answer questions about abortion risks to women, if people are keeping their abortions private.

A possible link between abortion and breast cancer raises the additional problem of measuring fatalities that do not happen right away. What if abortion is a time bomb that goes off ten, twenty, or thirty years after the surgery?

The CDC is only recording immediate deaths that happen at the time of the surgery, and that are reported to health officials as an abortion-related fatality. But an abortion when you're 16 might cause you to die from a miscarriage when you are 30, or die from breast cancer when you are 50. What if abortion is an invisible killer? If so, these fatalities are missed by our health officials, who are only tracking immediate deaths when the death certificate identifies abortion as the cause of death.

According to the Centers for Disease Control, out of every 100,000 abortions in the USA today, less than one of them will

---

[53] Mads Melbye, et al, "Induced Abortion and the Risk of Breast Cancer," *The New England Journal of Medicine* (January 9, 1997).
[54] *Supra* note 50.

result in the death of a woman.[55] Numbers like this is why the ACOG argues that abortion is "potentially" 23.3 times as safe as pregnancy and childbirth, and why Dr. Hern says that abortion is the indicated treatment for pregnancy. It is a statistical argument, based on reported fatality rates.

A new study out of Finland has embarrassed the ACOG, the pro-abortion media, and any Supreme Court Justice who relies on this faulty scholarship.[56] Finland, unlike the USA, has socialized medicine. This means that all pregnant women in Finland have a doctor, but it also means that patients have no real medical privacy. All your medical information is in a government database. So while that's bad for your privacy, it's quite good for medical research. Health officials can search the medical records of all the women in Finland, and find out who has been pregnant. They can even do a search and find the records of all the women who have had an abortion.

Finland commissioned a study that was performed by researchers working for STAKES, the statistical analysis unit of Finland's National Research and Development Center for Welfare and Health. The scientific researchers pulled the death certificates of all women of reproductive age (15-49) who died in Finland between 1987 and 1994, for a total of 9,192 women who had died.

After identifying these fatalities, the researchers went through the database and identified any pregnancy-related events in the 12 months prior to the deaths. If a woman gave birth to a child and died two months later in a car wreck, she would make it into the study. If a woman had an abortion and committed suicide six months later, she would make it into the study.

---

[55] *Supra* note 45.
[56] Mika Gissler, et al, "Pregnancy-Associated Deaths in Finland 1987-1994," *Acta Obsetricia et Gynecologica Scandinavica* (1997).

There was no attempt to prove causation between the pregnancy-related event and the fatality. The point here was to get accurate data. The researchers wanted to remove any subjective bias in the reporting of fatalities.

The results were striking. What we see in the STAKES study is a sizable increase in the number of fatalities from women who recently had an abortion. This suggests that American researchers have been undercounting the fatality risk from abortion.

The unadjusted mortality rate per 100,000 cases in Finland was 27 fatalities involving women who had given birth the previous year, 48 fatalities involving women who had miscarriages the previous year, and 101 fatalities involving women who had abortions the previous year.[57]

Note that these risks are still quite small. The odds that a woman in Finland who has an abortion will be dead within the year are one in a thousand. But the study does suggest that our CDC statistics in regard to abortion fatalities are quite bad.

Indeed, even this study might be under-counting a true abortion fatality rate. The STAKES study only measure fatalities in the year after abortion. It's quite possible that an abortion injures a woman's reproductive system, and increases her fatality risk down the road.[58]

In our own country, our health officials are reporting more pregnancy fatalities than abortion fatalities. Indeed, it's entirely possible that the official CDC statistics will always show more pregnancy fatalities than abortion fatalities. What if a woman who dies during an abortion is counted twice by the CDC? It's a

---

[57] *Id. See also* David Reardon, "Abortion Nearly Four Times Deadlier Than Childbirth," www.afterabortion.org (2000).
[58] *See* note 52.

pregnancy death (she was pregnant) and an abortion death (abortion made it into the death certificate). After all, the CDC is not doing a study. They're just collecting statistics. And the statistics for maternity deaths include surgeries.[59]

In the United States, there has been a remarkable increase in pregnancy-related fatalities in the years after *Roe v. Wade*.[60] According to the CDC, in 1987 we see 7.2 fatalities per 100,000 pregnancies. We should expect this number to go down over time, as it has gone down throughout the 20th century, due to improvements in healthcare.[61] Instead, over the last twenty years the number has risen dramatically. In 2009, the CDC reports 17.8 fatalities per 100,000 pregnancies.

What has caused this dramatic rise in pregnancy-related deaths? One possibility is that an abortion--far from protecting "reproductive choice"--actually injures a woman's cervix, or scars her uterus, and by doing so makes future pregnancies more dangerous.

---

[59] Both the CDC and the World Health Organization define a maternal death as "the death of a woman while pregnant or within 42 days of termination of pregnancy, irrespective of the duration and the site of the pregnancy, from any cause related to or aggravated by the pregnancy or its management..."

[60] *See* Carol Morello, "Maternal Deaths in Childbirth Rise in the U.S.," *The Washington Post* (May 2, 2014).

[61] Abortion rates might be the cause of a tremendous racial disparity in maternal mortality rates. *See* Mary Engel, "Abortion Rate Down, But Report Cites Racial Disparity," *The Los Angeles Times* (September 23, 2008). Engel reports that African-Americans "had abortions at five times the rate of white women." *Compare* Belle Taylor-McGhee, *High Maternal Mortality Rates for Black Moms Still a Mystery*, www.msmagazine.com (December 17, 2012). "(W)hen you ask why black women in the United States die from complications of pregnancy and childbirth at three to four times the rate of other ethnic/racial groups, the answer is usually the same: 'We simply don't know.'"

The *New York Times* reports that 5-10% of first trimester abortions are actually incomplete abortions.[62] This means the abortion doctor has accidentally left behind a few grams of the baby's tissue in the uterus. In some cases abortion doctors have left behind the whole fetal sac. If the *Times* is right, tens of thousands of women report to the emergency room every year to deal with this trauma.[63]

How does this happen? One difficulty is that abortion is a blind procedure. You are operating without a clear line of sight. When a doctor can't see what she is doing, it makes any surgery more dangerous. The doctor can perforate the uterus or lacerate the cervix, or accidentally leave tissue behind. As Dr. Hern says, "As a society, I think we've been in denial about the risks of abortion, both because of ideology, and because of economics."[64]

Many of these injuries are hidden from both patient and doctor. For instance, the abortionist has to violate the cervix in order to perform a surgical abortion. The cervix is a tight little muscle designed by nature to stay closed during the nine months of the pregnancy. The job of the cervix is to hold the weight of a large baby, who is sitting on top of the muscle. When an abortion doctor pries open the cervix, he is damaging that muscle.[65]

---

[62] Tamar Lewin, "A New Weapon in an Old War," *The New York Times* (April 9, 1995).

[63] A study in Finland reports that 20% of the women who abort via pill had significant complications. 15.6% had excessive bleeding, 6.7% had incomplete abortions, and 1.7% had an infection in their uterus. Maarit Niinimi, et al, "Immediate Complications After Medical Compared With Surgical Termination of Pregnancy," *Obstetrics & Gynecology* (October, 2009).

[64] *Supra* note 62.

[65] The American Pregnancy Association reports, "An incompetent or weakened cervix happens in about 1-2% of pregnancies. Almost 25% of babies miscarried in the second trimester are due to incompetent cervix." www.americanpregnancy.org. *See also* note 61 and the CDC report, "African-American Women and Their Babies at a Higher Risk for Pregnancy and Birth Complications," www.cdc.gov. "The infant mortality rate among black infants is 2.4 times higher than that of white infants, primarily due to preterm birth."

The doctor's hope is that the cervix will heal completely. If not, the woman's damaged cervix will open prematurely during her next pregnancy. This is one reason abortion has been linked to an increased risk of a premature birth in your next pregnancy. A massive study of 600,000 women in Scotland found that aborting your first pregnancy increased your risk of future premature births by 37%.[66]

Another medical risk from abortion is Asherman's syndrome, or a scarred uterus. Almost 90% of patients who suffer Asherman's syndrome were injured during a D&C surgery.[67] In the USA this surgery is most common after a miscarriage or an incomplete abortion. Asherman's, an under-reported condition, is implicated in the rise of miscarriages, infertility, and ectopic pregnancies.

Over 2% of pregnancies are now ectopic (i.e. happen outside the uterus). An ectopic pregnancy is an awful medical condition that is almost always fatal to the mother, unless she aborts naturally, or a doctor performs an abortion. In 1970, there were 4 ectopic pregnancies per 1000 pregnancies.[68] That number has increased six-fold since *Roe v. Wade*. A 2007 study reports 26.2 ectopic pregnancies per 1000 pregnancies.[69]

---

[66] Siladitya Bhattacharya, et al, "Reproductive Outcomes Following Induced Abortion," *British Medical Journal* (2012). *See also* Nick Collins, "Abortion Raises Risk of Premature Birth Next Time," *The Telegraph* (September 5, 2012).

[67] *See* www.ashermans.org.

[68] *See* The Centers for Disease Control, "Surveillance for Ectopic Pregnancy," www.wonder.cdc.gov/wonder/prevguid/m0031632/m0031632.asp. "From 1970 through 1989, more than one million ectopic pregnancies were estimated to have occurred among women in the United States; the rate increased by almost fourfold, from 4.5 to 16.0 ectopic pregnancies per 1,000 reported pregnancies." The CDC stopped this surveillance early in the Clinton administration.

[69] Britton Trabert, et al, "Population-Based Ectopic Pregnancy Trends, 1993-2007," American Journal of Preventive Medicine (May, 2011).

The STAKES study suggests that a woman who had an abortion in Finland was 3.5 times more likely to be dead in a year than a woman who decided to give birth to a baby.[70]

One of the surprising aspects of the study was that a woman who was not pregnant at all was twice as likely to be dead in a year as a woman who had given birth to a baby. That's an amazing finding. The STAKES study suggests that giving birth to a baby-- far from being dangerous to women--actually has a protective effect. Apparently it's healthier in Finland to have sex and have a baby than it is to be celibate.

We actually see a similar finding in breast cancer research. Medical researchers have known for centuries that giving birth to a baby actually decreases any future risk of breast cancer.[71] Pregnancy and birth has a protective effect. Thus celibate nuns, lifelong virgins, women on the pill and aborting women are all more likely to develop breast cancer than moms. One of the best things a young girl can do to decrease her future risk of breast cancer is to have a baby.[72]

---

[70] *Supra* notes 56 and 57.

[71] *See* Sarah Boseley, "How 18th Century Nuns Held Clue To Possible Breast Cancer Cure," *The Guardian* (October 5, 2008).

[72] And breast-feed your baby for two years or more. Bangladesh is known as a society where an overwhelming majority of women have a baby before the age of twenty, and breast-feed for two years or more. This explains the dramatic numbers in the Bangladesh study. *Supra* note 52. Aborting women in Bangladesh are twenty times more likely to get breast cancer because the control group are having babies and breast-feeding them. *See also* Yale News, "Breast Cancer Risk Reduced By 50 Percent By Breastfeeding for Two or More Years," news.yale.edu (January 25, 2001).

Chapter 3

The Supreme Court's failure to talk about the health risks to women suggests that perhaps it's not just unborn babies who are unseen. Maybe the Supreme Court does not see all the pregnant women who have had abortions, and has no idea what that surgery does to them. Maybe these women are invisible as well.

Why would a woman induce a miscarriage? One interesting study was summarized in a paper titled, *Abortion: The Least of Three Evils*.[73] It's an attempt to understand "the psychological dynamics of how women feel about abortion."[74] The conclusion of the paper is that aborting women "perceive the choice of abortion as the least of three evils (abortion, adoption, keeping the child) because it prevents the unwanted pregnancy from leading to the death of the self…"[75]

As Paul Swope writes in *First Things*, "Unplanned motherhood, according to the study, represents a threat so great to modern women that it is perceived as equivalent to a death of self. While the woman may rationally understand this is not her own literal death, her emotional subconscious reaction to carrying the child to term is that her life will be over. This is because many young women of today have developed a self-identity that simply does not include being a mother. It may include going through college, getting a degree, obtaining a good job, even getting married someday; but the sudden intrusion of motherhood is perceived as a complete loss of control over their present and future selves. It

---

[73] A summary of findings of a study conducted for the Vitae Society by Kenny & Associates. www.heartbeatinternational.org (August, 1994).
[74] *Id.*
[75] *Id.*

shatters their sense of who they are and will become, and thereby paralyzes their ability to think more rationally or realistically."[76]

In other words, the subconscious id is telling many women that this baby is a threat to their life. Thus many women see abortion as a life-or-death matter. Indeed, surprisingly all the women in the study (who characterize themselves as "pro-choice") agree that abortion is a killing.[77]

And the women in the study feel bad about it. Many aborting women believe they did a bad, but necessary, thing. They justify the killing on the subconscious grounds that their own life is at risk. As Swope writes, the aborting woman perceives her choice as either "my life is over" or "the life of this new child is over."[78] Thus, for many pro-choice women, abortion is a killing, but it's a killing in self-defense.

Obviously there are some analytical problems here. The id is notorious for being irrational and selfish. Aborting women may be in for some serious conflicts as their conscious self later realizes that a baby--except in rare medical emergencies--is not actually a threat to your life.

From the study:

> An unwanted pregnancy is at first met with disbelief and denial. There is a deep-seated rationalization that the current pregnancy is not real unless it is accepted by the pregnant woman. Respondents tell us a woman who has an unwanted pregnancy feels as though she has lost control of her life.

---

[76] Paul Swope, "Abortion: A Failure to Communicate," *First Things* (April, 1998).
[77] *Supra* note 73.
[78] *Supra* note 76.

'Choice' is an existing attitude offering a woman the illusion of control by implying a process of evaluation in which several options to an unplanned pregnancy are considered and then accepted or rejected. It offers these women a feeling that they are consciously regaining control by going through a decision-making process – "thinking it through." In reality, very little thought is given once they determine that there is no other way to "save their lives" than abortion.

The term 'choice' is used by these women to claim the deep seated belief that the decision is theirs alone and no one else can or should tell them what to do. "Choice" is a way of reflecting what they believe is the intensely personal nature of the decision that a woman with an unwanted pregnancy must make. The real meaning of the word 'choice,' these women tell us, is "no one else can tell me what to do." The psychological dynamics and beliefs underlying the use of the word 'choice' are emotionally intense and consistent among these women. And they tell us that most women in crisis feel that there is really no choice but to abort and "learn to live with it."

Making the decision to abort is not a battle between good and evil. It is a battle only among evils. These women say that the decision to have an abortion is a very difficult decision to make because they agree it does take a life, which is evil, but it is seen as a necessary evil because it is a means of self-preservation – preventing an unwanted pregnancy from leading to the death of the self. And that carrying

> an unplanned pregnancy to term and
> keeping the child threatens both the
> woman's present and future selves.[79]

Note how profoundly traumatic this decision-making process is for a pregnant woman. She is doing evil, and she recognizes she is doing evil. But she feels she has no choice. To keep the baby is an evil, too, because it would destroy who she is, her self-identity. And adoption, which would seem to be a way out--and historically was the way women dealt with an unwanted child--is now seen as the worst possible option.

> These women say they dismiss adoption
> as an alternative very early in the
> process of thinking through their
> options because it provides no
> resolution to their dilemma. In fact,
> they see adoption as an even greater
> evil than abortion. They contend it is a
> loathsome act because of their
> professed assumption that the adopted
> child would be abused or neglected.
> And they think any child "given up" for
> adoption would feel rejected, unloved
> or abandoned. Abandoning your own
> child to strangers is tantamount to
> "throwing the child to the wolves." It
> is too painful and reflects negatively
> upon a woman's character because it is
> a renouncement of her responsibilities
> as a mother.
>
> Adoption creates an unresolvable
> spiritual conflict for these women
> because in their minds adoption equals
> two deaths - the death of the child by
> abandonment and the death of the self
> by carrying the child to term - so it is
> an even greater evil than abortion. To
> these women, abortion saves the child

---

[79] *Supra* note 73.

> from the ominous fate of adoption, so
> abortion creates less guilt than
> adoption would.[80]

Of course our id is irrational. Our deepest and most selfish desires are often irrational. For instance, what about future pregnancies? When you are ready to be pregnant and have a baby, this would seem to create a potential for trauma as you think about the baby you aborted. How do you resolve that conflict?

> Because many women who abort
> pregnancies wish only to postpone
> assuming the role of motherhood until
> they are ready to be the kind of
> mother they want to be, there is
> widely held belief among these women
> that they are resolving their spiritual
> conflict between ending the life of the
> fetus and ending their own life because
> the aborted baby can be brought back
> later when the time is right.[81]

No wonder we don't talk about abortion in our society! Our subconscious is telling us that an aborted baby "can be brought back later." That's a deeply irrational thought.

> In weighing these options, abortion is
> seen as the least of three evils. They
> can see no option where good wins out
> over evil – a unique dynamic that
> explains why it is so difficult to deal
> with an unwanted pregnancy.
>
> Fear of remorse is at the heart of the
> spiritual conflict with which these
> women struggle in deciding to abort. In
> the absence of a clear and absolute

---

[80] *Id.*
[81] *Id.*

'good,' the women feel guilt at agonizing over the choice between three evils. They continually tell us how self-tortured the women feel who have had an abortion. It is clear that in many cases they do not resolve the spiritual conflict because most of them think of abortion as a sin for which they must seek God's forgiveness. To them, abortion equals a 'trespass' and those having had an abortion must do penance. Many of these women have felt, or known others who have felt, that they were being punished by God for having had an abortion.

These women tell us that a woman deciding to abort knows that she alone bears the burden of guilt for denying the potential life. Just as the fetus is a part of the woman, the abortion becomes a part of who the woman is. They believe that women who abort must "learn to live with the decision." And the abortion literally becomes a part of who they are – their self-identity. The guilt and remorse they face are tremendous which means they must expand their understanding of who they are in positive terms or allow their character to be eroded by guilt.[82]

Of course there are millions and millions of women who have abortions, and many women feel no guilt or trauma at all. But it should be equally clear that for millions of women, abortion is a huge, life-altering choice, and once you make that choice, there are no do-overs.

As Swope writes, "The terrible miscalculation of young women is that abortion can make them 'un-pregnant,' that it will restore

---

[82] *Id.*

them to who they were before their crisis. But a woman is never the same once she is pregnant, whether the child is kept, adopted, or killed. Abortion may be a kind of resolution, but it is not the one the woman most deeply longs for, nor will it even preserve her sense of self."[83]

It's rather obvious when you think about abortion that it implicates at least a possibility of emotional trauma.[84] For instance we celebrate the birth of a child in our society. Do we have any equivalent celebration for an abortion? No. Indeed, for many women the anniversary of an abortion can be a trigger for emotional upset.[85] Many women mark the date they had an abortion and, in private, feel awful remorse on that date. Future pregnancies and childbirths can also be a trigger. Abortion is a life-altering event for many women, a dark secret that becomes part of their identity.

In the *New York Times*, Emily Bazelon interviews Rhonda Arias, an abortion counselor.[86]

> "It was the year Roe v. Wade was decided, and I remember saying, 'No guy in Washington is going to tell me what to do with my body!' " Arias said with a sharp laugh as we were driving.

---

[83] *Supra* note 76.

[84] This is perhaps especially true when a woman does not want an abortion, and either circumstances or people are forcing her to abort against her will. For instance China, where forced abortions are common, has the highest rate of female suicide in the world. *See* Ma Jian, "China's Brutal One-Child Policy," *The New York Times* (May 21, 2012).

[85] David Reardon theorizes that Lorena Bobbitt's castration of her husband was motivated in part by an abortion she did not want. He points out that her attack occurred on the 3-year anniversary of her abortion. *See* David Reardon, "Their Deepest Wound: An Analysis," www.afterabortion.org (August 6, 1996).

[86] Emily Bazelon, "Is There a Post-Abortion Syndrome?" *The New York Times* (January 21, 2007). And note the impulse of many journalists to print articles on the anniversary of *Roe v. Wade*. Pro-lifers feel a similar impulse to mark the date. *Supra* note 155.

But after the procedure, she says, strange feelings washed over her. "I remember having evil thoughts, about hurting children," she said. "It was like I'd done the worst thing I could possibly do. A piece of evil had entered me."

In 1983, Arias became pregnant again and planned to keep the baby. But in the fourth month, she says, she became scared about raising a child alone. She called her obstetrician. He scheduled her for a second-trimester saline abortion the following morning. Arias said she woke up from the anesthesia to the certain knowledge that she had killed her child.

Because of this knowledge, she is now equally certain, she slipped into years of depression, drinking and freebasing cocaine. One night when she was in her early 30s, she got as high as she could, lay down in the dark in a bathtub filled with water and slit her wrists. In her mind, all of her troubles — the drugs, the suicide attempt, the third and fourth abortions she went on to have, the wrestling match of a marriage she eventually entered — are the aftermath of her own original sin, the 1973 abortion. It's a pattern she sees reflected everywhere: "In America we have a big drug problem, and we don't realize it's because of abortion."

Abortion counselors are finding that for many women, abortion implicates sin. As Swope puts it, "these women feel that God will ultimately forgive the woman, because He is a forgiving God, because the woman did not intend to get pregnant, and finally, because a woman in such crisis has no real choice, the perception is that the woman's whole life is at stake."[87]

As a matter of Christian theology, this is right. You can be forgiven for any sin. But in order for this healing process to happen, you have to admit that you killed a baby, and ask forgiveness for it. This is incredibly hard to do. Many women are ashamed of their abortions, and highly secretive about them.

The Catholic Church has long tried to reach out to aborting women with love. For instance, Pope John Paul II said this:

> I would like to say a special word to women who have had an abortion. The Church is aware of the many factors which may have influenced your decision, and she does not doubt that in many cases it was a painful and even shattering decision. The wound in your heart may not yet have healed. Certainly what happened was and remains terribly wrong. But do not give in to discouragement and do not lose hope. Try rather to understand what happened and face it honestly.
>
> If you have not already done so, give yourselves over with humility and trust to repentance. The Father of mercies is ready to give you his forgiveness and his peace in the Sacrament of Reconciliation. You will come to understand that nothing is definitely lost and you will also be able to ask forgiveness from your child, who is now living in the Lord.
>
> With the friendly and expert help and advice of other people, and as a result

---

[87] *Supra* note 76.

> of your own painful experience, you
> can be among the most eloquent
> defenders of everyone's right to life.
> Through your commitment to life,
> whether by accepting the birth of
> other children or by welcoming and
> caring for those most in need of
> someone to be close to them, you will
> become promoters of a new way of
> looking at human life.[88]

Why is the Catholic Church reaching out to aborting women? Because the pro-life accusation is that abortion kills a child. If women believe they might have done this, they will feel an incredible amount of guilt and remorse after the fact. Even women who are pro-choice can feel sad about their abortions, particularly on the anniversary of their abortion.

Contrast the healing approach of the Catholic Church with the former President of the American Psychiatric Association, Dr. Nada Stotland. She flatly denies that any woman has ever felt trauma after an abortion. She calls it a "myth." She writes, "Among the strategies employed by anti-abortion forces is an effort, apparently quite a successful effort, to convince the public, as well as legislators and the judiciary, that abortion damages women psychologically."[89]

Dr. Stotland is apparently oblivious to how bad it looks for her credibility that she opens her discussion with a political analysis of how finding any abortion trauma might help the pro-life movement. She is supposed to be an objective doctor who is

---

[88] Pope John Paul II, *Evangelium Vitae* (March 25, 1995).

[89] Dr. Nada Stotland, "The Myth of the Abortion Trauma Syndrome," *The Journal of the American Medical Association* (October 21, 1992). *See also* Dr. Nada Stotland, "Abortion Trauma: The Myth," www.huffingtonpost.com (October 30, 2010).

helping her patients. But how can you help your patients if you
refuse to see any trauma?[90]

Our medical establishment--implicated in **Roe v. Wade**--is in
denial mode. For instance, our medical authorities deny that
abortion can ever cause depression in a woman. The A.P.A. put
together a panel to study the issue. And what was there
conclusion? A first trimester abortion "does not pose a
psychological hazard for most women."[91]

That seems a rather bizarre way to frame your discussion. Our
blue ribbon panel appears to be talking about abortion through the
prism of a right to choose. Yet the question is not whether
abortion is a hazard for people to avoid, or whether it should be a
crime. The question is whether there are any women who are
traumatized by their abortions. That's a different question.

What difference does it make if "most" aborting women do not
feel trauma if you are treating someone who does feel it?

---

[90] Dr. Hern recounts the story of a pregnant 14-year-old girl, who clearly and
unmistakably does not want to have an abortion. "What brings you here?" "I
have to have an abortion." "Why?" "I'm not old enough to have a baby."
"But you told the counselor we should all be killed?" "Yes, you should all be
killed." "Why?" "Because you do abortions." "Me, too?" "Yes, you should
be killed, too." "Do you want me killed before or after I do your abortion?"
"Before." Upset at this encounter, Dr. Hern refused to do the abortion.
Afterwards the young girl's mother was very angry with the doctor for not
going through with the procedure. In his account, Dr. Hern is complaining of
his own trauma from dealing with this situation, and doesn't seem to realize the
likelihood that the underage girl was there under extreme duress and against
her will. **See** John Richardson, "The Last Abortionist," **The Guardian**
(January 23, 2010).
[91] **See** Nancy Adler, "Psychological Responses After Abortion," **Science**
(April 6, 1990). And why limit your discussion to first trimester abortions?
Over 6 million abortions have taken place in the second trimester, and many in
the third. If you were actually looking for trauma in aborting women, wouldn't
you start with those?

Imagine our medical authorities authoritatively stating, "the Vietnam war does not pose a psychological hazard for most men." That could be true, as a statistical matter. But it's a useless and rather absurd comment. We instinctively suspect that the author of that statement is a supporter of the war in Vietnam. Why else make the statement? You're obviously not doing psychiatry.

Our medical authorities denied for decades the possibility that men could be traumatized by war. In retrospect this is quite silly. We all know death and decapitation and dismemberment and killing people and watching your friends die is traumatizing.[92] As William Sherman put it, in the 19th century, "War is hell." What kind of soft science is psychiatry that it had no idea that war could cause emotional trauma in men?[93]

Post-traumatic stress disorder first appeared in the *Diagnostic and Statistical Manual of Psychiatric Disorders* in 1980. Before that it didn't exist![94]

Bazelon writes, "the scientific evidence strongly shows that abortion does not increase the risk of depression, drug abuse or any other psychological problem any more than having an unwanted pregnancy or giving birth."[95] Again this psychiatric finding is couched in terms of abortion politics. What difference

---

[92] Many men do not talk about their war experiences. And many women do not talk about their abortions. This repression might be a healthy response to an awful situation. But it seems quite odd to assume that this inability to talk about it signifies no trauma whatsoever.

[93] This is perhaps unfair. The people who do not recognize PTSD see the trauma. They just do not believe it's a mental disorder. They believe it's a normal human reaction to an abnormal situation (the atrocities of war). For instance, if you have schizophrenia, something is wrong with your mind. If you have PTSD, your mind is fine. *See* Sally Satel, "Posttraumatic Stress Disorder: Issues and Controversies," *Psychiatric Services* (June, 2005).

[94] Note that Dr. Stotland and the A.P.A. aren't just denying that post-abortion stress is a mental disorder. They're denying the existence of any trauma. They're denying that you can have any emotional upset after an abortion, and they are doing so before they hear what any of their patients have to say.

[95] *Supra* note 86.

does it make if you "prove" that abortion is just as depressing as birth? Even if you say that abortion and birth have identical psychological outcomes--a highly dubious assertion--medical science has long recognized the possibility of depression after the birth of a child. It's called post-partum depression.

Why are our medical authorities willing to recognize depression after childbirth, but are unwilling to recognize depression after an abortion?

It seems rather preposterous to say that childbirth is more depressing than abortion. And yet that is what our medical authorities seem to be saying, as they recognize one form of depression but fail to see the other. And it's particularly bizarre to say there's no evidence of psychological trauma after an abortion when our society is filled with women who cannot talk about their abortions.

Justice Ginsburg, in her dissent in the second *Carhart* case, cites our medical authorities when she denies the possibility that abortion can lead to depression. "The Court invokes an antiabortion shibboleth for which it concededly has no reliable evidence: women who have abortions come to regret their choices, and consequently suffer from severe depression..."[96]

The STAKES study from Finland suggests that seven times as many women commit suicide in the year after an abortion, as opposed to women who had given birth.[97] Indeed, non-pregnant women were twice as likely to commit suicide as women who had given birth to a baby.[98] The STAKES study suggests what most of us would intuit: giving birth makes women happy.

---

[96] *Gonzales v. Carhart*, 550 U.S. 124 (2007) (Ginsburg, J., dissenting).
[97] *Supra* notes 56 and 57.
[98] *Id.*

Obviously this statistical analysis should not hide the possibility of a wide variety of individual responses to birth, or abortion. As Mark Twain put it, there are lies, damn lies, and statistics. But pro-life people don't deny the possibility of post-partum depression. Why does our medical community refuse to recognize post-abortion stress syndrome?

It's not just Roman Catholics who have seen pain in aborting women. Afterabortion.com is a self-help website set up by women who felt traumatized by their own abortions.[99] They set up this website to talk about post-abortion stress syndrome, or PASS. These women want to avoid any partisan fight over abortion. They just want to help women who have had abortions. And one of the major complaints by these women is that medical authorities are denying that their trauma is real.

Pro-choice people should be listening to these women. Dr. Stotland, who is supposed to represent psychiatry in America, should be listening to her patients, not denying their trauma because of abortion politics. Justice Ginsburg, who says she's a feminist who supports women, should be listening to women, all women.

As Naomi Wolf put it, "At its best, feminism defends its moral high ground by being simply faithful to the truth: to women's real-life experiences."[100]

---

[99] This on-line resource was created by "Jilly," a woman who had five abortions. She denies that she is pro-life or that her website is pro-life. "PASS is a collection of physical and/or emotional issues that are common to women after an abortion. It is not experienced only by women who are prolife, or who regret their abortion. There are plenty of prochoice women who have experienced PASS. There are also plenty of women who feel their abortion was the right choice, and don't regret it, yet still have problems with PASS. PASS is a medical condition, and has nothing to do with politics or religion."
[100] Naomi Wolf, "Our Bodies, Our Souls," *The New Republic* (October 16, 1995).

In 1995, Wolf published an interesting and provocative article in the *New Republic* that discusses the emotional trauma of abortion for a number of women. She quotes one woman: "I had an abortion when I was a single mother and my daughter was two years old. I would do it again. But you know how in the Greek myths when you kill a relative, you are pursued by Furies? For months it was as if baby Furies were pursuing me."[101]

Wolf wants feminism to recognize and talk about the loss of a baby. "(W)e stand in jeopardy of losing what can only be called our souls. Clinging to a rhetoric about abortion in which there is no life and no death, we entangle our beliefs in a series of self-delusions, fibs and evasions. And we risk becoming precisely what our critics charge us with being: callous, selfish, and casually destructive men and women who share a cheapened view of human life."[102]

And what about the psychological ramifications of denial? After all, we abort our pregnancies in secret. And often we pretend there is no baby. Indeed, we pretend that the pregnancy itself never happened. Is it healthy to behave this way?

Denying the reality of the unborn child has wider implications. If we deny the baby, there is no father. And this is precisely what we hear from feminists. "It's my body, it's my choice." There is no baby in that rhetoric. There is no father in that rhetoric.

And it's not just feminism that dismisses the importance of the father. *Roe v. Wade* absolutely ignores the father. He is mentioned as an afterthought in footnote 67.[103] A few years later, in *Planned Parenthood v. Danforth*, the Supreme Court finds

---

[101] *Id.*

[102] *Id.*

[103] *Supra* note 1.

that a woman can abort a baby without regard to the father at all.[104] In regard to abortion, a man has no say. He has no choice.

In *Roe* the Supreme Court considers the pregnant woman in isolation, as if she impregnated herself, and she did so without creating a baby or anything like that. And yet every pregnancy has a baby, and every pregnancy has a father. When feminists, and the Supreme Court, deny the baby and the father, they are asking us to deny reality.

Consider the family unit: man, woman and child. That is what we have with a pregnancy. We have a father, we have a mother, and we have a child. Prior to *Roe v. Wade*, the importance of family was recognized. We would say a pregnant woman needs to be married. Mom needs a husband. Baby needs a father. And so often mom and dad would take a vow to love one another, and the baby they have created.

In our new world, we have given parents a right to opt out. *Roe v. Wade* is like a right to have a divorce. "I don't want to marry you." That's often the subtext as a single father and a single mother talk about an abortion. Whoever suggests an abortion loves the least. Imagine a divorce court that grants a man and a woman a right to divorce each other, get rid of the child, and pretend this never happened. That's *Roe v. Wade*.

The possibility for trauma is obvious, is it not? In many cases we are talking about young people, in puberty or barely out of it.

Imagine a young woman, 19 years old, who is in love for the first time. She is young and has no idea how vulnerable she is. She is sexually intimate with her boyfriend. And the sex is amazing. The orgasms are fantastic. She is so happy.

---

[104] 428 U.S. 52 (1976).

And then she is surprised with a pregnancy. And the father of her child, the man she loves, suggests that she should have an abortion.

It represents a failure. Certainly there is a birth control failure. But abortion might also represent a failure to love. She might be finding out, the hard way, that the man sharing her bed does not love her. She has discovered they are not a family, and they are not going to be a family.[105]

And our medical authorities say there is no possibility of depression here?

Roe v. Wade has fostered a society where many of us think of sex as no big deal.[106] And it's no big deal because of birth control, and the emergency back-up plan of abortion. We simply assume that our birth control will always work. And so we have no discussions about what we will do if there is a pregnancy. Sex is often not a big deal because pregnancy is averted--until it happens, and then it's a very big deal indeed.

Our media is awash in sexuality. Young people might not realize how much of this is sexual fantasy, and how different sexual reality can be. James Bond, to give one example, never seems to impregnate a woman. And if he did, his whole world would come crashing down around him. Once James Bond is a dad, it's a different movie. The male fantasy has been shattered.

Feminism has its own sexual fantasies: the super-woman who can do everything, and the fish who doesn't need a bicycle.[107]

---

[105] Ingmar Bergman's classic film, **Wild Strawberries** (1957) has a very ugly scene where a man tries to coerce his wife into having an abortion. How many American women are forced to undergo this same sort of ugliness?

[106] **See** Allan Bloom, **The Closing of the American Mind** (1987).

[107] A quote often attributed to Gloria Steinem: "A woman needs a man like a fish needs a bicycle."

Feminism declares that women are independent and fathers are unnecessary. And this anti-male dogma is quite common in our media.[108] There are countless modern examples of fathers portrayed as clueless, incompetent or useless. Father does not know best. From sitcoms to commercials, this is how we now see men. We attack fathers, and we disregard them.[109]

In 1970, 11% of births were to unmarried women.[110] *Roe v. Wade* talks explicitly about this problem ("the stigma of unwed motherhood") and offers abortion as a solution.

Deciding to be a single mom is often an economically disastrous choice, both for mother and child. Feminism is too proud, or too upset, to admit that pregnant women need husbands. And babies need fathers. *Roe v. Wade* has ushered in a world where inducing a miscarriage is normal, and being a single mom is normal, too.

Abortions skyrocketed after *Roe v. Wade*. And so did single moms. The birth rate to single moms doubled by 1992, and twenty years later it doubled again. Now, 40 years after *Roe v. Wade*, 41% of our births are to unmarried women.[111] Feminism shot at patriarchy and killed our fathers. And what about the Supreme Court's plan to free our society from all the single moms? *Roe* has to qualify as the worst centralized planning since Stalin's five-year-plan.

---

[108] *See* John Leo, "Anti-Male Bias Increasingly Pervades Our Culture," www.townhall.com (July 25, 2000).
[109] *See* Helen Smith, *Men On Strike* (2013).
[110] Kay Hymowitz, "The Single Mom Catastrophe," *The Los Angeles Times* (June 3, 2012).
[111] *See* The Centers for Disease Control, "Unmarried Childbearing," www.cdc.gov.

Chapter 4

One of the major criticisms of ***Roe v. Wade*** is that abortion is not mentioned in our Constitution at all. This is one of the main criticisms that conservatives use to attack the opinion.[112] And yet we can imagine some popular rights that are also not mentioned in our Constitution.

For instance, imagine if King George had made it a crime for people to marry in the colonies. Or imagine if he had tried to make it a crime for married people to have a baby. That would have been insane, would it not? Making marriage and pregnancy a crime is far more upsetting than any tax on tea!

Men and women have been marrying and having babies for tens of thousands of years. Of course we have a right to marry and have a baby.

In ***Griswold v. Connecticut***, Justice Douglas framed the right to use birth control as part of the right of a man and woman to marry. "We deal with a right of privacy older than the Bill of Rights--older than our political parties, older than our school system. Marriage is a coming together for better or for worse, hopefully enduring, and intimate to the degree of being sacred. It is an association that promotes a way of life, not causes; a harmony in living, not political faiths; a bilateral loyalty, not commercial or social projects. Yet it is an association for as noble a purpose as any involved in our prior decisions."[113]

---

[112] ***See*** John Noonan, ***A Private Choice*** (1979): "The makers of the Constitution of the United States do not appear to have contemplated the subject of abortion. There is no mention of it by name..."
[113] 381 U.S. 479 (1965).

Married people have a right to have sex in private. It's an unwritten right to be sure, but it's a right dating back to the dawn of man. And since marriage is a license to have sex, it follows from this that married people have a right to use birth control.[114]

Yet the focus on marriage in **Griswold** was largely a deception. A few years after that opinion, in **Eisenstadt v. Baird**, the Supreme Court said it was "irrational" for the state to favor married people over single people when it comes to birth control.[115]

It's like saying there is no difference between married people and single people when it comes to sex. But there are important differences. Married people have taken a public vow to love one another. Single people have not.

And what happens if our birth control fails?

Not surprisingly, one year after saying it was "irrational" to think that married people are different from single people when it comes to sex, the Supreme Court was complaining about all the young single moms, and insisting that there needs to be a new right to abort pregnancies. So the Supreme Court writes **Roe v. Wade**. And abortion is said to be one of our reproductive choices, just like birth control.

---

[114] The Ninth Amendment speaks on this issue. "The enumeration in the Constitution of certain rights shall not be construed to deny or disparage others retained by the people." The word "retained" is very likely a reference to rights we had under the common law of England. So unwritten rights (like marriage, or having a baby), date back hundreds or even thousands of years. One might say a right to contract is such a right. And yet many people are deeply critical of an unwritten right to contract. *See Lochner v. New York*. 198 U.S. 45 (1905) (Holmes, J., dissenting). And of course that is a major problem with any unwritten right. Even if it's traditional, modern society might want to change. And note the Ninth Amendment says that these rights must be majoritarian ("by the people"). *See* Akhil Amar, *The Bill of Rights* (1998). If these rights are unpopular (or become unpopular), then they are not "rights" at all. Instead they seem like wrongs imposed on a free people by an unelected body of rulers. *See* John Hart Ely, *Democracy and Distrust* (1980).

[115] 405 U.S. 438 (1972).

This comparison to birth control explains why abortion supporters are so willing to deny any emotional trauma after an abortion. Who gets depressed over a condom? Nobody.

This mindset, that abortion is just like birth control, is obviously absurd if you think about it. And yet the Supreme Court often talks as if they believe it. In **Planned Parenthood v. Casey**, for instance, the Supreme Court makes the rather astounding observation that "in some critical respects the abortion decision is of the same character as the decision to use contraception."[116]

Many pro-lifers argue that abortion actually involves the killing of an unborn child. But even people who support autonomy rights for women might be suspicious of a Supreme Court that makes a facile assertion that choosing to have an abortion is just like choosing to use birth control.

Birth control prevents a pregnancy. Abortion forces a woman's body to have a miscarriage. Birth control is often simple and easy, such as using a condom. Abortion requires that you terminate the life inside the uterus, and remove a tiny baby cadaver, or a not-so-tiny baby cadaver.

Indeed, one might criticize **Griswold** for the glib way it ignored any possibility of health risks from the use of birth control. What about the medical dangers of using pharmaceuticals? While marriage is an institution dating back tens of thousands of years, safe and effective birth control was quite new in 1965. And how safe was it?

Nowhere in the birth control case does the Supreme Court discuss or quantify any of the medical risks to people involved with the pharmaceuticals or devices you might use for birth control. After

[116] **Supra** note 7.

all, some forms of birth control aren't risky at all (condoms) while other forms of birth control are much riskier (birth control pills).[117]

The birth control pill was introduced in 1960. Because of health risks to women, the pill was actually illegal in eight states in 1964, the year before *Griswold*.[118] When you take the pill, you are taking a steroid. And you are doing so every day.[119] The original pill introduces potentially unhealthy amounts of estrogen into a woman's body.[120] Implicitly, under *Griswold v. Connecticut*, the right to birth control means that states cannot regulate the manufacture or sale of birth control pills.

None of the nine Supreme Court Justices (all men) who wrote *Griswold* can imagine any possible negatives to women from the daily use of a pharmaceutical that changes your reproductive system. Of course the statute in *Griswold* outlawed all forms of birth control. Yet the right to birth control issued by the Supreme Court overruled not only the silly Connecticut statute, but the not-so-silly eight states that were trying to protect women from the medical dangers caused by swallowing a steroid every day.

We often outlaw or regulate steroids that men take to increase muscle mass. And yet we are so happy about birth control, we rarely warn women about the dangers of taking an estrogen-based steroid on a daily basis. Perhaps our desire for birth control, and a

---

[117] In 1962 Searle, the original manufacturer of the birth control pill, received 132 reports of blood clots and heart attacks. 11 women died. The company said there was no conclusive evidence that its pill caused blood clots. Reported in *American Experience: The Pill* (timeline) www.pbs.org.

[118] *Id.*

[119] One of the startling facts about the birth control pill is that it actually remodels your brain structure. *See* Craig Kinsley and Elizabeth Meyer, "Women's Brains on Steroids," *Scientific American* (September 28, 2010).

[120] It's entirely possible that our rise in breast cancer rates has been caused by doctors. The argument is that birth control pills, abortion, and estrogen-replacement therapy all result in higher levels of estrogen in the bodies of women, and this increases the risk of cancer. *See* note 50.

free and open sexuality that goes along with birth control, corrupts us and keeps us silent on the risks to women from the pill.

Specifically, many studies have shown that taking a birth control pill every day will increase a woman's risk for breast cancer.[121] As a matter of basic biology, women are 100 times more likely to get breast cancer than men anyway.[122] That's because estrogen, the female sex hormone, is one of the main causes of the disease. And many birth control pills increase the amount of estrogen in a woman's body.[123]

Pharmaceutical firms have started introducing "mini-pills" that are not estrogen-based. Why are we introducing these new forms of the pill? One reason is that flooding a woman's body with estrogen increases her risk for cancer. This danger is widely known in the medical community. And yet many women have no idea of this possibility.

What if a birth control pill is dangerous to women? And just how risky is it?

In 2009, the Fred Hutchinson Cancer Research Center found that a girl who uses birth control pills before the age of 18 nearly quadruples her risk of triple negative breast cancer.[124] In another study, a Swedish oncologist, Hakan Olsson, concluded that using

---

[121] *See* "Oral Contraceptives and Cancer Risk," *National Cancer Institute at the National Institute of Health*. www.cancer.gov.

[122] *See* "What Are the Risk Factors for Breast Cancer?" *The American Cancer Society*. www.cancer.org.

[123] From 1976 to 2009, the breast cancer rate in women age 25-39 almost doubled. *See* Rebecca Johnson, et al, "Incidence of Breast Cancer With Distant Involvement Among Women in the United States, 1976-2009," *The Journal of the American Medical Association* (February, 2013).

[124] Jessica Dolle, et al, "Risk Factors for Triple-Negative Breast Cancer in Women Under the Age of 45 Years," *Cancer Epidemiology Biomarkers & Prevention* (April, 2009).

the original birth control pill before the age of 20 increases your risk for breast cancer by more than 1000 percent.[125] In 2005, the World Health Organization started listing birth control pills as a class 1 carcinogen.[126]

Griswold v. Connecticut, like *Roe v. Wade*, does a horrible job of evaluating the health risks of medical devices and procedures. There is no discussion in *Griswold* about cancer risks from estrogen-based birth control pills. Similarly, *Roe* is embarrassingly glib about the medical risks to women from abortion. These non-doctors are in over their heads. They are talking about autonomy and liberty and giving ideological arguments about freedom. But any factual discussion about the medical risks to women is utterly missing.

Of course the Supreme Court was not worried about fatalities in *Griswold v. Connecticut*. The idea that birth control might kill some people seems ridiculous. And yet it's largely undisputed that the pill increases a woman's risk for breast cancer. And this is particularly true if you're an underage girl.[127]

A young girl's body is naturally flooded with hormones during puberty. For instance, increased levels of estrogen will result in breast development. So it makes sense that adding even more estrogen to a girl's body might somehow skew this process, and make people more susceptible to breast cancer over time.

What's particularly damning about this is that other forms of birth control have no breast cancer risk whatsoever. And while health

---

[125] Hakan Olsson, "Early Oral Contraceptive Use and Breast Cancer Among Premenopausal Women," *Journal of the National Cancer Institute* (1989).
[126] "An IARC Monographs Working Group has concluded that combined estrogen-progestogen oral contraceptives and combined estrogen-progestogen menopausal therapy are carcinogenic to humans (Group 1), after a thorough review of the published scientific evidence." *International Agency for Research on Cancer* (July 29, 2005).
[127] *Supra* notes 124-25.

officials acknowledge the connection between birth control pills and breast cancer, their health warnings are muted and rather quiet. Apparently imposing a birth control regime on American society is more important than frank and honest discussion about safety risks to American girls.[128]

To be sure, most of us really like birth control. It's highly popular, for obvious reasons. None of us want the pill to cause breast cancer. But we should not allow wishful thinking to blind us from actual truth.

One might assume the Supreme Court in *Griswold* was only protecting birth control rights in the abstract. It's a right to use birth control. Perhaps the Supreme Court did not mean to make any finding in regard to the health risks of any particular form of birth control. After all, the Supreme Court is made up of experts in law, not medicine. Some forms of birth control, such as pharmaceuticals or intra-uterine devices, would still need to be regulated by health officials. One would hope, even after *Griswold*, the FDA still has authority to withhold approval of birth control pills that have a bad safety profile. In other words, under *Griswold*, if a certain type of birth control pill gives young girls breast cancer, the FDA can still order a safety recall or perhaps require a black box warning.

Or did the Supreme Court intend to impose a birth control regime on American society? What if, as Justice Ginsburg suggested, the Supreme Court was actually motivated by population control? Then the autonomy and safety of individuals is secondary. Maybe the Supreme Court is actually saying that drugs and surgeries that control reproduction are so important, the health risks to individual women are irrelevant.

---

[128] The Associated Press, for instance, reported that WHO added "hormone pills" to its list of class 1 carcinogens. www.nbcnews.com (July 29, 2005).

In *Griswold* the Supreme Court is utterly silent about health risks to women, and *Roe* barely mentions the subject. Are health officials denied the ability to protect the health and safety of Americans who are using pharmaceuticals or undergoing surgeries? That would be risky. After all, the health industry is an industry, motivated by financial considerations.[129] And if government is stripped of any regulatory oversight, that industry will unintentionally--or perhaps recklessly--inflict horrible damages on people.[130]

So is *Roe v. Wade* a pro-choice opinion, one that is protecting an abstract right of an individual woman to have a surgery that stops a pregnancy? If so, this would leave health officials free to regulate the abortion procedure, as it regulates all other forms of medical practice, to protect the health of women who undergo the surgery.

Or is *Roe v. Wade* actually a pro-abortion opinion, one that proclaims that abortion is safe, and cannot be regulated by health officials?

One might see the lack of discussion about health risks in *Roe v. Wade* as an implied assertion that abortion, like birth control, is safe. After all, it is fair to say that *Griswold* is a pro-birth control opinion. So why isn't it fair to say that *Roe* is a pro-abortion opinion? And both opinions largely omit any discussion of health risks.

---

[129] For decades many people were upset about an opinion called *Lochner v. New York*. *See* notes 114 and 251. In that case the Supreme Court overturned a health regulation in regard to the number of hours in which a baker worked. In *Griswold* the Supreme Court felt the need to distinguish its birth control opinion from *Lochner*. "We do not sit as a super-legislature to determine the wisdom, need, and propriety of laws that touch economic problems, business affairs or social conditions." Is the Supreme Court saying that pharmaceuticals and surgeries are non-economic? The health industry is not an industry?

[130] Undergoing a surgery is far more dangerous than baking bread. *Id.*

The Supreme Court often tries to tie *Roe* to *Griswold*, and argues that the right to abortion is quite similar to the right to birth control. If the two opinions are so similar, maybe their flaws are similar as well. Maybe the lawyers on the Supreme Court are not up to the task of dictating health policies to the nation. They want their abortion opinions to be about law, or ideology, or morality. Yet *Roe v. Wade* also involves very serious medical issues. And there is so little discussion in that opinion about health risks to women. The Court simply cites reported fatality data, and that's it.

What's shocking about this is that after this skimpy non-discussion about the health risks of abortion, *Roe v. Wade* proposes a rather astonishing rule of law: "With respect to the State's important and legitimate interest in the health of the mother, the compelling point, in the light of present medical knowledge, is at approximately the end of the first trimester."[131]

It seems that *Roe v. Wade* is doing far more than finding an abstract right of a woman to abort a pregnancy. The non-doctors on the Court are stripping health officials of any authority to oversee the surgery in the first trimester. Early abortions are assumed to be harmless, and so state health officials have no power to regulate the surgery at all.

Apparently, *Roe v. Wade* is creating a new abortion industry, and the idea is that these abortionists will operate without any government oversight during the first 13 weeks of the pregnancy.

According to *Roe*, health regulations can only start in the second trimester. This means there can be no regulations for a woman's health and safety in the first trimester. You can't protect her ability to reproduce. You can't guard her safety. You can't license an abortion clinic, or an abortion doctor. You can't

---

[131] *Supra* note 1.

regulate abortion at all in the first trimester. It is to be "an abortion free of interference by the state."[132]

This is breath-taking. It's shocking. It's unbelievable. And yet there it is, in black and white.

Did the Supreme Court have so much faith in the CDC statistics that it actually thought unregulated abortions are safer than pregnancies? Or was Justice Blackmun's opinion just an incredibly sloppy draft of an abortion super-statute? After all, the Supreme Court has no business writing super-statutes, and they have no real experience writing statutes at all.

The sharpest criticism of *Roe v. Wade* has come from pro-lifers, who claim the opinion has legalized infanticide. But even if we take the baby out of the equation, what the Supreme Court is doing here is still indefensible. Imagine if there is no baby at all. The doctor is just removing unwanted tissue. Wouldn't it be insane for the Supreme Court to strip health officials of any authority to oversee this medical surgery?[133]

This is far beyond anything the Supreme Court said in *Griswold*.

What is the evidence the Supreme Court has that an induced miscarriage in the first trimester of pregnancy is so safe that our Constitution requires it to be "free of interference by the state"? Justice Blackmun cites the "now-established medical fact…that, until the end of the first trimester mortality in abortion may be less than mortality in normal childbirth."[134]

May be less?

---

[132] *Id.*
[133] Imagine an unlicensed plastic surgeon operating on you.
[134] *Supra* note 1.

There's actually quite a bit of evidence that miscarriages are more dangerous for women than a healthy pregnancy. But aside from that, note what Blackmun is doing here. He is arguing that abortion in the first trimester is safer than birth. He cites social science from states like California and New York, where abortion was legal prior to *Roe v. Wade*. He's comparing the death rate from abortion in those states to the normal maternal death rate. And so he concludes that abortion is safer than birth.

Assuming that's true, how does it follow that there can be no health regulations protecting women in the first trimester?

After all, California and New York had legalized abortion, but they also had state oversight in place. Prior to *Roe v. Wade*, these states were regulating abortion clinics and abortion doctors. They had health inspections and licensing boards. It's normal state regulation of a dangerous medical procedure. And yet Justice Blackmun is citing the health record of abortion in states where the procedure is regulated for his argument that we can't regulate abortion at all in the first trimester.

It's a sloppy and horrible mistake to be making.

The Supreme Court goes on to list the sorts of health regulations that states can start doing in the second trimester: "Examples of permissible state regulation in this area are requirements as to the qualifications of the person who is to perform the abortion; as to the licensure of that person; as to the facility in which the procedure is to be performed, that is, whether it must be a hospital or may be a clinic or some other place of less-than-hospital status; as to the licensing of the facility; and the like."[135]

Reading this it appears that a state cannot even require that an abortionist is a medical doctor until the second trimester. We

---

[135] *Id.*

have no interest in the "qualifications of the person who is to perform the abortion" until the second trimester?

"This means, on the other hand, that, for the period of pregnancy prior to the compelling point, the attending physician, in consultation with his patient, is free to determine, without regulation by the State, that, in his medical judgment, the patient's pregnancy should be terminated. If that decision is reached, the judgment may be effectuated by an abortion free of interference by the State."[136]

It is true that Blackmun mentions that a "physician" will be doing these first trimester abortions that are to be free of interference by the state. But his opinion in *Roe v. Wade* also says, quite specifically, that states cannot have any requirements "as to the qualifications of the person who is to perform the abortion" in the first trimester. Even more damning, *Roe v. Wade* also says that we cannot require a medical license for any abortionist in the first trimester.

To get an idea of how radical this part of *Roe v. Wade* actually is, consider that a state has a lot more authority to regulate veterinarians than it has to regulate abortion doctors. Apparently the state has unlimited authority to protect the health and safety of dogs and cats. But not women! Under *Roe v. Wade*, even the most basic health requirement--that only a doctor should do this surgery--is apparently forbidden in the first 13 weeks of pregnancy.

The Supreme Court's silly bit of propaganda ("an abortion free of interference by the state") made the first couple of years after *Roe* a real fiasco for state health boards. Under *Roe*, health departments were apparently barred from inspecting newly formed abortion clinics that specialized in first trimester

---

[136] *Id.*

abortions. According to the Supreme Court, government oversight could only start in the second trimester. All 50 states suddenly had new abortion rules they had to interpret--Justice Blackmun's opinion. And because **Roe** had seemingly banned any health regulations in the first trimester, states had no idea if they still had the authority to punish non-doctors for doing abortions.

Was abortion really that safe? We can't regulate it at all in the first trimester?[137]

In defiance of **Roe v. Wade**, Michigan and New Jersey continued to punish non-doctors for doing abortions. In sharp contrast, at least three other states--Connecticut, Minnesota, and Pennsylvania--all tried their best to follow the Court's opinion. And since **Roe** said that health regulations for women couldn't start until the second trimester, these states said that non-doctors had a legal right to start performing abortions on women.

We know that's what those five states were doing, because the Supreme Court mentions them in a small, slight opinion that is **Connecticut v. Menillo**.[138] This tiny case was the very first abortion case decided after **Roe v. Wade**. It was an unsigned opinion, what's called a per curium ("by the court") opinion.

---

[137] On January 19, 1993, Alicia Ruiz Hanna performed an abortion on a woman who was in her first month of pregnancy. Hanna was not a doctor and had little medical training. She owned and operated her abortion clinic out in the open, under the license of a doctor who was rarely there. The patient, Angela Sanchez, went into seizures after Hanna injected her with an unknown pharmaceutical, and died. According to testimony, Hanna refused to call 911 and was seen stuffing her dead patient into the trunk of a car. She was convicted of 2nd degree murder and sentenced to 16 years to life. *See* Rene Lynch, "Clinic Operator Sentenced for Murder," **Los Angeles Times** (January 28, 1995).

[138] 423 U.S. 9 (1975).

One of the interesting things about this case is that nobody seems to know about it. The media did not cover it. It's not taught in law schools. It's a tiny, anonymous, unsigned opinion. And yet the issues involved would seem to be quite important. The question in *Menillo* is whether our health authorities can require, under *Roe v. Wade*, that the people doing abortions are doctors.

This might explain why there is no discussion about *Menillo*. Perhaps nobody wants to talk about the case because it is a real embarrassment for the Supreme Court and for *Roe v. Wade*. After all, the doctor question--which is clearly an important question--should have been resolved in the original opinion. In *Menillo*, the Supreme Court was forced to clarify what it said in *Roe* (a.k.a. fix its mistake). *Roe* has caused this problem, and *Menillo* has to make it right.

"In 1971, a jury convicted Patrick Menillo of attempting to procure an abortion in violation of Connecticut's criminal abortion statute. Menillo is not a physician, and has never had any medical training. The Connecticut Supreme Court nonetheless overturned Menillo's conviction, holding that under the decisions in *Roe v. Wade* and *Doe v. Bolton*, the Connecticut statute was null and void."[139]

In other words, Connecticut is reading *Roe v. Wade* to protect a right of non-doctors to perform abortions on women. That's actually what *Roe* says about first trimester abortions, so we can see why Connecticut is reading it this way. In doing their jobs, lawyers and judges have to read and follow the Supreme Court's opinions, and any new rules the Court might issue. Our Supreme Court is our highest court and what they say is the final word as a matter of federal law. So Connecticut should follow the Supreme Court's ruling, regardless of how reckless it might be to do so.

---

[139] *Id.*

"The Connecticut Supreme Court felt compelled to hold this (abortion) statute null and void, and thus incapable of constitutional application even to someone not medically qualified to perform an abortion, because it read *Roe* to have done the same thing to the similar Texas statutes. But *Roe* did not go so far."[140]

Here the Supreme Court denies that its opinion said anything of the sort. And yet *Roe* is a published opinion. Anybody can read it. The Court specifically said abortionists cannot be licensed by any state until the second trimester. The Court also said states had no rational interest in protecting the health of pregnant women from abortions that take place in the first trimester.

Confronted with the reality that its work is, at best, slipshod and dangerous to women, the Court denies that it said what it said.

"Jane Roe had sought to have an abortion performed by a competent, licensed physician, under safe, clinical conditions, and our opinion recognized only her right to an abortion under those circumstances."[141]

In her *New York Times* interview, Justice Ginsburg says, "I was surprised that the court went as far as it did in *Roe v. Wade*."[142] Apparently the Supreme Court was surprised by how far it went, too! It had no idea that it had found a constitutional right for non-doctors to do abortions in the first trimester. And in *Menillo* the Court denies that it ever said such a thing. So now the Supreme Court is rewriting history. It does not want to acknowledge that its opinion in *Roe* put the health and safety of women at risk.[143]

---

[140] *Id.*

[141] *Id.*

[142] *Supra* note 8.

[143] One of the *Roe* dissenters, Justice White, refused to join the Court's opinion in *Menillo*. "Mr. JUSTICE WHITE concurs in the result." It's an odd concurrence in that Justice White says nothing at all. It's a silent rebuke.

Menillo continues: "*Roe* teaches that a State cannot restrict a decision by a woman, with the advice of her physician, to terminate her pregnancy during the first trimester, because neither its interest in maternal health nor its interest in the potential life of the fetus is sufficiently great at that stage."[144] Yes, that's right. According to *Roe*, our society has no interest in the health of a woman having an abortion in the first trimester.

"But the insufficiency of the State's interest in maternal health is predicated upon the first trimester abortion's being as safe for the woman as normal childbirth at term..."[145] *Roe v. Wade* said that, too. The Court states its ideological belief that first trimester abortion is always safer than childbirth. And now, confronted with an unlicensed doctor performing abortions, the Supreme Court writes, "(A)nd that predicate holds true only if the abortion is performed by medically competent personnel under conditions insuring maximum safety for the woman."[146]

It's almost like "an abortion free of interference by the state" is a really stupid idea or something. Why would the Supreme Court assume that forbidding state health departments from regulating abortions in the first trimester would lead to "conditions insuring maximum safety for the woman"? Or that doing away with a licensing requirement would lead to "medically competent personnel"?

It was irresponsible for *Roe* to say that an abortion in the first trimester is so safe that it cannot be regulated by our health officials. And it was particularly irresponsible for *Roe* to suggest that non-doctors had a constitutional right to perform first

---

[144] *Supra* note 138.
[145] *Id.*
[146] *Id.*

trimester abortions. And if *Roe v. Wade* does not say that, why are three state supreme courts reading it that way?

At best *Roe v. Wade* is muddled and confused on this rather important point of criminal law.

The Supreme Court, it should be noted, is incredibly slow to revisit and fix any mistakes it makes. *Roe v. Wade* was decided in January, 1973. *Connecticut v. Menillo* wasn't issued until December, 1975, almost three years later.

According to the Guttmacher Institute, a private research group affiliated with the largest abortion provider in our country, there were an estimated 2.6 million abortions in this time frame.[147] Or, to put it another way, in *Roe v. Wade* the Supreme Court said that a woman has a right to a first trimester abortion "free of interference by the state." Then, 2.6 million abortions later, the Court issues a clarification, allowing states to make it a crime for a non-doctor to do an abortion.

40 years after *Roe v. Wade*, in 2013 the state of California would bring back Justice Blackmun's original vision of an "abortion free of interference by the state." Governor Jerry Brown signed a new law allowing nurses and other non-doctors to perform first trimester surgical abortions. Or, as the *New York Times* put it, "California Expands Availability of Abortions."[148]

This confidence in non-physician abortions is wishful thinking. California is apparently relying upon a single study. The name of the study is *Safety of Aspiration Abortion Performed By Nurse*

---

[147] *See* Guttmacher Institute, "Trends in the Characteristics of Women Obtaining Abortions, 1974 to 2004," (August, 2008).
[148] Jan Lovett, "California Expands Availability of Abortion," *The New York Times* (October 9, 2013).

Practitioners.[149] 13,807 pregnant women participated in the study. Of these, the results of 2,320 women were excluded from the study. Why? The authors of the study apparently did not want to give the complication rates for nurses who were learning how to do the surgery.[150]

Even more alarming, there was incomplete follow-up with patients after the surgery. The study relied upon women filling out a survey. "If patients did not return the survey, clinic staff made at least 3 attempts to administer the survey by phone." How were patients who had to go to the emergency room captured in this study? The authors of the study were only able to survey 70% of the women who had abortions from a nurse. They have no idea what happened to 30% of the patients in their study. And yet the study treats all these non-responders as "no complications."[151]

We know as a matter of capitalist economics what deregulating the abortion industry will do in California: it will make abortions cheaper. You don't need to go to medical school now. Nurses can take a class, get a certificate and start doing abortions. Non-doctors are now operating on people in California.

Does this increase the health risk to women who are undergoing the surgery? Absolutely. As capitalists like to say, "let the buyer beware."[152]

---

[149] Tracy Weitz, et al, "Safety of Aspiration Abortion Performed by Nurse Practitioners," *American Journal of Public Health* (October, 2014).

[150] *See* Matt Briggs, "Abortion Safety: Doctors v. Nurses & Physician Assistants & Midwives – Part II," www.wmbriggs.com (September 18, 2013).

[151] *Id.*

[152] RU-486 is a drug approved for abortions early in the first trimester. So far there are 14 reported deaths and 612 reported hospitalizations from the drug, and over 2000 adverse events. The FDA estimates that 90-99% of adverse events are unreported. *See* Julian Guthrie, "Monty Patterson Learns About RU-486 the Hard Way," *SFGate* (December 5, 2011). *See also* www.abortionpillrisks.org.

Chapter 5

The need of the Supreme Court to rewrite its opinion in
Connecticut v. Menillo makes clear that ***Roe v. Wade*** was sloppy.

Of course many pro-lifers are criticizing ***Roe*** because they hate
abortion. Yet even pro-choice law professors are criticizing the
opinion as reckless and irresponsible.[153] John Hart Ely's
scholarly criticism of ***Roe*** is one of the most cited law review
articles ever written.[154] But the necessity for ***Connecticut v.
Menillo*** is itself the most damning criticism one could make.
These state courts aren't trying to criticize ***Roe***, or fight it, or
undermine it. They're trying to follow it. And they can't.

You don't need to be pro-life to see incompetence in how ***Roe v.
Wade*** was drafted. Just the fact that state courts were ordering the
release of non-physicians to go out and do abortions suggests a
real problem with the Supreme Court's work.

Clearly, the Supreme Court was in a big hurry to legalize
abortion, and to make induced miscarriages a normal medical
practice. Abortion was to be taught in medical schools. It was to
be a usual, everyday part of what obstetricians do. The Supreme
Court saw unwanted pregnancy as a national problem, and
abortion was its proposed solution.

No doubt the Justices expected some criticism after ***Roe***,
especially from political conservatives. But it was not expecting
to be engulfed in criticism, to have hundreds of thousands of
protesters show up every year on the anniversary of the

---

[153] ***Supra*** note 2.
[154] ***See*** Fred Shapiro and Michelle Pearse, "The Most Cited Law Review
Articles of All Time," ***Michigan Law Review*** (2012).

opinion.[155] The Court was prepared to be called "dictators," they had heard that criticism before. But they were not expecting to be called baby-killers.

After the opinion, the Court started receiving boxes and boxes of letters from ordinary Americans who had gone through pregnancy and knew exactly what they were talking about. And these non-lawyers were outraged at what the Supreme Court had done. *Roe v. Wade* was compared to the death camps of Dachau, the mass killings of Stalin, and the atrocities of slavery.[156]

Instead of resolving a "case or controversy," *Roe v. Wade* appears to have ignited one.

What should the Court have done? Perhaps instead of drafting a super-statute for the entire country, the Supreme Court should have focused on a more narrow issue. For instance, Jane Roe had informed her attorneys that she had been raped.[157] And the Texas statute at issue in *Roe* did not make an exception for a woman who had been raped.

So that's a narrow issue, and quite an important one. In fact it's one of the strongest possible argument for abortion rights. If you are raped, you are not engaging in reproductive sex, and you are not responsible for your pregnancy. To outlaw abortion without any exception for rape means that a rape victim will be traumatized for an additional nine months.

---

[155] "The National Park Service no longer does crowd size estimates, but organizers believed the crowd to be considerably larger than last year's 400,000 number." Doug McKelway, "Abortion Opponents March in Washington," *Fox News* (January 25, 2013). The first march was just 30 people. *See* www.marchforlife.org.

[156] *See* Bob Woodward and Scott Armstrong, *The Brethren* (1979).

[157] Jane Roe is a pseudonym for Norma McCorvey. She set the record straight in testimony she gave before the United States Senate. "I made up the story that I had been raped to help justify my abortion." *Testimony of Norma McCorvey*, www.judiciary.senate.gov (June 23, 2005).

On the other hand, Jane Roe's rape claim was actually a false claim, a lie.[158] Why was she lying about a rape?

We feel outrage over a rape, and we feel sorry for the victim. Presumably this is why Jane Roe invented a rapist.[159] She is making a fierce appeal for a right to an abortion.[160] And a rape claim makes her more sympathetic than she would otherwise be.[161]

Yet the opinion in **Roe v. Wade** does not mention the issue of rape at all. Indeed, the trial court's published opinion does not mention the rape allegation. And the lead counsel for Jane Roe, Sarah Weddington, says that she never brought up the subject of rape.

---

[158] *Id.*

[159] Many states are re-defining the crime of rape. This is resulting in a huge increase in the number of reported rapes. *See* Niraj Chokshi, "Rapes Are Up Under New FBI Definition," *The Washington Post* (February 18, 2014). For 90 years, the FBI had classified rape as "forcible rape." However, under the FBI's new definition, the word "forcible" has been dropped. Now the only issue is non-consent. Many women might actually be rapists under this new standard. For instance, if you lie to a man to get him in bed, are you a rapist? (Why would consent obtained by fraud be thought of as "consent"?). Or what about sex when your partner is intoxicated? Is he sober enough to consent? (And if two people are having drunk sex, are they raping each other?) Contrast this situation to a date rape drug, when a victim is intoxicated against her will. Most of us have no problem seeing that as a rape. It's a secret attack that is akin to poison. So why is the FBI now defining rape as a non-violent crime? And how does this new definition of "rape" help actual rape victims--the women (and men) who are violently attacked? *See also* Jed Rubenfeld, "The Riddle of Rape-By-Deception and the Myth of Sexual Autonomy," 122 *Yale Law Journal* 1372 (2013).

[160] When pro-lifers passed a law requiring abortion doctors to share their ultrasounds with their patients, feminists claimed this was a "rape" of women. *See* Carole Joffe, "Crying Rape," *Slate* (February 29, 2012). It was highly effective rhetoric. But it was also ugly, dishonest, and very disrespectful to actual rape victims.

[161] On the other hand, making a false claim of rape is obscene. *See* Daily Mail Reporter, "Woman Is Finally Jailed After Five False Rape Allegations," www.mailonline.com (July 9, 2013).

Why not? Jane Roe is alleging she was raped. Of course, she was lying. So perhaps Weddington and the other attorneys doubted her veracity.[162] Or maybe they thought rape was irrelevant?

Rape is such a strong argument for a right to abortion, it's hard to believe the issue was not brought up by the attorneys, or by the court. And yet it seems our federal judges have simply skipped over the subject, as if it does not matter. The issue of rape, like the issue of infanticide, would be ignored by the Supreme Court in *Roe v. Wade*. Apparently our highest Court hoped to "resolve" the abortion controversy while ignoring two highly charged issues underlying our fight: the rape of women and the killing of babies.[163]

While rape is a very strong justification for abortion rights--so strong that many pro-lifers recognize exceptions in rape cases-- rape also narrows the issue. What happens if the Supreme Court mentions the situation of rape? Now we are no longer discussing all women who have an unwanted pregnancy. We are talking

---

[162] At least Jane Roe did not go to the police and allege that an innocent man raped her. Note the wide discrepancy between rapes that are reported to police officers (84,767 in 2010) and rapes that are reported to medical researchers (1.3 million in 2010). *See* Christina Hoff Sommers, "CDC Study on Sexual Violence in the U.S. Overstates the Problem," *The Washington Post* (January 27, 2012). The CDC researchers define an unwanted kiss as a sexual assault, and "repeatedly asking" for sex is called a sexual assault, too. Why not define an unwanted kiss as an unwanted kiss? How does it help actual rape victims when the CDC defines kissing, intoxicated sex, or unhappy sex as "sexual violence"? *See* Cathy Young, "The CDC's Rape Numbers Are Misleading," *Time* (September 17, 2014).

[163] The emotional upset that pro-lifers feel about the homicide of an unborn child is quite similar to the emotional upset that feminists feel about the rape of a woman. Both pro-lifers and feminists are motivated by a love and concern for other human beings. But this can also result in hate or anger felt for people who are on the other side. When pro-lifers talk about killing a baby, or feminists talk about raping a woman, they should remember that other people are on the other side of these allegations. And truth is very important.

about a rape victim who is not responsible for her pregnancy at all.

Narrowing the issue to rape victims would have caused the Court to write a narrow opinion. Does a rape victim have a right to emergency birth control? Does birth control ever work an abortion? Is a woman pregnant at conception, or implantation? Is there a right to use emergency contraception after sex? When does pregnancy begin? Would Texas prosecute a doctor for prescribing an IUD to a rape victim?[164]

Rape implicates emergency birth control, and the question of whether birth control can actually work an abortion. After all, pregnancy does not happen immediately after sex. It's possible that a sperm fertilizes an egg rather quickly, within an hour after intercourse. But what is far more common is that the sperm arrives in the fallopian tubes and there is no egg there.[165] Sperm can stay in the tubes for up to five days after sex. During this five-day period, if an egg comes into the fallopian tubes, a pregnancy might happen.

A birth control pill or an IUD can stop ovulation and keep a pregnancy from happening. This is why people sometimes use birth control after sex, to prevent pregnancy.

An IUD, or an intra-uterine device, is 99% effective as birth control if used in the 24 hours after sex or rape. Day-after birth control pills also have extremely high rates of effectiveness. These forms of birth control work by stopping ovulation, or by killing sperm. The IUD--and some birth control pills--also weaken the lining of the walls of the uterus. So it's possible, if

---

[164] The answer is no. *See* notes 167 and 170.
[165] *See* William Saletan, "The Birds and the B's," *Slate* (April 1, 2006).

you're already pregnant when you take the pill or insert an IUD, that it actually performs an abortion on a microscopic zygote.[166]

In their arguments in **Roe v. Wade**, the state of Texas argued that pregnancy begins at implantation, rather than conception.[167] Implantation is when the zygote attaches to the walls of the uterus. It happens 7-9 days after conception.[168]

Why is Texas redefining when pregnancy begins?[169] By arguing that pregnancy begins at implantation instead of conception, Texas hopes to avoid any argument that its criminal abortion statute might offend the right to birth control found in **Griswold v. Connecticut**.[170] Some forms of birth control--the pill, the IUD--if used after conception has happened, might destroy a microscopic zygote. Since these forms of birth control are already protected, Texas is arguing that its criminal law only applies once the microscopic zygote attaches to the walls of the uterus.[171]

---

[166] *Id.*

[167] *Supra* note 156.

[168] *Id.* At oral argument in *Roe*, the attorney for Texas, Jay Floyd, marked the beginning of the abortion statute at "seven to nine days after conception." Justice Marshall asked him about six days, and then remarked, "But this statute goes all the way back to one hour." The statute cited in *Roe* does not actually say that. Marshall is assuming that pregnancy begins at conception.

[169] Redefining a word, and particularly a word involved in a criminal statute, can cause a lot of strife. *See* note 159. On the other hand, there might be good reasons to redefine a word. *See* note 171.

[170] *See* Linda Greenhouse and Reva Siegel, **Before Roe v. Wade** (2012) (Brief for Appellee Henry Wade). While the Texas brief does mention conception, the main argument is that "the fetus implanted in the uterine wall deserves respect as a human life."

[171] How would you even do a criminal prosecution for the abortion of a zygote? Prosecutors would have to prove that a zygote existed, and that this was known at the time emergency contraception was used. But there is no way to find out if anybody has conceived at this stage. The chemical test for pregnancy is to check and see if you have the pregnancy hormone--human chorionic gonadotrophin (hCG)--in your body. Yet this hormone only shows up a week after conception, when the zygote implants itself in the walls of a woman's uterus. In other words, authorities could not prosecute anybody for an abortion based on the use of emergency contraception. It would be an

So while the abortion statute did not mention rape, Texas would not prosecute anybody for an abortion for giving emergency contraception to a rape victim. And a rape victim had at least a week to seek this remedy. At any rate, the Supreme Court could have written an opinion that made this quite clear.

Of course many people feel strongly that pregnancy begins at conception, and that all abortions are wrong.[172] Yet a focus on rape victims, on emergency contraception, on the possibility that some forms of birth control might actually abort a microscopic zygote, would have resulted in a far stronger opinion, albeit a far more narrow one. It would have tied the Court's abortion opinion in a much stronger way to the right to birth control found in *Griswold v. Connecticut*.

So why didn't the Supreme Court resolve Jane Roe's case on the narrow grounds of rape? It's an important motivation for an abortion, far more important than scheduling concerns or "the stigma of unwed motherhood."[173] And yet the Court's opinion does not mention rape, a far stronger rationale. Apparently it's irrelevant whether Jane Roe was raped, or had reproductive sex with her boyfriend.

Indeed, it's apparently irrelevant whether she is pregnant at all! One of the surprising aspects of *Roe v. Wade* is that Jane Roe was not actually pregnant when the Supreme Court heard the case.[174] Jane Roe had already given birth to a little girl, and had placed the

---

impossible prosecution, since you could not prove that any zygote had existed, or that an abortion had in fact occurred.

[172] *See* Michael Stokes Paulsen, "The Unbearable Wrongness of *Roe*," *Public Discourse* (January 23, 2012).

[173] *Supra* note 1.

[174] *Id.*

baby with an adoption agency.[175] The child was two years old at the time *Roe v. Wade* was decided.[176] She could have sat in Justice Blackmun's lap while he announced his opinion finding a right to abort her.

That's rather startling. *Roe v. Wade* is not resolving a case or controversy at all. Jane Roe had already given birth to her baby. The case was over. There was nothing to litigate. So why were the attorneys going forward with the case? Why was the Supreme Court hearing the matter?

The Supreme Court wanted to hear Jane Roe's case because they wanted a platform to issue abortion rules for our entire country. They wanted an opportunity to mandate a new set of abortion rules. So they deemed it irrelevant that Jane Roe was not actually pregnant anymore, and that the original case or controversy had disappeared.[177]

Occasionally the Supreme Court will use a case or controversy as a platform to enact sweeping change throughout our country. For instance, in *Miranda v. Arizona*, the Supreme Court freed a rapist because the police officers did not inform the suspect that he had a right to be silent and to call an attorney.[178] At the time, there was widespread objection by the public to *Miranda*.[179] And yet today there is little objection to the case.

---

[175] Alex Witchel, "At Home With Norma McCorvey; Of Roe, Dreams and Choices," *The New York Times* (July 28, 1994).

[176] Billy Hallowell, "Do You Know the Fascinating and Troubling Story About the Woman Behind the Roe v. Wade Case?" *The Blaze* (January 22, 2013).

[177] *See* David P. Currie, *The Constitution in the Supreme Court 1888-1986* (1990). "By all rights the case ought never to have been decided...the case was moot..."

[178] 384 U.S. 436 (1966).

[179] Senator Sam Ervin was so mad he wrote a law review article, "Miranda v. Arizona: A Decision Based on Excessive and Visionary Solicitude For the Accused," *American Criminal Law Quarterly* (1966-67). In 1968 Congress

So perhaps that's what the Supreme Court was hoping to do with *Roe*. They wanted to issue new abortion rules for our society. They knew these new rules would be highly controversial. And they hoped the controversy would die down.

Yet this misses what upset so many people about *Miranda*. Telling suspects about their rights is not a bad rule at all. The controversy over *Miranda* has gone away because the rule itself is quite good. What's objectionable about what the Court did in *Miranda* is that it released a rapist in order to give itself a platform to announce a new rule for our society. There was no evidence that the police had coerced a confession or done anything wrong. They simply had not read the suspect his rights. But why would they do such a thing, when *Miranda* warnings did not exist prior to *Miranda*?

In other words, it's highly dangerous--and possibly unconstitutional--for the Supreme Court to ignore the actual case and controversy before it. It's not the Court's job to make up new abortion rules for our entire country. Nor is it the Court's job to release a rapist because the police violated a rule that did not exist until the Supreme Court invented it.

In the case of *Miranda*, the Supreme Court was issuing a new rule that is actually quite good. But the injustice it did to the rape victim in *Miranda* is still outrageous.

Rape is a serious crime. The Supreme Court should have thought about rape in *Roe v. Wade*, and what rights a rape victim has. Does she have a right to avoid a pregnancy? *Roe* should have discussed the rape question, and how the Texas statute affects rape victims. And the Supreme Court should have written an

---

attempted to overrule the opinion by statute. *See* Yale Kamisar, "Can (Did) Congress Overrule Miranda?" 85 *Cornell Law Review* (May, 2000).

opinion that discusses emergency contraception. Such an opinion would have been a great boon to actual rape victims.

Instead the Court had another agenda on its mind. The Supreme Court had no interest in narrowing the case to rape victims. Rape is not even mentioned in the case as a motivation for the opinion. While the Supreme Court does mention other, secret possibilities: overpopulation, pollution, poor people, and race.[180]

The Court shrugs off rape victims in *Roe*, as it shrugged off the release of an actual rapist in *Miranda*. Similarly, the Court shrugged at the idea that abortion might kill a baby. The Court did not bother to refute the claim. Rather, the Court said it did not care. "We need not resolve the difficult question of when life begins."[181]

In *Miranda*, the Supreme Court had a shocking disregard for a victim of rape. But at least the new proposed *Miranda* rule was not shocking. Indeed, the state was able to retry Ernesto Miranda, and he was convicted of his crime a second time.

Roe v. Wade had a similar disregard for ordinary human beings, for Norma McCorvey and for the child she gave up for adoption.[182] But unlike *Miranda*, in *Roe* the disregard for humanity was not limited to the immediate case. In *Roe* the Supreme Court ignores rape, and infanticide, and attempts to "resolve" abortion without discussing either subject.

---

[180] *Supra* note 1.

[181] *Id.*

[182] Years after *Roe*, Norma McCorvey was furious with her attorneys for not telling her that she could travel to another state and get an abortion. They did not inform her of this because they wanted to use her for purposes of litigation. *See* note 175. In other words, her attorneys had no real interest in helping her. They were using her for their own agenda.

The results are predictable. Pro-lifers are horrified at the possibility that abortion kills a baby. ***Roe v. Wade*** does nothing to silence those fears. And since the Supreme Court fails to discuss or talk about rape, many feminists are afraid their fears are being minimized. Many people are horrified at the possibility that a woman might be raped and forced to carry a baby for nine months. Why is this issue irrelevant? And why is the baby's life irrelevant? The Supreme Court's opinion avoids the two main controversies driving our fight over abortion!

One might say that ***Roe v. Wade*** is protecting the autonomy of all women. This includes rape victims as well as women who have sex without using birth control. But are these people similarly situated? When men and women freely participate in reproductive sex, they know or should know they might be creating a baby.[183] And we are all responsible for our actions. A rape victim, on the other hand, is not like that at all.

And yet the Supreme Court's opinion disregards the issue of rape, as it disregards the issue of homicide. We might see this disregard as an institutional disregard for humanity. Consider that in ***Roe*** an unborn baby, from conception until birth, is defined as a legal non-person. She is sub-human. She is property. Indeed, as John Hart Ely pointed out, the unborn are actually lower in the Supreme Court's eyes than dogs.[184] We can protect dogs. But ***Roe v. Wade*** suggests we have no right to protect an unborn human child.[185]

This mirrors the Supreme Court's finding that we are not allowed to protect the health of a pregnant woman in the first trimester of

---

[183] Nor does the use of birth control allow us to be irresponsible about any child we create. Birth control might fail, and we should know that, too.
[184] ***Supra*** note 2.
[185] In ***Roe v. Wade*** the Supreme Court said an unborn baby has no right to life. ***Supra*** note 1. Thus any attempt to protect the unborn child's right to life is treated with suspicion.

pregnancy. The health and safety of a pregnant woman is said to be an illegitimate concern for the first 13 weeks of pregnancy. We can't even guard her safety when she's undergoing a surgery, or when she's using pharmaceuticals. It's as if pregnancy puts the woman outside the law as much as it puts the baby outside the law.

Defenders of **Roe** would argue that this is overstating the point. As Justice Blackmun writes, "a State may properly assert important interests in safeguarding health, in maintaining medical standards, and in protecting potential life. At some point in pregnancy, these respective interests become sufficiently compelling to sustain regulation…"[186] Yes, at some point in pregnancy, we will be allowed to protect the health of women. At some point in pregnancy, we will be allowed to maintain medical standards. At some point in pregnancy, we will be allowed to protect the baby's life.

But the first trimester is to be an abortion free of interference by the state!

And this inspires a question that **Roe** does not answer. Why is the end of the first trimester "compelling" for health purposes? The Supreme Court's opinion does not tell us. In fact the Supreme Court cannot tell us. The Constitution says nothing at all about the trimesters of pregnancy, any more than it talks about abortion or sex.

While the Supreme Court overlooks the non-pregnancy of Jane Roe, and it ignores the problem of rape victims, and it ignores the possibility of infanticide, the Supreme Court nonetheless hopes to resolve the abortion controversy by issuing a bunch of rules that appear to be made up out of thin air.

---

[186] *Id.*

Roe v. Wade identifies two important points: the end of the first trimester (13 weeks) and viability, a shifting point that is currently at 22 weeks.[187] What makes these two points so important? And how did the Supreme Court arrive at these points? After all, our Constitution says nothing at all about this. But what's even more damning is that the Court's made-up rules seem so arbitrary.

For instance, there is nothing actually compelling about the end of the first trimester. It is not medically relevant at all.[188] The trimester system is simply a calendar doctors use to mark time during a pregnancy. The end of one trimester, or the start of another, has no underlying importance at all. It's rather like the end of May and the start of June.

How odd would it be for the Supreme Court to insist that June is compelling but there can be no regulations in May? It would be rather like Nero dictating an arbitrary rule. Indeed, that's exactly what it is: an arbitrary rule.

When Justice Blackmun circulated an early draft of *Roe v. Wade*, he attached a memo describing his work.[189] Many pro-lifers consider this memo to be a smoking gun, a rather obvious example of a judicial scandal, and maybe even an impeachable offense. A pro-choice person might actually agree with this, if she thinks about a pregnant woman's health and safety.

---

[187] There is another important point: birth. A born infant is a citizen and has a right to life specifically protected by the Constitution. In *Roe* the Supreme Court defined the unborn as non-people. This is their legal status for the 39 weeks of pregnancy. *Id.*

[188] Medical dictionaries define "trimester" as a period of three months. The pregnancy is divided into thirds, the same way a school year might be divided. The first trimester ends at week 13, the second trimester ends at week 26, and the third trimester ends at birth (often at 39 weeks).

[189] Justice William O. Douglas, a firm believer in free speech and open government, ordered that his private papers by published after his death. *See* Bob Woodward, "The Abortion Papers," *The Washington Post* (January 22, 1989).

Supreme Court of the United States
Washington, D.C. 20543

CHAMBERS OF
JUSTICE HARRY A. BLACKMUN

November 21, 1972

MEMORANDUM TO THE CONFERENCE

Re: No. 70-18 - Roe v. Wade

Herewith is a memorandum (1972 fall edition) on the Texas abortion case.

This has proved for me to be both difficult and elusive. In its present form it contains dictum, but I suspect that in this area some dictum is indicated and not to be avoided.

You will observe that I have concluded that the end of the first trimester is critical. This is arbitrary, but perhaps any other selected point, such as quickening or viability, is equally arbitrary.

I have attempted to preserve Vuitch in its entirety. You will recall that the attack on the Vuitch statute was restricted to the issue of vagueness. 402 U. S. at 73. I would dislike to have to undergo another assault on the District of Columbia statute based, this time, on privacy grounds. I, for one, am willing to continue the approval of the Vuitch-type statute on privacy as well as on vagueness. The summary here attempts to do just that. You may not agree.

I apologize for the rambling character of the memorandum and for its undue length. It has been an interesting assignment. As I stated in conference, the decision, however made, will probably result in the Court's being severely criticized.

Sincerely,

H. A. B.

In his memo Blackmun writes, "I have concluded that the end of the first trimester is critical. This is arbitrary, but perhaps any other selected point, such as quickening or viability, is equally arbitrary."

Remember, in *Roe v. Wade* the Supreme Court strips health officials of any power to regulate the abortion surgery in the first trimester. According to *Roe*, in the first 13 weeks of pregnancy the health of the woman is an illegitimate concern. And here, in a secret memo, Justice Blackmun declares that his new rule, the end of the first trimester, is actually an "arbitrary" point.

Of course this slipshod and callous attitude drives pro-lifers up the wall. How galling is it that the Supreme Court "resolved" the life-or-death issue by defining the unborn infant as a non-person, as sub-human? And that's in the published opinion. And not only pro-lifers, but pro-choice people, are outraged by the idea that the woman's health is of no concern to us.[190] We can't protect women until the end of the first trimester? And that's in the published opinion, too.

And then, in a secret memo, Harry Blackmun acknowledges that his first trimester rule is, in fact, arbitrary, and any other point the Court might come up with is arbitrary, too.

It is true that this is just an early draft of his opinion. And yet his attitude is scandalous. It's not just that the Supreme Court is dictating a bad rule, or that innocent people will suffer under this bad rule. What really shocks us is that the Supreme Court knew at the time that its rule was arbitrary. The Court admitted as much in its internal documents.

---

[190] For instance, Sandra Day O'Connor, who is pro-choice, was nonetheless upset about *Roe v. Wade*. In particular she was hostile to the idea that a pregnant woman's health and safety are irrelevant when she's undergoing a surgery in the first trimester. *Akron v. Akron Center For Reproductive Health*, 462 U.S. 416 (1983) (O'Connor, J., dissenting).

When Justice Blackmun circulated this memo, all nine Supreme Court Justices were put on notice that they were not following the Constitution, and that this judicial opinion was a very basic violation of the oath of office. The word "arbitrary" was a rather obvious tip-off that Justice Blackmun had lost his way.[191]

As his memo suggests, Blackmun's first draft was a largely irrelevant research paper on world history and abortion.[192] Indeed, Blackmun's published opinion would contain pages and pages of irrelevant discussion about the political positions of the American Medical Association, the American Public Health Association, and the American Bar Association.[193]

In his memo, Blackmun writes, "I suspect that in this area some dictum is indicated and not to be avoided."

What Blackmun means by this is that he is forced to cite other authorities because he has no real legal authority for what he is

---

[191] And it's not just Blackmun who is not doing his job. *See* Clarke Forsythe, *Abuse of Discretion* (2013). Forsythe's 477-page book is focused entirely on the procedural irregularities of *Roe v. Wade*.

[192] English common law might be relevant. *See* note 114. And yet Justice Blackmun's analysis of our abortion history is very bad. He makes the untrue statement that "even post-quickening abortion was never established as a common law crime." *Supra* note 1. The exact opposite was the case. It was not only a crime; it was often deemed murder. *See* Joseph Dellapenna, *Dispelling the Myths of Abortion History* (2006). And when abortion was deemed less-than-murder, it was still a very serious crime. There was never a "right" to beat a pregnant woman, or poison her, or jam instruments into her cervix. Abortion was always a dangerous and violent act, and early feminists hated it. Even Margaret Sanger was opposed to abortion. *See* note 508.

[193] *Supra* note 1. If you're writing a Supreme Court case and there are medical issues, you might cite the AMA as a medical authority. But Harry Blackmun isn't doing that here. He's citing the AMA as if it's a deliberative body with some sort of statute-writing authority. Indeed, he goes through the history of the AMA, even citing AMA opinions from the 19th century. To get a sense of how inappropriate this is, imagine a Supreme Court opinion dealing with the right to bear arms. Now imagine that the opinions and deliberations of the National Rifle Association had a prominent place in the opinion.

writing. That's why he's citing the AMA and the ABA instead of our Constitution.

It's a rather astounding approach to Constitutional law. An individual's right to vote is irrelevant, apparently, unless you are participating in an ABA meeting. Blackmun is throwing out the very basis of our republic--the right to vote--and he's replacing the idea of equal citizens under the law with an elitist attitude that only the opinions of doctors and lawyers really matter.[194]

According to **The Brethren**, a wonderful journalist account of the inside activities of the Supreme Court in this time frame, some of the judicial clerks had taken to referring to Blackmun's opinion as "Harry's abortion."[195] The authors, Bob Woodward and Scott Armstrong, are silent as to which judicial clerks are responsible for this ghastly humor. The clerks aren't supposed to be talking to journalists. But Bob Woodward was a hero to them, because of his work covering the Watergate scandal of Richard Nixon.[196]

At the time of **Roe**, the new Chief Justice, Warren Burger, a Nixon nominee, was intensely disliked by some of the liberals on the Court. Burger was suspected of the unusual habit of joining

---

[194] Why is **Roe v. Wade** quoting the opinions of legal groups like the ABA or the ALI? These organizations have drafted model penal codes, or suggestions for what an abortion statute should look like. But Texas and Georgia have no obligations whatsoever to follow these suggestions. A model penal code is irrelevant to the Supreme Court's job of following an actual statute. Indeed, after citing the ABA and the ALI for what a "good" abortion statute would look like, the Supreme Court ignores their model penal codes entirely. The Court drafts its own model penal code, with "arbitrary" points, and then issues an order that all 50 states must follow it.

[195] **Supra** note 156. The book recounts a judicial clerk's reaction to seeing Blackmun's first draft in **Roe v. Wade**: "The clerk was astonished. It was crudely written and poorly organized. It did not settle on any analytical framework." The book later recounts Justice Potter Stewart's reaction. "Stewart was disturbed by the draft. Aside from its inelegant construction and language, it seems to create a new affirmative constitutional right to abortion that was not rooted in any part of the Constitution."

[196] **Id.**

opinions in which he did not agree so that he could control who got the assignment.[197] If this was the case, the maneuver was a spectacular backfire in *Roe v. Wade*. Burger joined the majority and assigned the case to his fellow Nixon appointee, Harry Blackmun. But instead of moderating the opinion, the assignment had the opposite effect: it radicalized Blackmun.

While the rules laid out in *Roe v. Wade* are quite shocking, the opinion itself is mild in tone. Once he started getting pushback from pro-lifers--along with, presumably, photographs of aborted infants--Blackmun became a dogmatic and doctrinaire feminist, and his opinions became increasingly shrill. In *Webster v. Reproductive Health Services*, Blackmun writes that the plurality "casts into darkness the hopes and dreams of every woman in this country…"[198] In *Planned Parenthood v. Casey*, Blackmun talks about "the darkness" in his opponents, while referring to his own opinion as a "light" of knowledge.[199] He ends his opinion with a deep regret: "I cannot remain on this Court forever."[200]

---

[197] *Id.* Note that the Chief joined the majority opinion in *Roe v. Wade*. And he's still trying to control what the opinion says! "Plainly the Court today rejects any claim that the Constitution requires abortion on demand." *Doe v. Bolton*, 410 U.S. 179 (1973) (Burger, C.J., concurring). It's unfathomable how anybody can read *Roe v. Wade* and come to that conclusion. It's a denial of reality. It's as if Burger can't believe this is happening, and so he's pretending that it's not happening.

[198] 492 U.S. 490 (1989) (Blackmun, J., dissenting). Justice Blackmun has to know that many women are pro-lifers, while many men appreciate abortion rights. And yet he claims that his opinion is speaking for women and empowering women. Is that a fair or accurate way to describe his actual opinion in *Roe v. Wade*? Or his arbitrary memo? *Supra* note 189. Is he listening to pro-life women? And note that Sandra Day O'Connor is sitting right next to him on the bench. Is he even listening to her?

[199] And of course it is a dark vision of *Roe v. Wade* to see infanticide in the opinion. The appropriate question is not whether this view of *Roe* is "dark." The appropriate question is whether this view of *Roe* is right. After all, many of the abolitionists had an angry view of the Constitution, calling it a "pact with the devil." Why did they hate our Constitution? Why did they hate the Supreme Court and its *Dred Scott* opinion? They hated these things because they hated slavery, that's why.

[200] It perhaps did not occur to Justice Blackmun that other people might not want him to stay on the Court "forever." His reference to immortality is his

Not surprisingly, a man who is that emotionally invested in the rightness of his opinion did not budge one inch. He refused to admit error in *Menillo*. Apparently he had forgotten that he had written a memo describing his own abortion rules as "arbitrary." (The rest of the Supreme Court was too polite--or too complicit-- to bring up the subject).

At the end of his career Justice Blackmun was still defending each and every part of *Roe*. He defended his first trimester point in *Webster*, and again in *Casey*. And of course this arbitrary rule ultimately had nothing to do with unborn babies. Justice Blackmun is insisting that we cannot protect the health and safety of pregnant women who are having surgeries.

What is feminist about that, exactly? How is the arbitrary stripping of any and all health regulations of an abortion clinic in the first trimester supposed to take women out of the dark ages?

What's tragic about all of this is that Harry Blackmun was very likely a nice man. And the other Justices who were deeply involved with the drafting of *Roe* were also nice people. William Brennan was nice. Thurgood Marshall was a hero.[201] And yet these three nice, liberal people were largely responsible for a set of rules that would lead to atrocities. For instance, even the supporters of *Roe* would call the *Carhart* abortions "brutal" and "horrifying" and "gruesome."[202] But the Supreme Court feels like they have to require even horrifying abortions, because of the rules laid down in *Roe v. Wade*.

---

own fervent wish. It brings to mind what Learned Hand once said about the Supreme Court. "For myself it would be most irksome to be ruled by a bevy of Platonic Guardians..." (Ironically, Justice Blackmun would cite Plato in several places in *Roe v. Wade*, perhaps not realizing that citing a pagan for the "viability" doctrine might not be a good idea).

[201] Marshall was the primary litigator in all the racial segregation cases, culminating in *Brown v. Board of Education*, 347 U.S. 483 (1954).

[202] *Stenberg v. Carhart*, 530 U.S. 914 (2000).

According to *The Brethren*, it was Justice Brennan who was responsible for the arbitrary idea that our Constitution protects a new right to abort pregnancies during the first trimester.[203]   And Justice Marshall was unhappy with this. He wanted to find a new rule allowing women to have abortions in the second trimester as well. So he suggested viability, which is a point late in the pregnancy. It was Marshall's December 12 memo that was the ultimate basis for the rules of *Roe v. Wade*.[204]

> Dear Harry: I am inclined to agree that drawing the line at viability accommodates the interest at stake better than drawing it at the end of the first trimester. Given the difficulties which many women may have in believing that they are pregnant and in deciding to seek an abortion, I fear that the earlier date may not in practice serve the interests of those women, which your opinion does seek to serve.

Obviously Marshall and Blackmun are not actually doing Constitutional law here. But aside from the procedural irregularities of what these two Justices are doing, as a substantive matter this discussion is really skimpy. The two men are both

---

[203] *Supra* note 156. Blackmun's original intention was to void the statute for vagueness, and ask Texas to write a new one.

[204] *Supra* note 189. Marshall's idea apparently came from one of his clerks, Mark Tushnet. *See* Jeffrey Rosen, "Court Marshall," *The New Republic* (June 21, 1993). After going through the Marshall archives at the Library of Congress, Rosen reports, "The *Roe v. Wade* file…includes a memo from Mark Tushnet, a Marshall clerk, urging the Justice to ask Harry Blackmun to draw the line for abortions at fetal viability, rather than the end of the first trimester." This is rather odd, a judicial clerk telling his boss to offer suggestions to another Justice about what his opinion should say. But of course many people feel strongly about abortion. Tushnet would later write a paper arguing that all cases should be decided by how they "advance the cause of socialism." *See* Mark Tushnet, "The Dilemmas of Liberal Constitutionalism," 42 Ohio State Law Journal 411 (1981).

ignoring the baby's development. (***Roe v. Wade*** would also ignore the baby's development). They are also ignoring any increase in health risks to women if doctors induce miscarriages later in the pregnancy. (***Roe v. Wade*** omits this discussion, too).

As the baby gets bigger, the health risks increase. Yet neither man is focused on any of the risks of moving the abortion point deep into the second trimester. Instead, in a rather patronizing fashion, the two men discuss the inability of women to grasp that they are pregnant, or to make a decision.

> At the same time, however, I share your concern for recognizing the State's interest in insuring that abortions be done under safe conditions. If the opinion stated explicitly that, between the end of the first trimester and viability, state regulations directed at health and safety alone were permissible, I believe that those concerns would be adequately met.

And that was the basis for ***Roe***. In the first trimester, abortion was to be free of interference by the state. In the second trimester, states could start protecting the safety and health of women. Once the baby was viable outside the uterus, states could start protecting the unborn child.

That is how the Supreme Court ranks the interests involved: abortion comes first, and second comes the health and safety of women, and the last concern is for the life of the unborn child.

The flaws of this approach are obvious. Abortion is the primary interest. Thus it is more important than the safety of women, and more important than the life of the unborn baby. This focus on the necessity of abortion in our society blinded the Court to the health risks to women from the surgery, as well as to the possibility of infanticide.

Indeed, the problem was not just "an abortion free of interference by the state" in the first trimester. The Court's pro-abortion emphasis would cause it to undercut any protections for the safety and health of women in the second trimester, too. And in a weird bit of jujitsu, Blackmun would flip the health of women around to allow for the abortion of viable babies for any medical purpose.[205] As long as health meant more abortions, the Supreme Court was all in favor of women's health.

The "stigma of unwed motherhood" would become a health consideration allowing for the abortion of a viable baby.[206] Any sort of psychological upset would qualify.[207] Handicapped children would routinely be killed in the third trimester.[208] And healthy children would be aborted, too.[209]

In *Planned Parenthood v. Casey*, the Supreme Court writes, "The woman's right to terminate her pregnancy before viability is the most central principle of *Roe v. Wade*."[210] We should not confuse

---

[205] What is the standard for aborting a baby in the 39th week? In *Doe v. Bolton*, Justice Blackmun writes, "the medical judgment may be exercised in the light of all factors--physical, emotional, psychological, familial, and the woman's age--relevant to the wellbeing of the patient." *Supra* note 38.

[206] *Supra* note 24 and text.

[207] Ronald Reagan, when he was governor of California, signed a bill allowing doctors to perform abortions if the "health" of the patient was at risk. The number of abortions performed in the state skyrocketed from 518 to 100,000 a year. *See* Paul Kengor & Patricia Clark Doerner, "Reagan's Darkest Hour," *National Review* (January 22, 2008).

[208] *Gonzales v. Carhart* describes the killing of a baby in the third trimester. 550 U.S. 124 (2007). The child had Down's syndrome.

[209] Killing a baby in the third trimester is incredibly dangerous to women. Despite this risk, Dr. Hern has announced that all abortions qualify as "health" abortions. "I perform many abortions as late as the 26th week, and some as late as the 34th week." Warren Hern, "Did I Violate the Partial-Birth Abortion Ban?" *Slate* (October 22, 2003).

[210] *Supra* note 7.

this assertion with the idea that *Roe* recognizes the humanity of viable infants, or that their lives are protected in abortion clinics. *Roe* denies the humanity of the unborn until birth, and they have no constitutional protections. And note also that the right to abortion "is the most central principle of *Roe v. Wade*," outweighing even the woman's own safety and health.

Casey was an attempt to fix *Roe*'s disregard for the health of women. In *Planned Parenthood v. Casey*, the Supreme Court would finally overrule its doctrine of an "abortion free of interference by the state." 19 years after *Roe*, the Supreme Court finally recognized the health of women as an important state interest throughout the pregnancy.

But in many ways, *Casey* would be too late. *Roe* had already divided our country over the subject of abortion. *Casey*'s attempt to moderate the opinion, and normalize abortion so that it is treated like every other medical practice, failed utterly to resolve the fight.

For instance, *Planned Parenthood v. Casey* came out of a lawsuit in Pennsylvania. After the Supreme Court's ruling in *Casey*, the state of Pennsylvania was finally given explicit authority to do health inspections in abortion clinics, and to regulate abortion doctors to protect the safety of women. And what happened?

Pro-choice people in the state government would refuse to do any health inspections in abortion clinics. Pro-choice people in the media would refuse to warn women about any possible dangers from inducing a miscarriage. One abortion clinic, the Women's Medical Society, had no health inspections for 17 years. The result was a disaster for the many women who went to see Dr. Kermit Gosnell.[211]

---

[211] The murder trial of Dr. Gosnell is recounted in chapter 19. His indictment gives us an idea what an abortion "free of interference by the state" looks like:

All of this is in the future, however. In 1973, the Supreme Court was quite happy with *Roe v. Wade*. Why wouldn't they be happy? It was a major advance in the cause of socialism.[212] Poor women had a new right to abort pregnancies, and escape the cancer of poverty.[213] The Supreme Court was proud of its work.

"The clinic reeked of animal urine, courtesy of the cats that were allowed to roam (and defecate) freely. Furniture and blankets were stained with blood. Instruments were not properly sterilized. Disposable medical supplies were not disposed of; they were reused, over and over again. Medical equipment--such as the defibrillator, the EKG, the pulse oximeter, the blood pressure cuff--was generally broken..." The district attorney's office keeps the indictment online. www.phila.gov/districtattorney/pdfs/grandjurywomensmedical.pdf.

[212] *Supra* note 204.

[213] *Supra* note 28.

Chapter 6

In 1996, President Bill Clinton gave a speech and he said, "Abortion should not only be safe and legal, it should be rare."[214]

That's an interesting comment. Why should abortion be rare? And if abortion becomes rare, what would that mean for all the abortion doctors and nurses who work in this industry? Imagine if Bill Clinton gave a speech to abortion providers and he said, "I want most of you to lose all your revenues and go out of business."

It's a weird way to talk to a billion-dollar industry, is it not? Planned Parenthood is a billion-dollar-a-year "non-profit."[215] It's the largest abortion provider, and yet it represents only slightly more than 30% of the abortion industry.[216]

It's hard to know with specificity how much money is being made in abortion services. IBISWorld estimates the size of the family planning and abortion clinic market to be $2 billion a year.[217] Yet

---

[214] Clinton was in the midst of his re-election campaign. The "rare" word would make its way into the Democrat platform in 1996, 2000, and 2004. It would disappear in 2008, as the party shifted to the left.

[215] Actually the number is $1.2 billion. www.plannedparenthood.org (annual report 2012-2013). The largest abortion provider in the world is also rather secretive about its business model. In a pie chart we are told that abortion is only 3% of its services. *See* Rachael Larimore, "The Most Meaningless Abortion Statistic Ever," *Slate* (May 7, 2013). What we are not told is how much of Planned Parenthood's money comes from abortion. Why this secrecy? And note how journalists simply repeat what Planned Parenthood tells them. *See* Ezra Klein, "What Planned Parenthood Does, In One Chart," *The Washington Post* (February 2, 2012).

[216] Planned Parenthood reports 327,166 abortions in 2012. *Id.* The national number for abortions in 2012 is estimated to be 1.04 million. *See* "U.S. Abortion Statistics," www.abort73.com.

[217] *Supra* note 41. An abortion can cost anywhere from $400 to $2000, with the price increasing later in the pregnancy. *See* www.fpawomenshealth.com.

here is Bill Clinton, hoping these abortion clinics will lose all this money.

Why is he talking this way? Obviously, it's because abortion is a weird industry, an industry that used to be a crime. Abortion is still forbidden by the Hippocratic Oath, many hospitals do not allow for elective abortions, and many people think you are killing a baby when you perform this surgery.

Bill Clinton is attempting to stake out a moderate position on abortion, or at least sound moderate on the issue. Clinton is said to be a master of triangulation.[218] His speech is a fine example of it. He wants to protect the abortion industry ("legal"), while simultaneously attacking the abortion industry ("rare"). He is distancing himself from the practice of abortion while promising that the surgery will be safe for any woman who has one.

Of course, all our abortion rules are actually mandated by federal judges, not by our elected representatives. Still, if President Clinton meant what he said, he would nominate judges to the courts like Sandra Day O'Connor. In **Planned Parenthood v. Casey**, Justice O'Connor upholds **Roe v. Wade**, and a woman's right to choose.[219] But she also upholds safety regulations designed to protect women from the dangers of the surgery. O'Connor's focus is on protecting the safety of women. She's not interested in protecting abortion clinics and their revenue streams.

Bill Clinton would nominate Ruth Bader Ginsburg and Stephen Breyer to the Supreme Court. Are they pro-abortion radicals in the style of **Roe**? Or will they allow states to protect the health of pregnant women, like Justice O'Connor? We will know the answer if they uphold any abortion regulations.

---

[218] Dick Morris was running the Clinton campaign in 1996, and triangulation was his idea. **See** "Triangulation Saves Bill Clinton!" www.dickmorris.com.
[219] **Supra** note 7.

For instance, many states are now requiring abortion doctors to have admitting privileges in a hospital.[220] If you think abortion should be "safe, legal and rare," you can't possibly object to this. It's a simple health regulation. Another type of safety regulation is requiring that second or third trimester abortions take place in hospitals, or that an abortion clinic meets the simple standard of a surgery center. Dr. Hern, in his book *Abortion Practice*, suggests that every abortion clinic should be located "within 5 minutes of a full-service hospital."[221] Why? He wants to protect the health and safety of the woman having the surgery.

Yet many judges want to strike down this sort of health regulation. This is how we might distinguish a pro-choice jurist (as in *Casey*) from a pro-abortion jurist (as in *Roe*). Both judges are denying the unborn child's humanity. But the *Casey* judge will allow abortion regulations that protect the health and safety of women. The *Roe* judge says we're not allowed to do that.

A pro-abortion judge does not want abortion to be "rare," and assumes as a matter of course that abortion is always safe. Pro-abortion judges can be counted on to strike down health and safety regulations that protect women. They seek to make abortion as widely available as possible, and as cheap as possible, so that poor women can have abortions, too. Indeed, pro-abortion people really want the poor to have abortions.

We can see what a pro-abortion mindset is like by going back to the days when the Supreme Court first passed *Roe v. Wade*. Some people were very excited about this new right to abortion,

---

[220] 11 states now mandate that abortion doctors have hospital privileges. Sarah Kliff, "Admitting Privileges: the New Abortion Battle, Explained," *Vox* (August 12, 2014). Many abortion doctors do not have hospital privileges. *See* Dr. Susan Berry, "Record 87 Surgical Abortion Clinic Closures in 2013," *Breitbart.com* (December 30, 2013).
[221] *Supra* note 42.

how easy and safe it was. In December, 1973, Jane Brody of the *New York Times* ran a story about a "Lunch Hour Abortion."[222] The reporter stressed how cheap this new surgery was. "It is now available in 45 states at a maximum cost of $50."

The Lunch Hour Abortion was also called a "mini-abortion" or menstrual regulation. Its inventor, Harvey Karman, had simply replaced the metal curette that surgeons used with a plastic one. According to the *Times*, "The essence of menstrual regulation is the use of a narrow, flexible plastic suction curette..."[223]

Karman's hope was that women would use his $50 plastic device to abort themselves.[224]

The *New York Times* article quotes some of the participants in the First International Conference on Menstrual Regulation. Apparently the advantage of the Lunch Hour Abortion was that it was simple, cheap, rapid, and could be performed by non-doctors. "It is something that we will be able to bring practically to the rice paddy," said a doctor from the Philippines.[225]

In many ways, Harvey Karman was the face of abortion in the 1970's. "Harvey Karman did more for safe abortion around the world than practically any other person in the world," said Dr. Malcolm Potts, who is the chair of Population and Family Planning at UC Berkeley. "Karman's name is not known, yet his

---

[222] Jane Brody, "Physicians Study Abortion Method," reprinted in the *Lakeland Ledger* (December 25, 1973).

[223] *Id*. The flexible curette was considered a breakthrough because the metal curette did horrible damages to women.

[224] *See* Elaine Woo, "Creator of Device for Safer Abortions," *The Los Angeles Times* (May 18, 2008). "His ultimate goal...was to make it possible for women to safely do their own abortions using the simplest possible equipment."

[225] *Supra* note 222.

ingenuity and to some extent his courage has made safe abortion available to literally millions of women around the world."[226]

Other abortion supporters are far more critical. Carol Downer, an abortion provider and co-founder of Feminist Women's Health Clinics, was taught how to perform abortions by Karman over 40 years ago. Yet she is also highly critical of him. "Harvey engaged in some very irresponsible experimentation on women's bodies," she told a reporter for the *Los Angeles Times*.[227] And that's putting it mildly.

Karman was not a doctor, and had no surgical training. Yet he performed abortions on women without hesitation. In 1955 he performed an illegal abortion on a pregnant woman in a motel room, using a speculum and a nutcracker. She died.[228]

Karman spent two and a half years in prison for killing this woman. In fact, Karman was arrested for nine felonies during this period, most of them abortion-related.[229] When abortion was legalized in California in 1967, Karman--still not a doctor--trained physicians and non-physicians alike on how to induce miscarriages in pregnant women.

In 1972 Karman started working on late-term abortions. He developed a cheap abortion device known as the "Super Coil." In a bizarre publicity stunt, Karman had a busload of poor pregnant women driven from Chicago to Philadelphia so they could have their abortions on Mother's Day.[230] These abortions were to be

[226] *Supra* note 224.
[227] *Id*.
[228] Michelle Goldberg, "How Abortion Changed the World," *Salon* (April 10, 2009).
[229] Christine Dunigan, "Somebody Wanted Harvey Karman, That Rogue Abortionist From the Past," *Real Choice* (February 9, 2006).
[230] *Id.* Karman invited a film crew to televise the event.

performed by Dr. Kermit Gosnell, assisted by Karman, who was using his new Super Coil technique.

Dr. Gosnell would later make headlines across the country for murdering newborns in his abortion clinic. But apparently these abortions that he performed in 1972 were so ghastly, the surgeries actually came up in testimony during his murder indictment 40 years later.[231]

At Gosnell's grand jury indictment, Randy Hutchins--who participated in many abortions with Gosnell--described how the Super Coil worked. "(T)here was a device that he and (Karman) were working on that was supposed to be plastic--basically plastic razors that were formed into a ball." The plastic razors were coated with a gel so the contraption would remain closed. Then it was inserted into the uterus of all 15 pregnant women who had bused in from Chicago. "(A)fter several hours of body temperature, it would then--the gel would melt and these things would spring open, supposedly cutting up the fetus, and the fetus would be expelled."[232]

After the Super Coil went to work, nine of the 15 women had medical complications. Three of those were major complications, two required surgery, and one woman had to have her uterus removed. The press referred to the fiasco as the Mother's Day Massacre.

Another notorious late-term abortion procedure used in the 1970's, and a favorite technique of illegal abortionists around the world, is saline amniocentesis.[233] It too is a highly dangerous type of abortion for women.

---

[231] *See* Matt Purple, "Gosnell and the Super Coil," *The American Spectator* (April 19, 2013).
[232] *Id*.
[233] The movie *4 Months, 3 Weeks, and 2 Days* (2007), is about an illegal abortion in Romania. It's a chemical abortion, although it's unclear if it's

In 1976, in **Planned Parenthood v. Danforth**, the Supreme Court is confronted with a Missouri statute that outlaws saline amniocentesis.[234] The state is outlawing this elective surgery because it harms and sometimes kills women. Indeed, now in the 21st century it is hard to find an abortion doctor in the United States who performs saline amniocentesis. That is because it harms and sometimes kills women.

Here are some of the known medical risks to a woman who undergoes a saline abortion. It may cause uncontrolled blood clotting throughout the woman's body, with a risk of severe hemorrhage.[235] Seizures, coma, or death may also result from saline accidentally injected into the mother's vascular system.[236] An article in the Journal of the American Medical Association noted that saline amniocentesis "has the highest fatality rate of any elective surgical technique, second only to cardiac transplantation."[237]

In **Roe v. Wade** the Supreme Court said that states could start protecting the health and safety of women in the second trimester. So in 1976, Missouri is trying to do that. They are outlawing a dangerous late-term abortion procedure in order to protect the health and safety of women.

Danforth was decided in 1976, six months after the Court had to write **Menillo** and affirm that it was okay to criminalize non-doctors for aborting women. That screw-up should have

---

saline or some other chemical. Non-doctors prefer this method because they do not have to operate.

[234] Supra note 104.

[235] Dr. David Halbert, et al, "Consumptive Coagulopathy With Generalized Hemorrhage After Hypertonic Saline-Induce Abortion: A Case Report," **Obstetrics & Gynecology** (January, 1972).

[236] Gary Berger, **Second Trimester Abortion** (1981).

[237] Dr. Norman Kaplan, "Hazard of Saline Abortion," **The Journal of the American Medical Association,"** (July 3, 1972).

indicated to some of the Justices that perhaps they went too far in **Roe**. **Danforth** was the Court's opportunity to fix **Roe**, and say that states could always protect the health and safety of people.

Or the Supreme Court could simply affirm what it had said in **Roe**, and say that states could indeed protect the health and safety of pregnant women starting in the second trimester.

But the Supreme Court had other ideas. They wanted to protect abortion in the second trimester. That idea came first. As the Court writes, "Appellants challenge this provision on the ground that it operates to preclude virtually all abortions after the first trimester. This is so, it is claimed, because a substantial percentage, in the neighborhood of 70% according to the testimony, of all abortions performed in the United States after the first trimester are effected through the procedure of saline amniocentesis."[238]

Thus the Supreme Court ruled in **Danforth** that saline amniocentesis is a constitutional right, regardless of how risky the surgery is. The Court's determination to protect abortion, no matter what, meant that the health and safety of women was a secondary concern.

In **Roe** the Supreme Court said "until the end of the first trimester mortality in abortion may be less than mortality in normal childbirth."[239] This claim that abortion may be safer than childbirth would become a dogmatic assertion by the Supreme Court: abortion is always safer than childbirth. Even induced miscarriages in the second or third trimester are said to be safer than the birth of a child.

---

[238] *Supra* note 104.
[239] *Supra* note 1.

Danforth flatly declares, "the mortality rate for normal childbirth exceeds that where saline amniocentesis is employed."[240] The Supreme Court is relying upon the trial court for its medical findings. Apparently the district court ruled that the mortality rate for normal childbirth is higher than the mortality rate for a saline amniocentesis abortion. But this is absurd. Recall that the "mortality rate" involves reported fatalities that are passively collected by the CDC from state health authorities. Apparently the *Danforth* Court is now requiring that the words "saline amniocentesis" somehow make it into the death certificate. Are we expected to believe that the name of the actual abortion procedure used by the doctor is listed as a cause of death?

This assumption by non-doctors that saline amniocentesis is safer than birth is really suspicious once we realize that this abortion results in a birth. Saline amniocentesis is a late-term abortion procedure that involves injecting high doses of salt into a pregnant woman's uterus. The salt burns the skin off the baby inside the womb, and a few days later the mother gives birth to a corpse.

What makes the *Danforth* opinion particularly awful is that the Supreme Court apparently has no idea that saline amniocentesis causes the mom to go into labor and give birth. How can you say that saline amniocentesis is safer than birth when the abortion procedure itself causes the mom to go into labor and give birth? Apparently the Supreme Court is saying that it is safer for a mother to give birth to a scalded dead baby than to give birth to a live one. Injecting high doses of salt into your uterus is safer than not injecting high doses of salt into your uterus.

Justice White, dissenting in *Danforth*, warned the Supreme Court that they were recklessly endangering the lives of pregnant women when the Court overruled state health officials. "The

---

[240] *Supra* note 104.

record of trial discloses that use of the saline method exposes a woman to the danger of severe complications regardless of the skill of the physicians or the precaution taken. Saline may cause one or more of the following conditions: disseminated intravascular coagulation or consumptive coagulopathy (disruption of the blood-clotting mechanism), which may result in severe bleeding and possible death; hypernatremia (increase in blood sodium level), which may lead to convulsions and death; and water intoxication (accumulated water in the body tissue which may occur when oxytoxin is used in conjunction with the injection of saline), resulting in damage to the central nervous system or death. There is also evidence that saline amniocentesis causes massive tissue destruction to the inside of the uterus."[241]

By the late 1970's, abortion doctors largely stopped doing saline amniocentesis in the USA, because of all the dangers to women (and the lawsuits). By 1983, even the non-doctors on the Supreme Court finally realized that saline amniocentesis is a risky medical procedure. Out of the blue, in *Simopoulos v. Virginia*, the Supreme Court sent a doctor to prison for doing a saline amniocentesis abortion on a patient outside a hospital.[242]

What happened to *Danforth* and the claim that saline amniocentesis is a constitutional right? Down the memory hole![243]

Here are the facts of *Simopoulos*:

> Appellant is a practicing obstetrician-gynecologist certified by the American Board of Obstetrics and Gynecology. In November, 1979, he practiced at his office in Woodbridge, Virginia, at four

---

[241] *Id.*

[242] 462 U.S. 506 (1983).

[243] A reference to *1984*, by George Orwell. *See also* note 378.

local hospitals, and at his clinic in Falls Church, Virginia. The Falls Church clinic has an operating room and facilities for resuscitation and emergency treatment of cardiac/respiratory arrest. Replacement and stabilization fluids are on hand. Appellant customarily performs first trimester abortions at his clinic. During the time relevant to this case, the clinic was not licensed, nor had appellant sought any license for it.

P.M. was a 17-year-old high-school student when she went to appellant's clinic on November 8, 1979. She was unmarried, and told appellant that she was approximately 22 weeks pregnant. She requested an abortion but did not want her parents to know. Examinations by appellant confirmed that P.M. was five months pregnant, well into the second trimester. Appellant testified that he encouraged her to confer with her parents and discussed with her the alternative of continuing the pregnancy to term. She did return home, but never advised her parents of her decision.

Two days later, P.M. returned to the clinic with her boyfriend. The abortion was performed by an injection of saline solution. P.M. told appellant that she planned to deliver the fetus in a motel, and understood him to agree to this course. Appellant gave P.M. a prescription for an analgesic and a "Post-Injection Information" sheet that stated that she had undergone "a surgical procedure" and warned of a "wide range of normal reactions." The sheet also advised that she call the

> physician if "heavy" bleeding began.
> Although P.M. did not recall being
> advised to go to a hospital when labor
> began, this was included on the
> instruction sheet.
>
> P.M. went to a motel. Alone, she
> aborted her fetus in the motel
> bathroom 48 hours after the saline
> injection. She left the fetus, follow-up
> instructions, and pain medication in
> the wastebasket at the motel. Her
> boyfriend took her home. Police found
> the fetus later that day and began an
> investigation.

Obviously pro-lifers want to outlaw this. But why is the Supreme Court sending this abortionist to prison?

It might be a little unfair to blame the doctor for the girl's decision to go to a motel. After all, he can't force his patient to go to a hospital. Nor can he force her to stay in his clinic. A saline abortion might take hours or even days to complete. This one took a couple of days. And remember, the Supreme Court has already said, in *Danforth*, that saline amniocentesis is a constitutional right.

Yet even the author of *Roe*, Justice Blackmun, is calling this doctor a criminal. Other *Roe* jurists, like Justice Brennan and Justice Marshall, also think this is a crime. John Paul Stevens is the only Justice who wants to release him. But the usual *Roe* supporters have nothing nice to say about Dr. Simopoulos.

This is rather surprising. Yes, Dr. Simopoulos is performing a dangerous abortion procedure, and it's outside a hospital. But abortion doctors do that all the time. And in *Danforth* the Supreme Court has already said that saline amniocentesis is safer than birth. In *Akron v. Akron Center for Reproductive Health*--

decided the same day as *Simopoulos*--the Supreme Court said it was a constitutional right for abortion doctors to stay out of hospitals, even when doing a dangerous late-term abortion.[244]

Why, then, is Dr. Simopoulos going to prison? Note that Dr. Simopoulos, unlike most abortion doctors, actually had hospital privileges.[245] Presumably he could have done this surgery in a hospital if he wanted to. Perhaps he did the abortion in his clinic in order to make it cheap, so the high school student could afford it. Isn't that what the Supreme Court wants, to expand abortion access to the poor? That's what Dr. Simopoulos is doing.

It's actually quite unfair to Dr. Simopoulos for the Supreme Court to change its abortion rules after the fact. In *Danforth* the Supreme Court insists that saline amniocentesis is safer than birth.[246] Well, imagine if P.M. had made her other choice. What if the doctor had simply induced labor so that she would give birth to her baby? Would the Supreme Court insist that the obstetrician go to prison then?

Why did the Supreme Court subvert the right to abortion in this case?

One possibility is that our Supreme Court was embarrassed by what this abortion doctor did. It appears from the recitation of facts in *Simopoulos* that the Supreme Court is actually upset. They are not at all happy that this high school student gave birth to a dead scalded baby in a motel room, and left the baby's carcass in a trash can.

Maybe the Supreme Court in *Simopoulos* is actually concerned about the health of this young girl in a motel room, finishing off

---

[244] 462 U.S. 416 (1983).
[245] *Supra* note 242.
[246] *Supra* note 104.

an abortion by herself. Or perhaps the Supreme Court is embarrassed that the police were called.

This abortion looks bad, and it's very public.

Perhaps the Supreme Court has abandoned Dr. Simopoulos, and *Danforth*, because they are embarrassed and chagrined at all the publicity this abortion is causing. The Supreme Court does not want dead babies ending up in motel room bathrooms. It looks bad for the Supreme Court and their prestige. They want abortion, and the results of abortion, to be private, to be hidden. They do not want police investigations and newspaper headlines.

The Court can't really admit to a mistake in any of its abortion opinions. The stakes are too high. A mistake implies that babies, or women, might have died because of Supreme Court sloppiness. Presumably this is why the *Simopoulos* Court does not mention *Danforth*, or its mistaken assertion that this quite dangerous abortion is safer than birth. In the context of abortion, the Supreme Court really can't say "oops."

So perhaps that's what the Court is doing. They are secretly trying to protect the health of women. So on the same day that *Simopoulos* was issued, the Court upheld the constitutionality of a new late-term abortion procedure, dilation and evacuation (or "D&E"), in *Akron v. Akron Center for Reproductive Health*.[247]

Saline amniocentesis is out, D&E is in.

Maybe the Supreme Court, like a national health board, is trying to nudge the entire abortion industry away from dangerous saline abortions, and move all the abortion doctors to this new surgery, the D&E, instead.

---

[247] *Supra* note 244.

And that's pretty much what happened. Abortion doctors stopped doing saline amniocentesis, and started doing the D&E.[248] After all, if you are an abortion doctor and you do a saline abortion after 1983, you might join Dr. Simopoulos in prison.

A dead baby in a motel room bathroom is entirely predictable from the very nature of a saline abortion. It causes a woman to give birth to a scalded baby many hours after the procedure. The Supreme Court in *Danforth* might have realized all this if they had done some factual research before they claimed that our Constitution protects a right for doctors to inject salt into the uterus of pregnant women in violation of state health authorities.

In *Akron*, the Supreme Court actually repeats the mistake it made in *Danforth*. In *Akron* the Court strikes down a hospital requirement for another late-term procedure, the D&E abortion.[249] Like it did in *Danforth*, the Supreme Court does not bother to describe the surgery or talk about any health risks to the patient. So a reader of the opinion has no idea why Ohio thinks this surgery should only be done in a hospital.

Instead of talking about the safety of the patient, the pro-abortion jurists on the Supreme Court are focused on cutting costs. The emphasis in *Akron* is on money. The *Akron* Court wants to make late-term abortion as cheap as possible.

"A primary burden created by the requirement is additional cost to the woman. The Court of Appeals noted that there was testimony that a second trimester abortion costs more than twice

---

[248] As Justice Breyer writes, "In the early 1970's, inducing labor through the injection of saline into the uterus was the predominant method of second trimester abortion. Today, however, the medical profession has switched from medical induction of labor to surgical procedures..." *Supra* note 202. The Supreme Court does not mention how it sent Dr. Simopoulos to prison for performing a saline abortion outside a hospital, or how involved the Supreme Court was in this shift in abortion practice.
[249] *Supra* note 244.

as much in a hospital as in a clinic. (An) in-hospital abortion costs $850-$900, whereas a dilation-and-evacuation (D&E) abortion performed in a clinic costs $350-$400."[250]

Obviously a clinic is cheaper than a hospital. And a hospital is safer than a clinic. The city of Akron is trying to protect and guard the safety of women who are undergoing a dangerous late-term abortion. Yet the Supreme Court strikes down this health regulation, saying our Constitution requires cheaper and not-as-safe abortions.

In the first two decades after *Roe*, the Supreme Court would often assume that abortion is safe and healthy. So the Court feels no need to discuss the abortion surgery or learn anything about it. In *Akron* the Supreme Court is talking about a new late-term abortion procedure, the D&E. This abortion procedure is quickly replacing the dangerous saline amniocentesis abortion in clinics around the country.

Wait a second, why are we replacing saline amniocentesis? You said saline abortions are safe. It's not safe?

The non-doctors on the Supreme Court, who failed to discuss the risks of saline amniocentesis in *Danforth*, now fail to discuss any health risks with the D&E procedure in *Akron*. Instead the Supreme Court is upset about the cost of a hospital visit. Can't we do it in a clinic? The Justices prefer a $350-$400 late-term abortion for women. That's the price they want.

And so our Supreme Court, this unelected, unofficial national health board of non-doctors, strikes down a hospital requirement for D&E abortions. And these lawyers are making this ruling without the slightest bit of discussion about the difficulties of the

---

[250] *Id.*

D&E, or why Ohio health officials might be requiring a hospital visit.

Where in the Constitution is the clause that says abortion has to be as cheap as possible? And if you are deregulating the abortion industry and tossing out safety regulations to save money, isn't that dangerous to people?

Of course our society makes all sorts of trade-offs between safety and costs. But when the Supreme Court in *Akron* says that our abortion rule has to be cheaper, and cannot be safer, then it is mandating a society where the abortion industry comes first, and the safety and health of women is a secondary concern.[251]

After all, the D&E is invasive medical surgery. Maybe there actually are risks to people when a doctor is carving into you with a knife.[252] And there is simply no discussion in *Akron* about any possible medical risks involved with this surgery. Indeed, while the Supreme Court is over-turning a safety regulation, it does not

---

[251] It is indeed *Lochner* all over again. *Supra* note 114. Indeed, it would not be difficult for a law student to rewrite *Lochner* and uphold the case under modern Supreme Court jurisprudence. You just declare the creation of bread is a fundamental right of humanity. Of course we have a right to bake bread! (Can the police invade the sanctity of our kitchens?) And you ignore economics entirely as you strike down the regulations. Or, like the *Akron* Court, you might do some back-of-the-napkin analysis in regard to how safety regulations cost money, and deprive the poor of bread.

[252] The year after *Akron*, Dr. Raymond Showery was charged with manslaughter in the death of Mickey Apodaca, a mother of four. Dr. Showery was performing an abortion in the 19th week of pregnancy. He accidentally tore a hole in her uterus, severed an artery, and his patient bled to death. Prosecutors charged Dr. Showery with a felony on the grounds that he had inadequately trained his staff, failed to properly treat the wound, and delayed transfer to a hospital. Dr. Showery refused to provide his patient's medical records to the grand jury on grounds that they might incriminate him. (And note that Showery botched this abortion while he was out on bail for murder for killing a newborn). *See* "Raymond Showery," *ClinicQuotes* (August 30, 2012); "Raymond Showery," www.kermitgosnellcrimes.wikispaces.com; "Raymond Showery," www.cemetaryofchoice.wikispaces.com; Richard Haitch, "Abortion Sequel 2," *The New York Times* (April 29, 1984).

even bother to describe what happens in the surgery that is being deregulated.

The Supreme Court would not bother to describe a D&E abortion until the 21st century. Finally, in ***Stenberg v. Carhart***, the Supreme Court describes this abortion. "D&E involves dilation of the cervix; removal of at least some fetal tissue using nonvacuum instruments; and (after the 15th week) the potential need for instrumental disarticulation or dismemberment of the fetus or the collapse of the fetal parts to facilitate evacuation from the uterus."[253]

And finally, 27 years after ***Roe*** found a right to "an abortion free of interference by the state," and 17 years after ***Akron*** struck down a hospital requirement, the Supreme Court in ***Carhart*** lists some of the health risks to a woman who undergoes a D&E abortion:

"sharp bone fragments passing through the cervix"
"uterine perforations caused by (the doctor's) instruments"
"infection-causing fetal and placental tissue in the uterus"
"potentially fatal absorption of fetal tissue into the (bloodstream)"

In retrospect, then, it's rather awful that the ***Akron*** Court did not discuss any of these risks when they said it was unconstitutional for a state to require that this surgery happen in a hospital.

Why is the Supreme Court listing all the health risks of the D&E in ***Carhart***? Because now the Court has to explain why abortion doctors have stopped doing the D&E. 27 years after ***Roe v. Wade***, the abortion industry has adopted a radical abortion practice that involves inducing the birth of the baby.

---

[253] ***Supra*** note 202.

Justice Breyer's opinion in **Carhart** is in regard to the notorious late-term abortion procedure many people call "partial-birth abortion."[254] In this procedure, a doctor pulls a child halfway outside the birth canal, and then stabs her to death. Obviously this upsets a lot of people.[255] When a baby is born, we can see the baby. You are no longer aborting a "fetus," but a child in the process of birth. The baby is no longer unseen, but seen. You are killing the baby in front of our eyes.

Pro-lifers say this is murder. But what should not be overshadowed by this murder accusation are the health implications for women in the Supreme Court's pro-abortion jurisprudence. The Supreme Court has been insisting for 40 years that abortion is safer than birth. Over and over they have said this.

In **Danforth** the Supreme Court said saline amniocentesis was safer than birth. They implicitly admitted this was a mistake in **Simopoulos**, when they sent an abortion doctor to prison for doing a saline abortion outside a hospital.

In **Akron** they said D&E was safer than birth. D&E was so safe we couldn't even require a hospital visit. And now in **Carhart** we discover that many abortion doctors have stopped doing the D&E. Why? They were being sued.[256] D&E is a dangerous abortion procedure, and women are sometimes injured by it. Just like Ohio said!

Why are these abortion doctors inducing birth in order to kill the child? Obviously, they want to abort the child, and they want to

---

[254] Abortionists prefer the term "D&X" or "intact D&E."

[255] "We all wish it was formless, but it's not…and it's painful. There is a lot of emotional pain." Mary Meehan, "The Ex-Abortionists--They Have Confronted Reality," **The Washington Post** (April 1, 1988).

[256] Dr. Kermit Gosnell, for instance, stopped doing D&E abortions after he accidentally killed Semika Shaw with that procedure. **See** note 698 and text.

do so in the safest possible way for the mother. These doctors feel that killing a baby during birth is safer for the mother than aborting the baby inside the uterus.[257] Abortion doctors are in the business of making babies disappear. If you want to protect the mother's safety, you do not perform a D&E and run the risk of leaving baby parts in the uterus. And you certainly do not inject dangerous amounts of saline into her body.

You induce birth. Birth is safer than abortion at this stage.[258] You deliver the baby.

Of course, as pro-lifers point out, killing the child is medically unnecessary.[259] Once you start inducing birth, there is no ethical reason why the baby should be killed. A Caesarean section aborts the pregnancy just as well as any killing procedure, and has the

---

[257] Many doctors, including abortion doctors, argue this point. "I would dispute any statement that this is the safest procedure to use," Dr. Hern said. In particular, turning the baby around in the uterus is "potentially dangerous." You might cause "amniotic fluid embolism or placental abruption if you do that." Dr. Pamela Smith, the director of medical education in obstetrics at Mt. Sinai Hospital, adds two more dangers: you might damage the cervix when you forcibly dilate it for three days, and rotating the baby might cause a uterine rupture. *See* Diane Gianelli, "Outlawing Abortion Method," *American Medical News* (November 20, 1995).

[258] *See* Julie Rovner, "Obstetricians Challenge Partial-Birth Abortion Ban," *All Things Considered*, www.npr.com. Rovner quotes an abortionist, Dr. Steve Chabot. (One of the weird aspects of abortion politics is how abortionists hate to be called "abortionist," preferring the term "obstetrician"). Dr. Chabot states his belief that the D&X surgery is safer than D&E. And of course many abortion doctors feel that way, which is precisely why the D&X replaced the D&E in many clinics. What they don't talk about is why D&X is safer. It's birth that makes it safer.

[259] What is the health benefit to mom when you deliver a dead baby, as opposed to a live one? This is the real objection that obstetricians have to partial-birth abortion. The argument that the baby needs to die is a lie, in the vast majority of cases. In any event the criminal statutes allow for doctors to make that defense. For instance, the federal partial-birth abortion ban reads, "A defendant accused of an offense under this section may seek a hearing before the State Medical Board on whether the physician's conduct was necessary to save the life of the mother whose life was endangered by a physical disorder, physical illness, or physical injury, including a life-endangering physical condition caused by or arising from the pregnancy itself."

added benefit of keeping the baby alive.[260] It's quite dishonest for abortion supporters to say that homicide is medically necessary in these cases.[261]

Aside from the morality of killing a baby, why is birth the best mechanism for doing so? Isn't birth supposed to be incredibly risky to women? The Supreme Court has been telling us this for 40 years. And now we know for sure the Court's social science is bad.[262] We know it's bad, because abortion doctors themselves started inducing birth in order to avoid the health risks of an abortion inside the uterus.

---

[260] Even if there's a genetic issue with the baby, partial-birth abortion is an unnecessary surgery. "We, and many other doctors across the United States, regularly treat women whose unborn children suffer these and other serious conditions. Never is the partial-birth procedure medically indicated. Rather, such infants are regularly and safely delivered live, vaginally, with no threat to the mother's health or fertility. Sometimes, as with hydrocephalus, it is first necessary to drain some of the fluid from the baby's head. And in some cases, a cesarean section is indicated. In no case is it medically necessary to partly deliver the child vaginally, and then terminate his or her life before completing the delivery." Physicians' Ad Hock Coalition for Truth (PHACT), a coalition of more than 230 physicians, mostly professors and other specialists in obstetrics, gynecology, and fetal medicine. (In particular this coalition was upset at an ACOG statement that was actually written by the Clinton White House). *See* note 633 and text.

[261] *See* notes 632-633 and text.

[262] *Supra* note 39 and text.

Chapter 7

Partial-birth abortion shocks us, because the procedure implicates murder. The baby is outside the birth canal, we see the homicide, and we are upset. Yet some pro-abortion minds have been advocating the killing of newborns for quite some time.

One pro-abortion intellect is Peter Singer, who teaches at Princeton University and is the head of its bioethics department. As he writes in 1979, "Human babies are not born self-aware, or capable of grasping that they exist over time. They are not persons…"[263] After defining a newborn infant as sub-human property, Singer goes on to argue, "the life of a newborn is of less value than the life of a pig, a dog, or a chimpanzee."[264]

As in Justice Blackmun's *Beal* dissent, we see a valuation going on here, an economic argument that reminds people of socialism.[265] Singer values animal life quite highly--he is a notable fighter for animal rights--and is engaging in a cost/benefit analysis, comparing a newborn baby to an adult animal. And he's suggesting that parents have a right to kill any child if they are unhappy with their baby.

---

[263] Peter Singer, *Practical Ethics* (1979).
[264] *Id*.
[265] One of the minds behind Obamacare apparently believes that people over 75 should die. *See* Ezekiel Emanuel, "Why I Hope To Die At 75," *The Atlantic* (October, 2014). "Dying at 75 will not be a tragedy." Note that the Supreme Court (who currently has four people over the age of 75) has been far more vigilant about protecting the old than protecting the young. *See Washington v. Glucksberg*, 521 U.S. 702 (1997).

In 1993, Singer suggests that no newborn should be considered a person until 30 days after birth.[266] He also says that the attending physician should kill disabled babies on the spot.[267]

Singer's views are shocking and upsetting to both pro-life and pro-choice people. Pro-choice people respect a woman's autonomy, but killing newborns? Once a baby is born, the vast majority of pro-choice people are now pro-life people. Dr. Kermit Gosnell found this out when he was convicted of murder for killing newborns in his abortion clinic.[268]

Yet despite the shocking nature of what Peter Singer is advocating, it should give us pause that he has been given a highly prestigious job at an Ivy League university. And he was given this job in order to teach and instruct young minds.

Note that in most cases, Professor Singer is backing away from a state-run solution. He does not advocate that the state kidnap young healthy children from their parents and murder them. He recognizes the autonomy of parents. It is up to mom and dad to decide if they love their baby, or want to kill her. And Singer will give the parents 30 days, after the baby's birth, to make that

---

[266] *See* Scott Klusendorf, "Peter Singer's Bold Defense of Infanticide," **Christian Research Journal** (April 16, 2009). When Professor Singer was invited to speak in Germany, his glasses were broken during a melee, with a mob chanting, "Singer raus! Singer raus!" ("Singer out! Singer out!"). The Wall Street Journal compared Singer to Martin Bormann; a U.S. Congressman said he had taken the "Joseph Mengele chair in bio-ethics" (at Princeton!) *See* Johan Hari, "Peter Singer: Some People Are More Equal Than Others," **The Independent** (July 1, 2004).

[267] "He is the man who wants me dead. No, that's not at all fair. He wants to legalize the killing of certain babies who might come to be like me if allowed to live." *See* Harriet McBryde Johnson, "Unspeakable Conversations," **The New York Times** (February 16, 2003).

[268] The judge dismissed anybody who was pro-life from the jury pool. *See* Heather Clark, "Judge Dismisses Pro-Life Citizens During Jury Selection For Trial of 'House of Horrors' Abortionist," **Christian News Network** (March 6, 2013).

decision. So Singer is trying to hide a kill-right within a broader argument of autonomy and choice.

But Singer is also advocating what may be deemed medical autonomy. In Singer's universe, doctors are to have the option to kill handicapped children, even against the wishes of the child's parents.[269]

Singer's proposal has a remarkable similarity with the killing of handicapped people in Nazi Germany. These people were also killed against the wishes of their families. As the website for the United States Holocaust Museum puts it, "At the beginning of World War II, individuals who were mentally retarded, physically handicapped, or mentally ill were targeted for murder in what the Nazis called the 'T-4' or 'euthanasia' program. (It) required the cooperation of many German doctors, who reviewed the medical files of patients in institutions to determine which handicapped or mentally ill individuals should be killed. The doctors also supervised the actual killings."[270]

---

[269] "Some parents want even the most gravely disabled infant to live as long as possible, and this desire would then be a reason against killing the infant." Peter Singer, *Practical Ethics*, 2nd edition (1993). Note that Singer is not saying that parents have a right to keep their baby alive. And since the baby's humanity is denied, no murder charges can be brought. The doctor--and any other person, apparently--is allowed to make an independent determination whether to kill the child. "I do not deny that if one accepts abortion...the case for killing other human beings, in certain circumstances, is strong."

[270] *See* "The Murder of the Handicapped," www.ushmm.org. Singer denies that he is a national socialist. He is perhaps an international one. As Jonah Goldberg has argued, the two ideologies have a lot of similarities, not the least of which they are both forms of socialism. *See* Jonah Goldberg, *Liberal Fascism* (2008). And what should we make of Singer's suggestion that socialists should "swap Marx for Darwin"? *See* Peter Singer, *A Darwinian Left* (2000). Singer's focus on identifying inferiors through biology and killing them sounds very much like what the Nazis believed. "Underlying the Nazis' belief in race laws as the expression of the law of nature in man is Darwin's idea of man as the product of a natural development which does not necessarily stop with the present species of human beings..." Hannah Arendt, *The Origins of Totalitarianism* (1951).

In the United States a baby is a citizen when she is born, and is entitled to the equal protection of the laws. Some of the abortion cases--particularly *Stenberg v. Carhart*, which deals with partial-birth abortion--may undercut this understanding.[271]

Understandably, the Supreme Court has been quite reluctant to discuss homicide in the context of abortion. The Court has never referenced our death statutes, which are designed to resolve any medical dispute in regard to whether a patient is alive or not. Indeed, by defining the unborn child as a legal non-person, the *Roe* Court is suggesting that an unborn baby is sub-human property who is beneath our concern.

Even more problematic are the frequent references to Plato and Aristotle in the *Roe* opinion. Plato and Aristotle, like Peter Singer, are advocates of killing newborns.[272] Justice Blackmun acknowledges as much in footnote 22. "Aristotle's thinking derived from his three-stage theory of life: vegetable, animal, rational. The vegetable stage was reached at conception, the animal at 'animation,' and the rational soon after live birth."[273] Peter Singer's 30-day rule for killing newborns is an idea that is simply rehashing what Aristotle already said. The pagans of Greece and Rome were an ancient, baby-killing society.[274]

On its face, modern day abortion rights should not implicate the killing of newborns. Abortion is about the autonomy of a woman and her right to control her body. A newborn baby is independent of his mother, and has a right to life. Indeed, a newborn is a

---

[271] *Supra* note 202.

[272] Indeed, Professor Singer cites Plato and Aristotle in his book. *Supra* note 269.

[273] *Supra* note 1.

[274] *Roe v. Wade* cites Plato and Aristotle in many places, and they are the first cites the Supreme Court has for the viability doctrine. *See* notes 306-316 and text.

citizen of the United States. Killing a newborn means that the doctor, nurse or parent may be prosecuted for murder.

It's understandable why the Supreme Court would not want to discuss murder in any of its abortion opinions. Perhaps the Court feels that it's obvious that killing newborns is murder, and so there is no need to discuss it. And yet this failure to talk about murder might also imply that the Supreme Court is motivated by self-concern. It looks bad when you have to distinguish the crime of murder from your unenumerated constitutional right, and the Supreme Court does not want to look bad. A discussion about the murder statutes might get people thinking about the life of the unborn child. And the Supreme Court does not actually want people thinking about the life of the unborn child, since the Court has defined that child as outside of humanity.

This, by the way, is a unanimous rule among all the Supreme Court Justices, including all the dissenting Justices. All of them have defined the unborn baby as a non-person. And thus none of them bring up the death or murder statutes in any abortion case. While there are plenty of arguments made against *Roe v. Wade*, none of these arguments are actually pro-life. Nobody has said that a unborn baby has a right to life, or that this right has been violated by *Roe v. Wade*. Nobody on the Court has argued that an unborn baby is a person who has a right to the equal protection of the laws.[275]

To do so would be quite rude. The dissenting Justice would be calling his opponents baby-killers. And there is not a polite way

---

[275] Instead the abortion dissenters argue that the Court is being undemocratic, that the right to abortion is nowhere to be found in our Constitution, and that the majority has violated the principle of federalism. Note that these arguments can be made against many of the Supreme Court's opinions. They are entirely procedural in nature. Nobody on the Supreme Court has raised the substantive objection that abortion kills a baby. That is, until doctors started killing babies outside the birth canal. *Supra* note 202.

to make this argument. It would ruin relationships. It would strain the Supreme Court's hand-shaking ceremony.[276] You can make all sorts of arguments in the world of the Supreme Court. But saying that *Roe v. Wade* kills a baby is not one of them.

So the dissenters tiptoe around it. In his *Doe v. Bolton* dissent, Justice Byron White writes, "The Court apparently values the convenience of the pregnant mother more than the continued existence and development of the life or potential life that she carries."[277] Is that a homicide charge? He's not sure.

In his majority opinion in *Roe*, Justice Blackmun writes, "We need not resolve the difficult question of when life begins."[278] So are you saying abortion is not a homicide?

The Supreme Court abortion cases circle around and around and around the issue, with the pro-*Roe* Justices insisting they need not resolve the issue, and the *Roe* dissenters politely suggesting that maybe other people should decide if this is a homicide.

"Maybe it's a homicide."

"We need not resolve the issue."

"Maybe it's a homicide."

"We need not resolve the issue."

---

[276] "The 'Conference handshake' has been a tradition since the days of Chief Justice Melville W. Fuller in the late 19th century. When the Justices assemble to go on the Bench each day and at the beginning of the private Conferences at which they discuss decisions, each Justice shakes hands with each of the other eight. Chief Justice Fuller instituted the practice as a reminder that differences of opinion on the Court did not preclude overall harmony of purpose." www.supremecourt.gov/about/traditions.aspx

[277] *Doe v. Bolton*, 410 U.S. 179 (1973) (White, J., dissenting).

[278] *Supra* note 1.

So polite, so friendly, so nice! Meanwhile, our country is losing its mind over the abortion issue. Abortion doctors are shot.[279] Abortionists are tried for murder.[280] And the Supreme Court acts like nine absent-minded professors in an ivory tower, gently dithering back and forth, always polite, determined to be civil.

The Supreme Court actually did address the possibility of murder at oral argument in *Roe v. Wade*. Justice Potter Stewart asked this question: "There is no state, is there, that equates abortion with murder? Or is there?"[281]

So that's an interesting question. Justice Stewart, who would sign on to *Roe v. Wade*, is asking the attorneys at oral argument whether abortion is murder. First he states his certainty that no state is defining abortion as murder. Abortion can't be murder. No way. And then he has this voice in the back of his mind that reminds him that he doesn't actually know what all the states are doing in this area. So he has this flash of uncertainty, this panic that maybe some crazy state somewhere has defined abortion as murder. It's not murder. Or is it?

This certainty/doubt seems to plague Supreme Court jurisprudence in regard to abortion. Nobody on the Supreme Court wants to jump to the conclusion that abortion is not murder. And yet they also want to avoid saying that it is murder. They want to avoid the dogmatism of either side. So they waffle and

---

[279] Vigilantes who have murdered abortion doctors include Eric James Kopp, Paul Jennings Hill, Scott Roeder, and Michael Griffin. Eric Rudolph went on a bombing campaign in the 1990's, injuring many people and killing an off-duty police officer.

[280] At least 15 abortionists have been charged with murder since *Roe v. Wade*: Dr. William Waddill (twice), Dr. Raymond Showery, Dr. David Benjamin, Alicia Ruiz Hanna, Dr. Bruce Steir, Dr. Gordon Goei, Dr. Joseph Melnick, Dr. Kermit Gosnell, Steven Massof, Lynda Williams, Adrienne Moton, Sherry West, Dr. Douglas Karpen, Steven Brigham and Dr. Nicola Riley. *See* note 659.

[281] Transcript: *Roe v. Wade* (first oral argument) (December 13, 1971).

wonder why hundreds of thousands of protesters show up every January 22nd.

And note the awesome swing in the mind of Justice Stewart. At oral argument he's asking the attorneys if abortion is murder, the most awful crime there is. And then he signs on to *Roe v. Wade*, which says that abortion is a constitutional right. This is the same Justice Stewart, by the way, who said there was no right to use birth control in *Griswold*. And now he goes from wondering if abortion is murder to saying it's a right thing to do.

Roe suggests that nobody can answer the infanticide question, not doctors, not philosophers, not priests, and not judges. "When those trained in the respective disciplines of medicine, philosophy, and theology are unable to arrive at any consensus, the judiciary, at this point in the development of man's knowledge, is not in a position to speculate as to the answer."[282] Here the Supreme Court is talking about when life begins. But of course that question implicates the question of whether abortion kills a child. And *Roe* is suggesting that we can't answer that question. Nobody can.

Apparently, according to the Supreme Court, the unborn is a maybe-baby, and so abortion is a maybe-murder. The Supreme Court not only does not answer the question in *Roe*, they say that nobody else can answer it, either. Do we need to answer it? Maybe somebody else should answer it. But if we let somebody else answer it, it will look like we didn't answer it. Did we answer it? Do we need to answer it?

All of the Justices take this attitude. Even the Justices who hate *Roe v. Wade* talk like this. Justice Antonin Scalia, a fierce critic of *Roe*, writes a dissent in *Casey*. And he says this: "The whole argument of abortion opponents is that what the Court calls the

---

[282] *Supra* note 1.

fetus and what others call the unborn child is a human life. Thus, whatever answer *Roe* came up with after conducting its 'balancing' is bound to be wrong, unless it is correct that the human fetus is in some critical sense merely potentially human. There is of course no way to determine that as a legal matter; it is in fact a value judgment. Some societies have considered newborn children not yet human, or the incompetent elderly no longer so."[283]

A pro-lifer might wonder, suppose Peter Singer has his way, and Washington starts killing newborns. Would Scalia strike this down as unconstitutional? Would Scalia recognize a newborn child's right to life? He does not say. But the invitation is there. The implication is that newborns might not be people, too.

Pro-lifers warned about this. They warned about a slippery slope.[284] The failure to protect the lives of the unseen has put in jeopardy the lives of the babies we do see.

Roe v. Wade might give doctors the wrong mindset, and might open the door to the killing of newborns. For instance, suppose a pregnant mother pays a doctor to abort her pregnancy. And so the doctor injects the woman's uterus with saline solution. And the mother gives birth to a scalded infant.

Now suppose this newborn child does not die right away. The baby is alive, she's crying, she's horribly injured. What should the doctor do?

---

[283] *Planned Parenthood v. Casey* 505 U.S. 833 (1992) (Scalia, J., dissenting).
[284] In 1982, in Bloomington, Indiana, a child ("Baby Doe") was born with Down's Syndrome and a blocked esophagus. A simple operation would have opened the esophagus so the child would live. The physician advised the parents not to do the operation. The child starved to death. *See* Jeff Lyon, "The Death of Baby Doe," *Chicago Tribune* (February 10, 1985).

Should he place the baby in a neonatal intensive care unit? Abortion clinics do not actually have neonatal intensive care units, so this is not a possibility for most abortion doctors. But suppose this abortion takes place in a hospital. The doctor could place the scalded baby in a NICU and try to keep her alive. But then he might be sued if the baby survives.[285] The mother will sue, since she is now a mother against her will. And now she has a live baby who was injured by the doctor.

Or maybe the doctor should keep the baby out of the NICU, and hope the baby is unable to get oxygen, or dies of dehydration. If the child is neglected and simply left to die, is the physician responsible for this death? Is the mother?

What if the doctor strangles the baby to death?

The murder prosecution of Dr. William Waddill is quite illuminating. In 1977, Dr. Waddill, an obstetrician, was charged with strangling a baby to death in front of many witnesses.[286]

It's rather unusual behavior in a hospital. Why did Dr. Waddill murder a newborn? He wasn't related to the child. He wasn't a father who was trying to get rid of a financial obligation. The baby was a stranger to him.

Apparently, Dr. Waddill murdered the child in a desire to follow through on his abortion attempt.

---

[285] A couple in Washington was awarded $50 million dollars for the "wrongful birth" of their son. If they had known about his genetic defect, they would have aborted him. The hospital did not cause the injury or harm the child in any way. The hospital was held responsible for its failure to discover the genetic defect, and was blamed for the birth of a baby. *See* Carol Ostrom, "$50M Awarded Over Birth Defect; Test Said Baby Would Be Okay," *The Seattle Times* (December 10, 2013).

[286] *See* Christina Dunigan, "William Waddill and the Killing of Baby W," *Real Choice* (November 12, 2006).

In 1977, a high school student, Mary W., sought out an abortion with Dr. Waddill. She was in the third trimester.[287] According to *Roe v. Wade*, a doctor can perform an abortion up until birth for purposes of the mother's health.[288] And so Dr. Waddill agreed to abort her pregnancy. Yet there is nothing in the record of the Waddill trial suggesting that there were any health risks in this pregnancy, or that anything was wrong with the baby or the mother's health.

That does not seem to matter. *Roe* suggests that "the stigma of unwed motherhood" might justify a late-term abortion. "Psychological harm may be imminent." Apparently a "health" abortion is rather like getting a note from your doctor. As long as you can find a doctor willing to do it, you can have a third trimester abortion under *Roe*.

Mary had already visited one obstetrician, who had told her that she was too far along for an abortion and advised her to consider adoption.[289] A week later, she visited with Dr. Waddill, who agreed to perform a late-term abortion. The baby's age was now estimated at 29 weeks.[290]

On March 2nd, 1977, in a surgical room at Westminister Community Hospital, Dr. Waddill performed a saline amniocentesis abortion on Mary W.

Many hours after the salt was administered, Mary gave birth to an infant. The baby was 2 pounds and 8 ounces. She did not appear to be badly burned by the saline and her color was described as

---

[287] *Id*.

[288] *Supra* note 205.

[289] *Supra* note 286. The obstetrician estimated the baby's age at 28 weeks on February 22nd.

[290] Adding a week to the first obstetrician's estimate. *Id*. One newspaper reported the baby was "anywhere from 20 weeks to 30 weeks old." *See* Jeanne Wright, "Matters of Life and Death," *The Los Angeles Times* (February 2, 1993). At trial Dr. Cornelsen estimated the baby's age at 32 weeks.

pink. A nurse clamped the umbilical cord and was about to put the baby in a bucket when the child started to cry.

The nurses had no idea what to do. One nurse suggested that they should put the baby in the bucket anyway. Yet another nurse testified that she had seen the baby moving but had not said anything to avoid distressing the mother. The nursing supervisor was called. She sent the baby to the nursery, made a notation that the baby was alive, and called for Dr. Waddill.

At the nursery, the baby was placed in a neonatal intensive care unit. A nurse charted a heart rate of 88. Another nurse began providing respiratory assistance to the little girl, and asked for help performing an intubation to help the child breathe.

Dr. Waddill arrived. He cleared all the nurses from the room and instructed them "not to do a goddamn thing for the baby."[291] An ER doctor testified that he saw Dr. Waddill squeeze the umbilical cord. The child jerked her body and gasped for air.

Under the law, Dr. Waddill was required to call a pediatrician to assist when a newborn was in distress. He called Dr. Ronald Cornelsen. When Dr. Cornelsen arrived, the baby was still breathing and had a heart rate of 60-70. There were visible bruises on her neck. Cornelsen watched as Dr. Waddill tried to strangle the baby in front of him. "I can't find the goddamn trachea," said Waddill. "This baby won't stop breathing."[292]

Dr. Waddill told a nurse to get potassium chloride to poison the baby. Dr. Cornelsen told her not to. Dr. Waddill then asked for a bucket to drown the baby in. Dr. Cornelsen asked, "Why not just

---

[291] *Supra* note 286.
[292] *Id*.

leave the baby alone?" Dr. Waddill responded, "The baby can't live or it will be a big mess."[293]

Dr. Cornelsen and several nurses stood and watched as Dr. Waddill strangled the baby to death.

At the baby's autopsy, the pathologist determined that the baby had been alive for thirty minutes, and she had died from manual strangulation. The autopsy also found that the saline injuries had been minimal. The solution had only burned the baby's placenta and small bowel.

Somebody on the hospital staff notified the police. After talking to the witnesses, officers arrested Dr. Waddill and charged him with murder. He was prosecuted in a trial that lasted over three months. There was a bit of a media circus, with both pro-life and pro-choice protesters outside the court. The defense attorney often arrived to court in a limo.

The jury was unable to agree on a verdict, and the judge declared a mistrial. The district attorney again prosecuted Dr. Waddill for murder. A second jury was also unable to reach a verdict, and the judge dismissed all charges.

Mary W. sued Dr. Waddill for not telling her the baby was alive, and for killing her child.

Perhaps, we might conclude, **Roe v. Wade** is not implicated in this murder. For whatever reason, Dr. Waddill decided to strangle a newborn. That has nothing to do with the Supreme Court or its right to abortion. Indeed, Dr. Waddill knew he had committed a crime. Why else would he be trying to cover it up?

---

[293] *Id*.

At the trial there was testimony that indicated Dr. Waddill wanted help from Dr. Cornelsen in hiding what he had done. An audio tape of a phone call between the two doctors was entered into evidence.

Dr. Waddill: "If we all tell the same story, there will be no trouble…so long as we stand together, no one anywhere can make any accusations anywhere…do not get squirrely. Just tell them exactly as we've discussed. Just say you went in, there was no heartbeat and you left."[294]

Obviously, this tape suggests that Dr. Waddill knew that killing a newborn was a crime. That's why he wants Dr. Cornelsen to lie and say the baby was stillborn. Waddill is aware of the difference between abortion and murder.

Yet this might be too glib. After all, Dr. Waddill had no history of strangling newborns. What would make an obstetrician flip out and start killing a child in a room full of people?

The facts suggest that Dr. Waddill strangled this baby because his abortion had failed. Perhaps he felt a duty to his patient, the mother, who was paying him to abort her pregnancy. He wanted to finish that job.

Note too that he strangled the baby in front of witnesses, without any fear that he might be prosecuted for a murder. It was only later, after the police were called, and started investigating the murder, that he began to panic. He realized that newborns are citizens, protected under our law, and so it was really important that Dr. Cornelsen say the right thing. The baby had to be born dead.

---

[294] *Id*.

And look at the reaction of all the witnesses. One nurse sees the baby move, but doesn't want to say anything because it might upset the mother. Another nurse suggests that they just put the baby in a bucket. These nurses are not sure how to treat a newborn infant.[295] They are not sure if they should try to keep the baby alive, or pretend the baby is dead. The patient is paying for an abortion. But the baby's alive. What should they do?[296]

Consider too the odd reactions of the hospital staff to the actual murder itself. They watch. The baby is helpless and defenseless. None of the witnesses--doctors and nurses who are trained to save lives--do anything to stop a murder of a defenseless baby. Do they even object? "Why not just leave the baby alone?" suggests Dr. Cornelsen. It's unclear if Dr. Cornelsen, a pediatrician, is objecting to the murder, or is suggesting they just wait for the baby to die on her own.

After the murder trial, there would no longer be abortions performed at Westminister Community Hospital. This would be replicated in hospitals across the country. Abortion, by and large, has been kicked out of hospitals.[297]

---

[295] **See** Liz Jeffries and Rick Edmonds, "The Dread Complication," **The Philadelphia Inquirer** (August 2, 1981). "When nurse Marilyn Wilson flicked on the lights and pulled back the covers, she found, instead of the still born fetus she'd expected, a live 2½-pound baby boy, crying and moving his arms and legs there on the bed." The nurse called the abortionist at home. "He told me to leave it where it was," the head nurse testified in court, "just to watch it for a few minutes, it would probably die in a few minutes."

[296] **The Philadelphia Inquirer** reports that live births "are little known because organized medicine, from fear of public clamor and legal action, treats them more as an embarrassment to be hushed up than a problem to be solved." The newspaper quotes Willard Cates, the former head of the Centers for Disease Control. "It's like turning yourself in to the IRS for an audit," Cates said. "What is there to gain? The tendency is not to report because there are only negative incentives." **Id**.

[297] "Hospitals provide just 4% of abortions in the U.S…and many facilities limit the procedure to rare cases…The majority of hospitals perform fewer than 30 abortions per year. Others refuse to provide the procedure at all." Grace Wyler, "Doctors Urge More Hospitals To Perform Abortions," **Time** (August 23, 2013).

Why did Westminister Community Hospital kick abortion out, if abortion had nothing to do with this murder?

No doubt the hospital did not like all the publicity of a baby's murder performed by one of their doctors, in a room filled with doctors and nurses. And obviously they would not want a repeat of these events. And doctors make mistakes. Abortion is weird in that a doctor's mistake can result in a live baby.[298] Not just a live baby, but a scarred or mutilated baby, and a lawsuit.

So perhaps that's why abortion was kicked out of the hospital. It's a fear of lawsuits and bad publicity.

But there's another possibility. Many doctors look at the way Dr. Waddill acted, and how all the other nurses and doctors acted, and they are concerned about medical ethics. Specifically they are concerned that *Roe v. Wade* has given Dr. Waddill a bad mindset. He should not have done a third trimester abortion on a healthy child. Indeed, why kill the baby at all? Why not induce labor, deliver the child, and put her in a neonatal intensive care unit?

Roe v. Wade is supposed to be about terminating a pregnancy. But birth terminates a pregnancy, too. Why not simply give birth to a child, particularly a viable child? Why does Dr. Waddill have this determination to poison her, drown her, or strangle her?

Roe v. Wade seems to have given some doctors the mindset that they are not just aborting pregnancies, but that they are in a new business of aborting babies. And it is this mindset ("abort the

---

[298] "Hundreds of times a year in the United States, an aborted fetus emerges from the womb kicking and alive. When such a baby is allowed to die and the incident becomes known, the authorities often try to prosecute the doctor. But interviews with nurses, some of them visibly anguished, uncovered dozens of similar cases that never reached public attention. In fact, for every case that does become known, a hundred probably go unreported." *Supra* note 295.

baby") that has caused Dr. Waddill to strangle the child, and get himself charged with murder.

Yes, he should have realized the difference between an unborn baby and a born infant. But perhaps our legal authorities--who refuse to discuss murder in any of their abortion cases--have opened the door to this sort of moral confusion. *Roe v. Wade* has confused the doctors and nurses as to their duties and responsibilities to an unwanted child.

In other words, abortion is incompatible with medical practice. This is why abortion has to be kicked out of hospitals. It's corrupting doctors and medical ethics.

The Supreme Court's dream in *Roe v. Wade* was that abortion would be a normal part of medical practice. Obstetricians would help mothers give birth, if they want to do that, or abort pregnancies, if they want to do that. *Roe* suggests a hope that doctors might guide their patients into making the "correct" choice. At any rate, the idea in the opinion was for abortion to be a normal part of medical practice.

It didn't work out that way. Abortion was pushed out of the hospitals and into clinics. The Supreme Court in *Akron* tries to spin this as a positive. "(A) second trimester abortion costs more than twice as much in a hospital as in a clinic."[299] Yes, abortion is cheaper when hospitals refuse to do them. But *Akron* also noted a negative. "Moreover, the court indicated that second trimester abortions were rarely performed in Akron hospitals."[300]

Pushing abortion into the clinic would take away any medical oversight. Now the abortion doctor is free to strangle, drown, or drug any accidental newborn to death. There is nobody to object,

---

[299] *Supra* note 244.
[300] *Id*.

or challenge what the doctor wants to do. In most cases there will not be an autopsy performed. There is no more issue about the appropriate mindset of doctors and nurses. In the hospital, doctors and nurses have a life-saving mentality. The mindset of William Waddill ("the baby can't live or it will be a big mess") is segregated away from the hospital, and into an abortion clinic.

Chapter 8

As the Supreme Court admits in ***Roe v. Wade***, the Hippocratic Oath forbids doctors from performing abortions. Part of the Oath reads: "I will neither give a deadly drug to anybody if asked for it, nor will I make a suggestion to this effect. Similarly, I will not give to a woman an abortive remedy."[301]

Let's count all the violations of the Hippocratic Oath in Dr. Waddill's behavior. He's performing an abortion on an unborn child (violation), he's injecting saline solution into the uterus of a healthy patient (violation), and he's murdering a newborn (violation). We are told by the Supreme Court in ***Roe*** that the first two violations can be ignored. And yet it's entirely possible that these earlier violations of the Hippocratic Oath have paved the way to the murder of a newborn child.

In ***Roe v. Wade*** the Supreme Court dismantles the Hippocratic Oath, and frees abortion doctors from any obligation to follow it. This is a serious problem, since it's the Hippocratic Oath that describes the mindset we want our doctors to have. We want our doctors to respect the sanctity of human life, to do nothing to put the lives of women or babies in danger. Certainly we do not want our doctors strangling infants.

In his opinion, Justice Blackmun has lots of nice things to say about Hippocrates. "What then of the famous Oath that has stood so long as the ethical guide of the medical profession and that bears the name of the great Greek…who has been described as the Father of Medicine, the 'wisest and the greatest practitioner of his art,' and the 'most important and most complete medical personality of antiquity,' who dominated the medical schools of

---

[301] ***Supra*** note 1.

his time, and who typified the sum of the medical knowledge of the past?"[302]

And yet, after saying all these nice things about Hippocrates, Blackmun goes on to criticize his Oath ("strict…a matter of dogma…uncompromising…apparent rigidity…").[303] Why is the Supreme Court attacking the Hippocratic Oath? We have one obvious possibility: the Oath explicitly forbids abortion, and the Supreme Court wants doctors to abort pregnancies.

The Supreme Court is asking doctors to reject the sanctity of life arguments of Hippocrates. The idea is to replace this mindset with the viability doctrine of Plato and Aristotle.

In *Roe v. Wade*, Justice Blackmun attacks the Hippocratic Oath by pointing out how often it was ignored by the rest of the physicians in ancient Greece. "(T)he Oath originated in a group representing only a small segment of Greek opinion, and…it was certainly not accepted by all ancient physicians."[304] Yes, Hippocrates was in the minority. The majority of ancient Greek physicians had no reverence for the sanctity of life. That's why Hippocrates started his school in the first place.

Blackmun then contrasts the life-affirming Hippocrates with the aborting society of ancient Greece. "Most Greek thinkers, on the other hand, commended abortion, at least prior to viability."[305] This is the first mention of the viability doctrine in *Roe v. Wade*.

---

[302] *Id*.

[303] *Id*. It is quite bizarre to say all these nice things about Hippocrates while you attack his oath. The oath is what we like about Hippocrates. We certainly do not cite Hippocrates for his medical knowledge! And this disregard for a doctor's oath might make us wonder about our unelected judges. You too swear an oath, a promise that you will follow our Constitution. Is this your attitude about your oath of office?

[304] *Id*.

[305] *Id*.

It's actually quite odd, if you think about it. The Supreme Court is citing the ancient pagans for viability?

And it's truly bizarre once we look up his cites. Justice Blackmun is relying upon Plato's **Republic** and Aristotle's **Politics**. And when we read these works, what do these ancient Greek philosophers actually say?

Aristotle writes, "As to the exposure and rearing of children, let there be a law that no deformed child shall live…"[306] Clearly Aristotle is not talking about a surgical abortion. There was no way for an ancient Greek to determine if a child was "deformed" until she was born. And "exposure" is a direct reference to the ancient Greek practice of exposing a baby to the elements so the child would die.

Roe v. Wade cites Aristotle, and Aristotle is defending the murder of newborns. In fact, he's not just defending infanticide; he's requiring it. It's not like you get to choose whether to love your handicapped child. As a matter of Athenian law, you are required to kill her.

This is the citation Harry Blackmun puts in **Roe v. Wade**?

Aristotle has more to say. "On the ground of an excess in the number of children, if the established customs of the state forbid this (for in our state population has a limit), no child is to be exposed…"[307] What Aristotle is saying is that if the established customs in a Greek city-state forbid killing babies, then no child is to be exposed. But what he's also saying is that in his state, "population has a limit." Thus, in the city-state of Athens, kill away. Kill healthy babies. Aristotle is a population control nut.

---

[306] Aristotle, **Politics**, VII, 1335b.
[307] **Id**.

Blackmun also cites the fifth volume of Plato's *Republic*, page 461. Has he actually read Plato? On page 460, Plato argues "the offspring of the inferior, and any of those of the other sort who are born defective, they will properly dispose of in secret, so that no one will know what has become of them. That is the condition of preserving the purity of the guardian's breed."[308]

Plato argues for marriages arranged by the state, in order to make sure the superior people are breeding. Plato also sought to keep the inferior citizens from having any children. He was a strong proponent of eugenics. And both Plato and Aristotle were passionate defenders of the ancient Greek practice of abandoning newborns to die.

Aristotle writes, "(W)hen couples have children in excess, let abortion be procured before sense and life have begun."[309] Aristotle's use of the word "abortion" is broader than how we use it today. An abortion in ancient Greece was often a reference to the killing of a newborn child. As footnote 22 in *Roe v. Wade* makes clear, Aristotle thought newborns were not capable of rational thought, and so they may be killed.

All of this discussion seems alien to us, of course, because it's a violation of Judeo-Christianity. Jews and Christians believe it is deeply immoral to kill a baby, regardless of how weak and helpless she might be.

Why is Blackmun citing Plato and Aristotle in regard to "viability," anyway? It's not as if the ancient Greeks had neonatal intensive care units. No, the Supreme Court is talking about viability in the broadest possible sense. It is survivability. Are you independent of your mother? Can you survive on your own?

---

[308] Plato, *Republic*, V, 460.
[309] *Supra* note 306.

Viability, or survivability, is a measure of independence, strength, and power. A baby has none of those characteristics. Babies are vulnerable, weak, and helpless. A baby cannot feed herself. A baby will not seek shelter.

That was the philosophical basis for exposing an infant to the elements. In the ancient Greek view, you were not guilty of murder. You were simply freeing yourself of your baby and walking away. If the baby died, she died of her own weakness, her failure to be autonomous and take care of herself. She would cry herself to death.[310]

Of course the ancient Greeks were not the only ones who would abandon babies to die. The Romans were well known for it.[311] Remember, there was no effective birth control in ancient Greece or Rome. And ancient Rome was a place where the orgy was a common practice. If you have a society where there's no birth control, and lots of orgies, you're going to have a high number of unwanted pregnancies.

The ancient city of Rome was said to be founded by Romulus and Remus, two babies who had been abandoned in the wild. The story was that these two babies survived, as they were suckled by wolves.[312] Thus the myth about Romulus and Remus assumed the infanticide of the age. The idea is that Romulus (he later killed

---

[310] "(T)he practice of infanticide was widespread and commonplace in the classical world." Emmet Scott, "The Role of Infanticide and Abortion in Pagan Rome's Decline," *New English Review* (October, 2012). "Christians had large families and were noted for their rejection of infanticide."

[311] As one Roman wrote to his wife, "I beg and plead with you to take care of our little child, and as soon as we receive wages, I will send them to you. In the meantime, if (good fortune to you!) you give birth, if it is a boy, let it live; if it is a girl, expose it." Lewis Naphtali, "Papyrus Oxyrhynchus 744," *Life in Egypt Under Roman Rule* (1985).

[312] *See* Stephanie Pappas, "Ancient Roman Infanticide Didn't Spare Either Sex, DNA Suggests," *Live Science* (January 24, 2014).

his brother) was so strong that he survived his early abandonment. To use Supreme Court's language, Romulus was "viable."

Even under the myth of Romulus, animals had to milk the child. A baby can't feed himself. A baby is, by definition, helpless. The baby's vulnerability is why the pagans defined newborns as sub-humans. This small child is weaker than the rest of us. The viability doctrine of Plato and Aristotle is a measure of a baby's vulnerability and helplessness.

Bizarrely, the Court's opinion in **Roe** omits the infanticide practices of ancient Greece and Rome. It's odd to be talking about ancient Greece and Rome, anyway. But it's really strange and unusual to wrench the viability theories of Plato and Aristotle--theories created as a rationale for the murder of newborns--and cite them in an argument for your modern right of abortion.

Has Blackmun not read his own cites? Does he actually not know that the ancient Greeks and Romans killed newborn infants, all the time, as a part of their culture?[313]

It is rather embarrassing that **Roe v. Wade** is citing Plato and Aristotle in its abortion opinion. These philosophers were discussing the killing of newborns, a fact that either escaped Blackmun's attention, or he knew and wanted to hide. But this begs the question, why cite Plato and Aristotle for the viability doctrine? Indeed, why go back over 2000 years in the first place?

The Supreme Court is citing these ancient pagans because there is no legal authority for what it is saying. For 2000 years, Judeo-Christianity had resolved the abortion issue by thinking about the baby's life or death. Is the baby alive? Is this a homicide?

---

[313] **See** Jennifer Viegas, "Archaeologists Document Ancient Baby-Killing," **NBC News** (May 5, 2011).

Before 1973, that's how the abortion issue was always resolved, throughout the common law, throughout our history.[314]

In *Roe v. Wade*, the Supreme Court jettisons this standard. "We need not resolve the difficult question of when life begins."[315] The life-or-death question is deemed irrelevant, and so the Court skips it. In its place the Court adopts a new standard, "viability," which is actually a very old standard. It is the standard of the ancient pagans. Can the baby survive?

It's quite odd to be discussing ancient attitudes about abortion, as *Roe v. Wade* does. But it's really odd to omit any discussion of infanticide in ancient Greece and Rome. Justice Blackmun writes, "Greek and Roman law afforded little protection to the unborn."[316] An honest Supreme Court opinion would have said "babies" here, instead of "unborn," since newborns were killed all the time. Indeed, such an opinion might have mentioned that both infanticide and slavery were widespread in these societies. Women were bought and raped, and there was no birth control.

Justice Blackmun also fails to mention how unsafe abortion was in ancient Greece and Rome. "Abortion was practiced in Greek times as well as in the Roman Era and…it was resorted to without scruple."[317] Who has no scruples? The doctor who feels no pain and is getting paid? Imagine a barber performing an abortion without anesthesia. Or a "doctor" who gives you poison.[318]

---

[314] *Supra* note 192.
[315] *Supra* note 1.
[316] *Id*.
[317] *Id*.
[318] "Barber-surgeons would normally learn their trade as an apprentice to a more experienced colleague. Many would have no formal learning, and were often illiterate. The red and white pole which is still used to identify a barber's shop was originally intended to reflect the blood and napkins used to clean up during bloodletting. This treatment was one of the main tasks of the barber-surgeon, as well as extracting teeth, performing enemas, selling medicines, performing surgery and, of course, cutting hair." www.sciencemuseum.org.uk.

People died from surgery all the time in the B.C. era. Blackmun might have mentioned how painful and dangerous the surgery was, or how the pagans often resorted to the practice of killing newborns because of this danger. Instead Justice Blackmun whitewashes this history. He neglects to talk about the killing of newborns, or any dangers to pregnant women from an abortion.

When Justice Blackmun writes, "Ancient religion did not bar abortion," he might distinguish between the ancient pagan societies he is describing and Jews and Christians, who had the unique view of insisting that all human life has value and infanticide is evil. Indeed, Jews and Christians took a tough stance on human sexuality--outlawing fornication and prostitution, not to mention the orgy--in part because of strong moral objections to all the baby-killing that was happening in the wider pagan society.[319]

What's really shocking is how the *Roe* opinion adopts a viability standard out of the blue. "With respect to the State's important and legitimate interest in potential life, the 'compelling' point is at viability. This is because the fetus then presumably has the capability of meaningful life outside the mother's womb."[320]

The Supreme Court is saying that a baby's life inside the uterus has no meaning. The child only has value if she is born, or if she could be born. Yet very basic questions are left unanswered by the *Roe* opinion. For instance, is it a homicide to kill an unborn child who is viable?

---

[319] In our modern birth control culture, we do not associate sex with pregnancy (much less with infanticide). So many of us are confused as to why the word "fuck" is such a bad word. The word is likely an implicit reference to all the babies who were murdered prior to the rise of Judeo-Christianity.

[320] *Supra* note 1.

Roe v. Wade does not answer the question of whether an unborn baby is alive inside the uterus, or whether an abortion kills her. The opinion seeks to move us off that standard entirely. Instead of asking whether the baby is alive, the only question is whether the baby could survive outside the uterus.

In other words, the viability doctrine measures whether an unborn baby could survive in a harsh environment outside the womb. And this is exactly the same attitude the ancient Greeks had. Could the baby survive if you left her on a hillside somewhere? Viability is exposure.

In *Planned Parenthood v. Casey*, the Supreme Court writes, "The woman's right to terminate her pregnancy before viability is the most central principle of *Roe v. Wade*."[321] In the modern context, when the Court talks about "viability," it is a reference to a baby's ability to survive in a neonatal intensive care unit. This doctrine assumes a roomful of adults who have a moral duty to sustain the child. And yet the Supreme Court has undercut this duty with its subversion of the Hippocratic Oath.

How can any baby survive, if the adults in the room decide that she should not?

Abortion clinics do not have neonatal intensive care units. A very premature infant needs to be placed into a NICU if she is going to have any chance of survival. That's what the nurses who were concerned about Mary W's daughter did--they placed the preemie in an incubator to help her breathe. So if viability is "the most central principle of *Roe v. Wade*," why is it that our abortion clinics do not actually have this life-saving equipment for viable infants?

---

[321] *Supra* note 7.

A neonatal intensive care unit is expensive, that's why.[322] If you're going to have a neonatal intensive care unit, you might as well be in a hospital. And, as its abortion cases make quite clear, the Supreme Court is heavily invested in making abortion as cheap as possible. Keeping viable infants alive makes abortion expensive. So viability is not "the most central principle of *Roe v. Wade*" after all.

Why not a constitutional right to put a baby in a neonatal intensive care unit? Why did the abortion cases develop as they did, with a kill-right, instead of a right to "remove a trespasser" or something like that? Why not induce birth, finish the delivery and put the tiny baby in an incubator? The pregnancy is still aborted. Mom is no longer pregnant. And in that scenario, the doctors are making very best efforts to keep the baby alive. What's wrong with that?[323]

And yet the Supreme Court's focus has always been on making unwanted babies disappear. Thus they are not interested in a rescue-right. It's always been a kill-right.

When does an unborn infant become viable? Obviously it depends greatly if a baby is born into a hospital or an abortion clinic. Abortion doctors violate the Hippocratic Oath every time they perform an abortion. Abortion doctors do not have the mentality to keep babies alive, and they have the wrong equipment for baby care.

---

[322] *See* Spencer Ante, "Million-Dollar Babies," *Businessweek* (June 11, 2008).
[323] Of course it's not a practical suggestion. Putting a premature infant in a NICU is very stressful for the child. In many cases she will die, or she will be disabled. And putting a baby in a NICU is a very expensive solution. People are already complaining about the health costs of all our premature infants. The Institute of Medicine put a $26.2 billion price tag on them. What the Institute of Medicine might want to talk about is how abortion has been linked to premature births. *See* notes 65-66 and text. *Roe v. Wade* is actually responsible for many of these billions that we are spending.

Do abortion clinics even have bottles of milk?

In a hospital, a baby can survive outside a uterus at 21 weeks and 6 days, because Amillia Taylor did it.[324] She was so tiny, she weighed 10 ounces at birth. She was born and survived in a hospital, in a NICU. Yet she only survived because the adults in the room made an effort to keep her alive. And the horrible truth is that these doctors and nurses would have let this baby die, if Amillia's mom had not lied to them about her age.[325]

At the time of Amillia's birth, in Florida hospitals any baby younger than 24 weeks was denied access to a NICU. Apparently the viability doctrine of **Roe v. Wade** has corrupted medical practice in hospitals. Even newborns can be deemed non-viable, and left to die by doctors and nurses. Medical care is sometimes denied premature infants, even against the will of the parents.[326]

This focus on the cost of the premature infant leaves desperate parents in a moral quandary. If you are going into premature labor, your doctors might ask you when your last period was. This is because the viability doctrine is based on the baby's size and weight, but also the number of weeks in the pregnancy. And many doctors will let your baby die if you say the wrong thing.[327]

---

[324] **See** Amanda Cable, "The Tiniest Survivor," **The Daily Mail** (May 22, 2008).

[325] **Id**. "It was the next morning, when pediatricians scanned Sonja's unborn child, that she made the split second decision to lie, giving her unborn baby a fighting chance."

[326] **See** Rahul Parikh, "In Preemies, Better Care Also Means Hard Choice," **The New York Times** (August 13, 2012). Dr. Parikh recounts a deep divide between doctors and parents. "Saving lives this young is not benign." That's Dr. Parikh's opinion. "Parents hold to a far more consistent ethos…a significant majority believed that attempts should be made to save all infants…" In contrast, Dr. Parikh reports that "just six percent of health professionals said the same."

[327] **See** "Baby Denied Medical Treatment and Handed Back To His Mother To Die," **The Daily Mirror** (September 9, 2009).

So Amillia's mom lied. She lied, and lied, and lied. And Amillia survived. Now she is a happy and healthy child.

The survival of Amillia Taylor in a NICU at 21 weeks and 6 days establishes the viability line at 21 weeks and 6 days. How many babies are aborted past that marker?

It's a hard question to answer. An estimate of survivability depends on a baby's size and age. Doctors can judge the baby's size via ultrasound, and age by the mother's answer in regard to when she had her last menstrual period. But these are just estimates. When we say a baby is 22 weeks, we can be off by 2 weeks in either direction.

According to the Guttmacher Institute, 1.2% of abortions take place after 21 weeks, or right at the age of Amillia Taylor.[328] If this number is accurate, 16,800 viable or potentially viable infants are killed every year. And over the 40 years of *Roe v. Wade*, 672,000 viable or potentially viable infants have been killed.

If viability is so important, why are so many babies who might survive in a NICU knifed or poisoned under *Roe v. Wade*?

While many abortion clinics self-regulate at 20 weeks, other abortion clinics routinely do abortions until 24 weeks, and some "specialists" perform abortions all the way until birth.[329] Dr. Waddill, for instance, was attempting to kill a viable baby (29 weeks) in the uterus in 1977, and nobody in the hospital seemed to blink at that. The baby who died in *Simopoulos* was at 22

---

[328] *See* "Induced Abortion in the United States," www.guttmacher.org (pie chart). Pro-lifers argue that Guttmacher is a biased source. *See* notes 11-12. The numbers may actually be higher. And consider that many abortion clinics (and the Guttmacher Institute) resist the ultrasound as an unnecessary expense. *See* notes 527-528 and text. Without an ultrasound the estimate of the baby's age might be off by two months or more. *See* note 538 and text.
[329] *See* note 658.

weeks. The baby whose murder Justice Kennedy describes in
Carhart II was at 26 weeks. Dr. Carhart, an abortion doctor who
is so prolific he has two Supreme Court cases named after him,
has no idea when viability is.[330]

In *Roe v. Wade*, the Supreme Court writes, "If the State is
interested in protecting fetal life after viability, it may go so far as
to proscribe abortion during that period, except when it is
necessary to preserve the life or health of the mother."[331] This is
why so many late-term abortions happen in our society. The
Supreme Court says viability is important, and yet there is a
health exception. If a doctor decides, in his medical judgment, to
abort an unborn baby, state law is irrelevant. That's a rather
broad exception!

Mom's health overrides the baby's maybe-life. And Mom's
health is defined quite broadly, to include the stigma of unwed
motherhood, financial concerns, and psychological well-being.

In *Casey* the Supreme Court tell us that viability is the "central
principle" of *Roe v. Wade*. And yet the Court's secret memos
indicate that the *Roe* Justices really thought that viability is as
arbitrary as any other point. The only reason it was mentioned at
all was because Justice Marshall wanted to ensure that abortions
could be had late in the term.[332]

No, the "central principle" of *Roe v. Wade* is that an unborn
infant is a non-person who has no right to life. Birth is the
important line, the line that distinguishes abortion from murder.

---

[330] "He performs abortion throughout pregnancy, including when he is unsure
whether the fetus is viable." *Stenberg v. Carhart*, 530 U.S. 914 (2000)
(Kennedy, J., dissenting). This would seem to contradict the Supreme Court's
opinion that "viability" is some sort of law that abortion doctors are following.
Are abortion doctors following the viability doctrine? If not, shouldn't the
Supreme Court revisit its opinion in *Casey*?

[331] *Supra* note 1.

[332] *Supra* note 204 and text.

As long as the child is unborn, an abortion can be had one way or another. After all, it is the abortion doctor who is defining whether the baby is viable. And he is allowed to ignore the viability rule whenever he deems it medically proper to do so.

Aside from the embarrassing number of violations of the rule, and the contradiction between the Court's public and private statements, viability is a rather odd idea. It's actually a comment on the state of our technology as much as anything.

Viability is a measure of man's ability to develop an artificial respiratory system, what we call a neonatal intensive care unit or NICU. But why does man's artificial incubator have moral value? And why are we supposed to value it more than mom's uterus? It's like the Supreme Court is suggesting that our life is unimportant as a Constitutional matter unless technology sustains us.

What does a neonatal intensive care unit do? It helps a premature infant breathe. So is lung capacity the important biological criterion?[333] Perhaps this is why we are so bigoted against a baby in the womb--she is not breathing. The womb is this weird place where a baby's lungs are filled with liquid. You're not breathing, you're sub-human!

Not only does our Supreme Court dehumanize the unborn child, their very definition of when a baby's life has value is dehumanized and unnatural. Apparently an unborn baby's life only has value when she can survive in a machine. A woman's uterus dehumanizes any baby inside it, while man's neonatal intensive care unit gives humanity to a weak and helpless baby.

---

[333] At the time of **Roe v. Wade**, in most states heart-and-lung function was the important biological factor in regard to whether a human being was alive. By the time of **Casey**, all 50 states had switched to a new standard, brain activity. **See** note 405.

You can tell **Roe v. Wade** was written by nine men!

It's just a huge flaw to take the viability theory of the ancient pagans--a theory used to justify the killing of newborns--and attempt to use that theory to justify aborting a baby inside a uterus. Whether or not the unborn can survive outside the uterus is a rather hypothetical question to be asking. She's not outside the uterus; she's inside the uterus.

Is she viable where she is? Yes! Nature has designed the perfect neonatal intensive care unit--the mother's womb. We know a baby is viable if you leave her in your uterus. So if the baby's viability outweighs the mother's right to control her uterus, then why isn't the baby's viability inside the uterus a factor?

Viability is a hypothesis, based on a hypothetical situation. It's a fantasy. The Supreme Court is pretending that we live in a world where born infants are autonomous individuals who can survive on their own. But they cannot. No baby is viable, which is why Plato and Aristotle invented a viability doctrine for unwanted children in the first place. All babies need an adult to care, if the baby is going to survive.

But if that's our rule, whether or not babies can survive if an adult is caring for the baby, then an unborn baby is viable too. An unborn baby can survive perfectly fine inside your uterus.

Has the Supreme Court's viability doctrine upset and undermined our treatment of newborns? Some premature infants are kept out of NICUs, against the will of the parents. Why do doctors do that? Are you trying to save money?[334]

---

[334] While our medical and legal authorities talk about "viability," the secret motivation seems to be money. How strongly were Blackmun, Brennan, and Marshall motivated by economics? *See* note 25 and text. Apparently the primary reason for the selection of viability was so the poor would have every opportunity to abort their pregnancies. *Supra* note 204 and text. Indeed,

Imagine a mom's anguish when her premature infant is sentenced to die by hospital administrators.[335] In many cases the baby was premature because the mother had a previous abortion, which she was told was healthy and safe.[336] In actuality it has weakened her cervix, caused a premature birth, and endangered a baby that she wants very much indeed. So **Roe v. Wade** is responsible for the deaths of unborn children, but also the deaths of many preemies who die gasping for air.

The viability doctrine has had an unforeseen side effect--it has corrupted how we treat newborns.

Perhaps we will keep sliding down this slippery slope. What about a mom who abandons her baby, who frees herself from her obligation and walks away? Does she have a right to do so? A newborn is independent of his mother. And yet simultaneously, a newborn is utterly dependent. The baby will die if you abandon him. According to the viability doctrine, this inability to survive outside the uterus means the mother may kill the child.

In 1997 the media was filled with stories about the notorious "Prom Mom" case.[337] A young high school student named Melissa Drexler hid her pregnancy for nine months. She wore baggy clothes, and nobody knew she was pregnant. Not her family, not her boyfriend, and not her classmates.

---

money might be the secret motivation for much of our aborting society. Why do men walk away from a woman they have impregnated? What makes a woman so desperate she induces a miscarriage? Why do doctors poison or stab small babies in violation of the Hippocratic Oath? And when we refuse to even try to save a baby's life, what is the motivation?

[335] "In the United States in 2006, about 19,000 babies died in their first month." www.marchofdimes.org.

[336] *Supra* notes 65-66.

[337] *See* Robert Hanley, "New Jersey Charges Woman, 18, With Killing Baby Born at Prom," *The New York Times* (June 25, 1997).

On the way to her senior prom, Melissa's water broke. She managed to keep that a secret, too. Melissa gave birth by herself, in a toilet stall at the dance.

She fished her baby out of the commode and cut the umbilical cord with the serrated edge of a sanitary napkin dispenser. She wrapped several garbage bags around her child, and dropped her baby into the trash.

Then Melissa went out on the dance floor and joined her friends.

When all the kids went back to school on Monday, blood was noticed on the floor of the ladies bathroom. The janitor was called, and he discovered an infant wrapped in garbage bags. Paramedics tried to resuscitate the baby for two hours, but it was too late. The child was dead.

Melissa Drexler was charged with murder. She pleaded guilty to aggravated manslaughter and was sentenced to 15 years in prison. She served three.

It is quite common for people to say that moms who kill their newborns have nothing to do with women who have abortions, or *Roe v. Wade*. But in fact there are many similarities. Often there is the same isolation. There is the same desire to keep the pregnancy secret. There is sex and pregnancy and a father and a desperate girl who does not want to be a mom.

The only real difference is that we recognize this action as a homicide. She abandoned her baby to die. We see the dead baby, and we are outraged.

Our society is not ready to adopt the Supreme Court's viability rule and apply this standard to newborns. *Roe v. Wade* cites Plato and Aristotle. And Melissa Drexler is following the rules of Plato

and Aristotle. And we do not care. Our society rejects
infanticide.

Chapter 9

What is the Prom Mom doing? She is denying her pregnancy and hiding her pregnancy. She is denying the factual reality of pregnancy. And when her baby is born--the baby who is the cause of all her distress--she abandons the child to die. The similarities between the Prom Mom and the pregnant teenager in the *Simopoulos* case are obvious. Both girls hid their pregnancies from their family, and both girls left the baby in the trash.

In many of these cases, abortion is like a cover-up. You are avoiding a high school sex scandal.[338] And so you deny that you are pregnant. You deny the pregnancy, you hide it, and you get rid of the evidence.

In *Roe v. Wade* the Supreme Court writes about "the stigma of unwed motherhood." That is the scandal that we are trying to avoid. And the Supreme Court offers abortion as a right so that people can avoid a sex scandal.[339] You can hide your pregnancy and deny your pregnancy and no one will know. That is the promise of *Roe*. We will help you hush up this scandal. We will keep it quiet.

---

[338] Pregnancy is odd in that it starts off private and becomes public. Early in the pregnancy, you can keep it private. But as the baby gets bigger, it is more obvious that you are pregnant. As your pregnancy becomes public knowledge, your sex life becomes public knowledge, too. Thus an urge to hide your pregnancy might be an urge to hide your sex life.

[339] One of the strangest ideas in *Roe v. Wade* is this argument that we outlaw abortion because sex is bad. "It has been argued occasionally that these laws were the product of a Victorian social concern to discourage illicit sexual conduct." *Supra* note 1. This is exactly backwards. If sex is original sin, it's because sex is a creation story. Sex is how babies are made. And God wants us to love the children we create.

In offering abortion as a solution, the Supreme Court is like an accomplice to a cover-up. They are helping pregnant women hide their pregnancy and get rid of the baby. When challenged on this, the Supreme Court denies that there was a baby. What pregnancy? What baby?

From the very beginning the Supreme Court denied that a pregnancy involves a baby. The baby's humanity disappears in *Roe v. Wade*. She's defined as a non-person. Obviously the word "fetus" is very important here. We did not kill a baby. We just got rid of a fetus, that's all. But sometimes even the pregnancy itself is denied. For instance, in *Casey* the Court writes, "in some critical respects the abortion decision is of the same character as the decision to use contraception."[340]

Who confuses birth control with abortion? That's a very basic denial of the reality of pregnancy.

To be sure, in the first trimester babies are very tiny. The unborn might just be an inch or two from head to rump. It's easy to see why people are willing to dehumanize this child. She's so tiny!

Maybe that's why the Supreme Court sees no problem in conflating abortion with birth control. The unborn is so small, it's like the doctor is removing nothing from the uterus. How hard can it be to remove a tiny little nothing from the uterus?

Actually, as Dr. Hern has suggested, abortion is often a difficult procedure, even for highly respected doctors. It's a blind medical procedure, you can't see what you are doing, and in a minority of patients, tissue will be left behind in the uterus, causing a visit to the emergency room.

---

[340] *Supra* note 7.

And *Roe* also involves not-so-tiny abortions. These are abortions that are illegal in almost all of Europe.[341] And yet *Roe v. Wade* requires them, too. A late-term abortion often results in major health risks to women, and medical issues, and sometimes the Court has to get into facts it would rather not think about, or discuss.

For instance, in *Catholic League v. Feminist Women's Health Center*, Justice Rehnquist is faced with thousands of tiny baby cadavers.[342] This is one year after *Simopoulos*, when the Supreme Court was embarrassed by a scalded dead baby left in a motel room trash can. Now Rehnquist is faced with the remains of over 16,000 abortions.

"Appellants ask that I stay an order of the California Court of Appeals, Second Appellate District, which determines, under state law, the disposition of some 16,000 aborted fetuses presently in the custody of the Los Angeles County District Attorney. Because I am satisfied that this appeal raises no substantial questions of federal law, I will deny the application."[343]

It's rather odd to say these 16,000 aborted infants have nothing to do with our federal law. Notably Justice Rehnquist's short little opinion fails to mention *Roe v. Wade* at all. One might see Justice Rehnquist's framing of the issues in *Catholic League* as a willful act of repression. He doesn't mention the Supreme Court's involvement in the case!

This is interesting because William Rehnquist was a dissenter in *Roe*. His opinion is a good example of how even the *Roe* dissenters might be doing a savage act of injustice to the unborn.

---

[341] *See* Mary Ann Glendon, *Abortion and Divorce in Western Law* (1989).
[342] 469 U.S. 1303 (1984).
[343] *Id.*

Justice Rehnquist, like all the dissenters, objects to the idea that our Constitution protects a right to abort a pregnancy. And yet Justice Rehnquist is nonetheless defining the unborn as sub-human, as property. This position is unanimous among all the Supreme Court Justices. They automatically dehumanize these infants, and have no regard for them. This prejudice will affect how Rehnquist talks about the unborn, and how he resolves the case.

"The fetuses were discovered by a container company on the premises of a defunct pathology laboratory, and were turned over to the District Attorney's office."[344]

That's a rather skimpy discussion of the facts. And it's not actually true! Malvin Weisberg, the owner of the pathology laboratory, had removed the giant steel container from outside his pathology lab. He was now keeping the container on his own giant estate in Woodland Hills. It was in his backyard, right behind his private tennis courts.[345] (Authorities would later find additional bodies in his garage).[346]

When Weisberg stopped making payments, the container company went to his property and used a winch to recover their container, not knowing what was inside. The container company would open the container the next day.

Here is one of the employees, Ron Gillette, describing what happened next: "One of them fell down and hit me, right in front

---

[344] *Id*.

[345] *See* "Evidence of the American Holocaust, Part 2" *California Catholic Daily* (December 2, 2012).

[346] *See* "Fetus Memorial Service Is Endorsed By Reagan," *The New York Times* (May 27, 1982).

of my feet. And it was opened up. And there it was. It was a mutilated body."[347]

Another employee, Hank Stolk said, "I saw them myself. I couldn't believe it. It was just…little itty babies, you know, all torn to pieces. The heads chopped off, arms, legs. It just makes you sick, to see something like that. It makes you want to cry."[348]

The aborted remains were packaged in formaldehyde. The manager, Nick Martin, said, "They say they're just fetuses, but they sure look like humans to me."[349] The workers were appalled and distressed. The smell coming from the spilled remains was horrible. At least one of the men vomited.

Are these facts irrelevant as a matter of law? Maybe. On the other hand, we might say that perhaps Justice Rehnquist is too embarrassed to discuss these issues in any detail. After all, the Supreme Court is implicitly responsible for the treatment of these 16,000 bodies.

And, just like in *Simopoulos*, somebody called the police again!

Why do people keep calling the police? In *Roe v Wade*, Texas was defining abortion as a crime, with a punishment similar to manslaughter. The Supreme Court denied it was a crime, and said it was a right thing to do. And yet people keep calling the police when they see one.

When a maid in a motel finds a 22-week aborted infant in the trash, she calls the police. When a janitor at a school finds a dead newborn in the bathroom, he calls the police. When a container

---

[347] The workers were interviewed by Jane Chastain. They are visibly upset. *See* "17,000 Bodies Found in Shipping Container," www.youtube.com.
[348] *Id*.
[349] *See* Nick Thimmesch, "Can a Fetus Be Called Medical Waste?" *Observer-Reporter* (February 18, 1982).

company finds 16,000 dead bodies floating in formaldehyde inside one of their containers, they call the police. What else are you going to do?

Justice Rehnquist does not talk about this. He does not mention how his own Court is responsible for this case. The Supreme Court is implicated in these 16,000 human cadavers that ended up in the custody of the district attorney's office. Justice Rehnquist is embarrassed and does not want to hear the case. And he's sure the Supreme Court does not want to hear the case, too.

"After a period of indecision concerning the disposition of the fetuses, during which the District Attorney's office was contacted by several groups, religious and otherwise, offering various means of disposal, the District Attorney made public his decision to turn the fetuses over to a religious organization for the purpose of holding a burial service, and subsequently arranged for interment in a private cemetery that had offered its space to the State free of charge."[350]

Once the bodies are in the public domain, they are really embarrassing. What do you do with them? The D.A. decides to give them to a church to bury them. An abortion clinic sues, claiming it is an establishment of religion to bury the dead in a cemetery.

It's an irrational legal argument, really. Where are we supposed to bury people? When the district attorney dies, is it an establishment of religion to bury him in a Catholic cemetery? Or is that okay?

One suspects the real objection is to the idea that these abortions are people who have died. The abortion clinic wants to squash that idea.

---

[350] *Supra* note 342.

The abortion clinic is suing to stop a funeral service, and asking state authorities to seize the bodies. Imagine the police showing up, interrupting a funeral service, seizing the deceased and taking the body away. According to Rehnquist, there's no free speech issue here, no free exercise issue. "(T)he First Amendment does not entitle applicants to have the State enhance the impact of their speech by providing the subjects of a funeral service."[351]

Is that true, that we have no right to hold a funeral service? Or is *Catholic League* all about denying the baby's humanity? And of course it's *Roe* that denied the baby's humanity in the first place. So maybe *Catholic League* is all about the Supreme Court denying its own involvement.

Clearly Rehnquist has no regard for the humanity of these babies. For instance, he is not thinking of this as a funeral service. His opinion assumes these dead bodies are just props we are using for free speech. They are a visual aid. And of course the visual image of a dead baby is quite powerful. A funeral is an important symbol to the pro-life movement. That's why the abortion clinic wants to squash the service--it wants to censor the idea.

And yet, defining a dead baby as a prop, or speech enhancement, is dehumanizing. In the same way that jamming thousands of dead bodies into containers is dehumanizing, or dumping a baby into the trash is dehumanizing. The abortion clinic and the state of California have stripped these babies of their humanity. As did the bankrupt pathology lab. We don't keep dead people in jars behind our tennis courts. Do we?

Roe v. Wade says abortion is right because our society does not recognize the unborn as human beings. But what happens when we see the body of a baby who has been aborted? We are upset.

---

[351] *Id.*

The unseen is now seen. Humanity is recognized. Thus the Supreme Court's "privacy" jurisprudence, in the context of abortion, is rather like we are covering up a scandal. We hide the bodies because we are ashamed of the bodies. We are ashamed of what we do.[352]

So the Supreme Court is rather like the Prom Mom. Both want to avoid a scandal. She wants to avoid a sex scandal. You're pregnant in high school? That's a scandal. So this young girl denies she's pregnant and hides her pregnancy and gives birth in a bathroom and gets rid of the baby.

Justice Rehnquist wants to avoid a scandal, too. He wants to avoid any implication that his Supreme Court is involved with any of these dead bodies. The right to avoid a high school sex scandal has become a possible infanticide scandal involving our unelected officials.

You discover a dead body. So you call the police. It looks like a crime, so the police investigate. Prosecutors get involved, and they realize this implicates the judges. And by the time the dead body reaches the judges, there is no dead body. What dead body? That's just a speech prop for your advocacy and there are no federal issues in this case.

The Supreme Court is not the only one who is avoiding this scandal. Where is our national media? You'd think the discovery of a giant steel container holding the bodies of 16,000 abortions would be news. And yet there was barely a peep in our media.

---

[352] When we protect privacy, we are thinking of innocent people who are doing good things. For instance, we might want to keep our sex lives private in order to foster intimacy and love. Or, as Justice Douglas put it, we are guarding "the sacred precincts of marital bedrooms." *Supra* note 113. But our right to privacy does not apply to crimes of violence. A man cannot beat his wife and hide behind a right to privacy. A woman cannot kill her baby and hide behind a right to privacy.

There were many articles in the local paper (the **L.A. Times**), a brief mention by the wire services, and random articles in newspapers in places like Ottawa and Orlando.[353] A syndicated columnist, Nick Thimmesch, wrote about it, and Cal Thomas did too.[354]

But the overwhelming majority of Americans never heard a word about it. Why is that? Why wasn't the national media interested in this scandal?[355]

Pro-lifers suspect that our media is biased. After all, overwhelming majorities of journalists identify as "pro-choice" in opinion polls.[356] Is it possible this ideological belief affects how an abortion story is perceived, and written about?

If you're an abortion rights supporter, you might hope that this appalling story would be suppressed and hidden. After all, that's why the abortion clinics are suing. They want to kill this story. It looks bad for **Roe v. Wade** and the Supreme Court. It looks bad for feminism and a woman's right to choose. Not to mention how it looks for the doctors who are involved. So it's entirely possible that journalists want to kill this story out of sympathy.

And yet, if this is the case, then isn't our media actually complicit in this scandal? They are helping to hide the bodies, similar to the way **Pravda** (and the **New York Times**) covered up Stalin's homicides in the Ukraine.[357]

---

[353] "17,000 Fetuses May Get Burial," **Ottawa Citizen** (August 20, 1983); "Aborted Fetuses Get Religious Burial, Reagan Sends Message To Ceremony in Los Angeles," **Orlando Sentinel** (October 7, 1985).
[354] **Supra** note 349.
[355] Jane Chastain interviewed most of the people involved with the discovery, and shot footage of the victims. **See** note 347. None of the networks would run it. **See** note 552.
[356] **See** note 545.
[357] **See** notes 601-608 and text.

Or perhaps there is a more innocent explanation. Feminist groups are characterizing the bodies as "medical waste." If this is accurate, then our media is not covering up a scandal. What scandal? Medical waste isn't a scandal. It's not even newsworthy. Officials discovered medical waste stored in a container. So what?

Of course, pro-lifers--millions of them--are insisting that abortion is infanticide.[358] So they are claiming that over 16,000 dead people have been jammed into this steel container. If this is true, it's obviously newsworthy.

Even if it's not true, the allegation is newsworthy. And it would seem to be in the interest of truth to try to find out the answer, one way or the other. Why not publish photographs of the remains, if only to disprove the allegations?

The overwhelming majority of the aborted infants were very tiny. In fact, authorities originally estimated that the body count was in the hundreds. It was only after the autopsy team (led by the celebrity-coroner-to-the-stars Dr. Thomas Noguchi) painstakingly went through and sorted out all the remains that they came up with an official tally: 16,431.[359]

Obviously many of these babies were tiny embryos. But 193 of the children were estimated to be older than 20 weeks when they were aborted. Dr. Eva Hauser and Dr. Joseph Wood performed autopsies on 43 of them. One baby was estimated to be in the 30th week when she was killed.[360]

---

[358] The discovery of the bodies inspired a Pat Boone song, "16,000 Faces," which includes a rather sharp criticism of the Supreme Court.
[359] *See* Ted Rohrlich, "D.A. Will Not File Charges in Deaths of 16,431 Fetuses," *Los Angeles Times* (August 20, 1983).
[360] *Id*. At least 31 of the babies weighed four pounds or more. *See* note 349.

Why not publish a photograph of the tiny embryos, and another photograph of one of the larger infants?

A fair-minded journalist should also question the characterization of the remains of these babies as "medical waste." Even if extremely tiny, they are developing human beings. Medical waste makes an aborted baby sound like discarded tissue. That would make an abortion similar to what you might see after a liposuction.

If this is the fact of the matter, then an abortion doctor is simply removing tissue from the woman's body. Is this a fair or accurate way to write about abortion? Is it really analogous to plastic surgery?

Describing the remains as "medical waste" seems rather flippant and unreal. It seems like rhetoric, as opposed to an accurate attempt to describe what we are talking about.

And there's a logical flaw with arguing that this is a non-event that is not worthy of our time. Why are the abortion and feminist groups suing to stop a burial service? If this is, in fact, "medical waste," what do you care if Roman Catholics want to have a funeral service and say a few words? Why are you going to all the expense (three and a half years of litigation!) to control the disposition of medical waste?

An unbiased reporter should be wondering about this. Even as the abortion clinics are claiming that it's just medical waste, and these pro-lifers are ridiculous, the actions of the abortion clinics do not seem to agree with their rhetoric. The lawsuit seems like an attempt to control the disposition of the deceased. It's almost like they really do want to hide the bodies.

The litigation itself appears to be an implicit acknowledgment that these pro-lifers have a point. If having a funeral service for "medical waste" is ridiculous--and it would be--then the appropriate response is to either ignore the silliness, or mock it. Yet the abortion clinics are fighting a desperate battle to regain control of the tiny cadavers.

And the fight in the courts wasn't over after Justice Rehnquist wrote his brief opinion in **Catholic League v. Feminist Women's Health Center**. The district attorney was still determined to hold a funeral service. So the California authorities found a non-denominational cemetery and planned to hold the burial service there.

And the abortion clinic sued again![361]

Obviously the argument that a funeral service for the babies is an establishment of religion was a charade. The real goal was to keep the babies from being recognized as human, and to stop any funeral service at all. This second round of litigation failed, however, since the plaintiffs didn't have a leg to stand on. The establishment clause argument was itself rather frivolous. But now that the authorities were planning to bury the babies in a non-denominational service, the judicial case for censorship had utterly fallen apart.

This time around, the courts refused to interfere.

On February 4, 1982, the bodies were discovered. 44 months later, on October 6, 1985, the babies were buried.

Over two hundred people went to the funeral service, including Hank Stolk, one of the workers who first discovered the bodies.[362]

---

[361] Dorothy Townsend, "Feminist Center Challenges Planned Burial of Fetuses," **Los Angeles Times** (September 14, 1985).

Mike Antonovich, the county supervisor, read a telegram sent by President Ronald Reagan.

> Just as the terrible toll of Gettysburg can be traced to a tragic decision of a divided Supreme Court, so also can these deaths we mourn. Once again a whole category of human beings has been ruled outside the protection of the law by a court ruling which clashed with our deepest moral convictions.[363]

President Reagan was famous for calling the unelected Communist regime in the Soviet Union an "evil empire," and would later tell Mr. Gorbachev to tear down the Berlin Wall. Now he was throwing down a gauntlet to our own unelected rulers, the Supreme Court, and reminding them of the humanity of the unborn. Like many pro-lifers, Reagan was making an analogy between *Roe v. Wade* and *Dred Scott*.[364] He was criticizing the Supreme Court for dehumanizing these infants. And implicitly he was holding the judicial branch responsible for their deaths.

Ironically, one of the attorneys who was working in the White House at the time, John Roberts, would go on to become Chief Justice of the Supreme Court. At his confirmation hearing, the Reagan telegram would became noteworthy, as Roberts wrote a memo on it, agreeing to its release.[365]

Shortly after the bodies were discovered, Dr. Philip Dreisbach, a doctor in Palm Springs and the secretary for the California Pro-Life Medical Association, wrote to the President about the circumstances of the discovery, and asked if they might bury the

---

[362] "Evidence of the American Holocaust, Part 6," *California Catholic Daily* (December 27, 2012).

[363] *Id.*

[364] *Dred Scott v. Sandford*, 60 U.S. 393 (1857).

[365] Amy Goldstein and Jo Becker, "Memo Cited 'Abortion Tragedy,'" *The Washington Post* (August 16, 2005).

babies in Arlington National Cemetery. The President wrote back to Dr. Dreisbach, expressing his "great horror and sadness" at the discovery. While implying that he would not be able to attend any funeral, Reagan also suggested that Dr. Dreisbach pursue his plan to have a funeral service for the infants.[366]

> Your decision to hold a memorial service for these children is most fitting and proper. On such an occasion we must strengthen our resolve to end this national tragedy.
>
> I am hopeful that evidence like that found in California will move those who have thus far preferred silence or inaction and encourage them to agree that something must be done.[367]

The pro-life group in California started using Reagan's letter in its fund-raising materials. This made some of the attorneys in the White House mad. (Specifically, they were mad that photographs of aborted babies were also included in the materials). In a memo that Roberts drafted with co-counsel, he would disparage the "gruesome anti-abortion display" of the pro-life group.[368]

Ironically, once John Roberts became Chief Justice of our Supreme Court, he would participate in a "gruesome anti-abortion display" himself (a.k.a. the second *Carhart* opinion).[369] After the Roberts Court issues a judicial opinion describing in graphic detail how doctors are killing babies outside the birth canal, John Roberts really can't complain about pro-lifers who are uncouth.

---

[366] *Supra* note 346.
[367] *Id.*
[368] R. Jeffrey Smith and Jo Becker, "John G. Roberts Jr.: In His Own Words," *The Washington Post* (August 17, 2005).
[369] *Supra* note 208.

Chapter 10

Catholic League is a fight over a funeral service. It might be hard to see how *Catholic League* involves a woman's choice at all. Why are these abortion clinics fighting so hard to hide the tiny bodies of aborted children?

And yet denying the humanity of the unborn is a very basic part of *Roe v. Wade*. Indeed, that principle underlies the entire case. In *Roe* the Supreme Court writes this: "The appellee and certain amici argue that the fetus is a 'person' within the language and meaning of the Fourteenth Amendment. In support of this, they outline at length and in detail the well-known facts of fetal development. If this suggestion of personhood is established, the appellant's case, of course, collapses, for the fetus' right to life would then be guaranteed specifically by the Amendment."[370]

As in much of *Roe v. Wade*, this conclusion is sloppy and overbroad. Recognizing the humanity of an unborn baby does not mean that life begins at conception. Maybe life begins when the baby's heart starts beating, or when she has activity in her brain. Maybe early abortions are not homicides. That would be one of the questions a competent opinion dealing with abortion would have to resolve. You have to address the infanticide issue. You can't just skip over it. You have to think about rape. You can't just omit any discussion.

Obviously many of our citizens are intensely divided over abortion, and we are arguing past one another. Pro-lifers are mad about infanticide and the killing of unwanted children. Feminists

---

[370] *Supra* note 1.

are angry about rape and the violation of a woman's freedom.[371] And the Supreme Court makes our fight far more awful than it has to be, by refusing to discuss either subject.

Read *Roe v. Wade*. There is no discussion of these topics. It is quite damning of *Roe*--and all the opinions that follow it--that there is no in-depth discussion anywhere about the baby in the womb and her development. No discussion of her heartbeat, her brain, her lungs, her movement. We don't even have a discussion of how big she is.

People who are worried about infanticide would be discussing this, and thinking about it. The Supreme Court should be asking if the baby is alive, how the state defines death, and so on. An opinion that did this would pay particular attention to the baby's development. Such an opinion would give us a discussion of biological factors. Does the baby have a heartbeat? Is the baby moving? Is this movement voluntary, or reflex? Is there brain activity? Is there an EEG? Are the baby's lungs working, or capable of working? These are criteria a doctor might use to determine if a baby is alive or not, in accordance with state law.

Resolving the infanticide issue is important. The Supreme Court's failure to resolve the infanticide issue simply left the infanticide issue unresolved. Pro-lifers accuse the Supreme Court of killing babies under *Roe v. Wade*. And the Supreme Court's response is that it does not know what a person is.

It's such a shocking way to behave. Imagine you are the police, investigating a crime. You want to know how that dead baby ended up in the trash. And you're questioning a suspect. And the suspect tells you that he has no idea what you're talking about.

---

[371] And both sides can be over-protective. Pro-lifers often claim that all abortions are homicides (but what about our death statutes?) Feminists say that any unwanted sex is rape (but isn't rape a crime of violence?) Both sides need to be careful of false allegations.

What baby? And then, in the middle of this interrogation, the suspect tells you that he has no idea what a person is.

In *The Adventures of Huckleberry Finn*, Mark Twain writes of a conversation between Aunt Sally and Huck Finn.

"Good gracious! Anybody hurt?"

"No'm. Killed a nigger."

"Well, it's lucky; because sometimes people do get hurt."[372]

That's one of the problems with *Roe v. Wade*. We all know infanticide is bad. We're not arguing about whether killing a baby is bad. We're arguing about reality. If pro-lifers win this fight, our society will have a massive shift, like our society did after slavery. One day, slavery is normal, and the next day you're a monster. One day, abortion is normal, and the next day you're a baby-killer.

Millions of American women have had abortions. Our mothers, our daughters, our sisters, our girlfriends, our wives--all of us know somebody who has had an abortion. We might not know who they are, because we are so secretive about our abortions. But we all know somebody who has had one. And these are nice people, people who give to charity and help others.

Does this mean abortion is right?

Or perhaps we might think of abortion as just like slavery. After all, our first President was a slave-owner, the author of our Declaration of Independence was a slave-owner, and the architect of our Constitution was a slave-owner.

---

[372] Mark Twain, *The Adventures of Huckleberry Finn* (1884).

George Washington, Thomas Jefferson, James Madison, these are
our best and brightest. They are the founders of our country, our
smartest citizens, children of God and fighters for freedom.
These are our heroes. And yet in regard to slavery they had a
moral blind spot. They did not see the humanity of the people
they were oppressing. And when you do not see the humanity,
even nice people can do horrific things.

To us, the humanity of a slave is obvious. We don't understand
how people could own slaves. Future generations might ask us
similar questions. How could we kill our own baby? How could
we induce a miscarriage and pretend that was a normal thing to
do? How could we make unwanted people disappear?

And we won't know what to say.

We should not blame any woman who has had an abortion.[373] We
all live in a media culture that says nothing about abortion, other
than it's a right thing to do. It's one of your options, one of your
choices. We hide any evidence of infanticide from women. We
don't want women to see an aborted baby, or to think about what
it means to abort your child.

But of course all this supposes that pro-lifers are right. Maybe
they are not right. Maybe abortion is not an infanticide. Maybe
it's analogous to birth control. But we can't answer these
questions unless we talk about it and think about it. So let's start
by trying to answer the question the Supreme Court is asking in
Roe: what is a person?

---

[373] Many pro-lifers do not see the aborting mom as the primary criminal. She
is seen as an accomplice, or in some cases another victim. Pregnancy is seen
as a mitigating factor. For instance, the criminal statute at issue in *Roe* made it
a crime to perform an abortion, not undergo one. And when Dr. Gosnell's
abortion clinic was raided, none of the moms were arrested. Only the doctor
(and non-doctors) who did the actual killings would be prosecuted for murder.
The moms, many of whom were accomplices-after-the-fact, were not
prosecuted at all.

A person is a live human being.[374]

In *Roe v. Wade* the Supreme Court is making this rather fantastic claim that they have no idea what the Framers of our Fourteenth Amendment meant when they used this "person" word. The Court is playing semantic games with a very basic, two-syllable word we use to describe humanity.

As if you need to go to law school to know who people are!

Roe v. Wade discusses the word "person" like it's a legal term of art. Humanity is some weird legal doctrine, apparently.[375] So Justice Blackmun is scouring the Constitution, looking for examples to see how the word is used in a sentence. In *Roe v. Wade* the Supreme Court catalogs every use of the word "person" in our Constitution.

> The Constitution does not define
> "person" in so many words. Section 1 of
> the Fourteenth Amendment contains
> three references to "person." The first,
> in defining "citizens," speaks of
> "persons born or naturalized in the
> United States." The word also appears
> both in the Due Process Clause and in
> the Equal Protection Clause. "Person" is
> used in other places in the
> Constitution: in the listing of

---

[374] *See* www.dictionary.com; www.freedictionary.com; www.merriam-webster.com.

[375] This idea the Supreme Court has that some live human beings can be defined as non-people leads to disregard for authority, unrest, and even outbreaks of violence. The very basis of law is a deep respect for words. *See* James Boyd White, *Justice As Translation* (1990). When our authorities play semantic games with language--when they lie--our authorities are not only subverting our laws, but undermining their own authority. You cannot speak for the Constitution if you cannot read the Constitution. And ultimately a disregard for the language of law dashes any hope for a peaceful resolution of conflicts.

> qualifications for Representatives and
> Senators, Art. I, § 2, cl. 2, and § 3, cl.
> 3; in the Apportionment Clause, Art. I,
> § 2, cl. 3; in the Migration and
> Importation provision, Art. I, § 9, cl. 1;
> in the Emolument Clause, Art. I, § 9,
> cl. 8; in the Electors provisions, Art. II,
> § 1, cl. 2, and the superseded cl. 3; in
> the provision outlining qualifications
> for the office of President, Art. II, § 1,
> cl. 5; in the Extradition provisions, Art.
> IV, § 2, cl. 2, and the superseded
> Fugitive Slave Clause 3; and in the
> Fifth, Twelfth, and Twenty-second
> Amendments, as well as in §§ 2 and 3
> of the Fourteenth Amendment. But in
> nearly all these instances, the use of
> the word is such that it has application
> only post-natally. None indicates, with
> any assurance, that it has any possible
> pre-natal application.[376]

The Court is attempting to prove that the authors of the 14th Amendment did not specifically intend to protect the unborn. And so Blackmun argues that none of the provisions in the Constitution seem to apply to unborn infants.

Using the same logic, one might also conclude that the Framers did not intend to protect newborns. Is a baby going to be extradited for crimes? No, because babies do not commit crimes. So we might deduce that the Framers were not specifically thinking of babies when they wrote our Constitution.[377]

---

[376] *Supra* note 1. It's quite odd that our Supreme Court insists that an unborn baby is not a person while it simultaneously claims that a corporation is one. *Supra* notes 437-439 and text.

[377] If we are going to define a class of inferior people, a baby would seem to be an obvious candidate, since babies are so helpless and vulnerable. Indeed, babies need affirmative action if they are to survive. *See* Stephen Carter, *Reflections of an Affirmative Action Baby* (1992). Is it dangerous for the Supreme Court to define a class of inferior people? And once we start this

On the other hand, babies are people and people are protected. Even if states have authority to discriminate against children, that is not a power to dehumanize them. Can we discriminate against six-year-olds? Yes. Can we murder them? No.

There is nothing in our Constitution that suggests a kill-right.

One of the most blatant and ugly aspects of Supreme Court abortion jurisprudence is the use of the word "fetus" to describe an unborn infant. It's a Latin word that actually means "baby." So why not use the baby word, at least some of the time?

It seems Orwellian, as if the purpose is to dehumanize.[378] Using the Latin word makes our child sound like an alien in a B movie. It's *The Fetus Inside Me*. Of course you want to stop it, that's the idea.

If the Supreme Court was serious about reproductive choice, it would often use the word "baby" in its abortion opinions, to remind people of our other choice. You can abort the fetus or you can keep your baby. But the Supreme Court never talks this way, because reminders of the baby's humanity undercut the right to abortion.

We say "baby" when we want the baby and "fetus" when we do not. And litigation is always in regard to unwanted infants, so the Supreme Court says "fetus" all the time. We know with complete assurance just by the use of the word "fetus" that we are reading an abortion opinion. It is a very powerful word, a quasi-scientific

---

project of identifying people who are inferior, how should we regard them? Should we be hostile? Or should we love?

[378] George Orwell, *1984* (1950). Orwell describes an "unperson" as a person who has not only been killed, but every trace of their existence disappears. In the context of "choice," you abort the pregnancy and then pretend as if you were never pregnant at all.

word, much like "Negro," a word that is used to dehumanize other human beings. And the baby must be dehumanized if **Roe v. Wade** is to work. That is why the Supreme Court is very careful to always use the Latin.

Of course an obstetrician might use the word "fetus" in an innocent way, as a medical term. It is a medical word, after all, common in medical texts. But obstetricians also use the medical term "gravida," which is Latin for a pregnant woman.[379] If you're using Latin, it's gravida and fetus. If you're using English, it's pregnant mom and baby.

So we might ask, why has the Supreme Court never used the word "gravida"? Don't you want to be medically accurate?

Imagine a pro-life jurist who kept writing about "the gravida and the baby." That's what we have, in reverse, from the Supreme Court all the time. It's the pregnant woman and her fetus. They use the cold Latin, the medical terminology, to dehumanize a human infant. While they use regular English to describe a pregnant woman.

It's upsetting to ponder how much of our abortion regime relies upon this rhetorical trick. One suspects that if the Supreme Court used the English word instead of the Latin word, our abortion rules would be quite different.

And can we honestly say that nobody uses the word "baby" to talk about the unborn? What words do obstetricians use when they talk with happy pregnant mothers? What word do all the pregnancy websites use?[380]

---

[379] In his abortion textbook, Dr. Hern describes the mother as a "gravid female" and the baby as a "fetoplacental unit." **Supra** note 42.

[380] **See** www.babycenter.com; www.whattoexpect.com; www.webmd.com; www.pregnancy.com; www.americanpregnancy.org; www.thebump.com.

The baby/fetus dichotomy suggests a kind of baby segregation in our minds. We are discriminating against the babies we do not want. The unborn babies we do want--same age, same weight, same location--we identify those babies as "babies." Yet the Supreme Court never does.

It's rather shocking when you think about it. For instance, what words do we use when we talk about an accidental miscarriage? Baby. We always say baby. It would be vicious and cruel to tell a crying woman that she lost a fetus. Who does that?

Here is Ariel Levy, writing about her miscarriage in the pages of *The New Yorker*.

> I felt an unholy storm move through my body, and after that there is a brief lapse in my recollection; either I blacked out from the pain or I have blotted out the memory. And then there was another person on the floor in front of me, moving his arms and legs, alive. I heard myself say out loud, "This can't be good." But it *looked* good. My baby was as pretty as a seashell.
>
> He was translucent and pink and very, very small, but he was flawless. His lovely lips were opening and closing, opening and closing, swallowing the new world. For a length of time I cannot delineate, I sat there, awestruck, transfixed. Every finger, every toenail, the golden shadow of his eyebrows coming in, the elegance of his shoulders--all of it was miraculous, astonishing. I held him up to my face, his head and shoulders filling my hand, his legs dangling almost to my elbow. I tried to think of something maternal I

could do to convey to him that I was,
in fact, his mother, and that I had the
situation completely under control.[381]

Ariel's baby, born prematurely at 19 weeks, died right after birth. Her grief is haunting.

I was so sad I could barely breathe. On
five or six occasions, I ran into mothers
who had heard what had happened,
and they took one look at me and burst
into tears. (Once, this happened with
a man). Within a week, the apartment
we were supposed to move into with
the baby fell through. Within three,
my marriage had shattered. I started
lactating. I continued bleeding. I
cried ferociously and without warning--
in bed, in the middle of meetings,
sitting on the subway. It seemed to me
that grief was leaking out of me from
every orifice.[382]

This human suffering is real, and the Supreme Court's phony use of the "fetus" word is a sham. It's a sham and a disgrace. How many babies have we aborted that are just like Ariel Levy's miraculous and wonderful baby? And are we really supposed to say that the baby's status as a human being depends on our feelings?

We have no trouble recognizing the humanity of the unborn when we want a child. Here is Naomi Wolf, writing in the *New Republic*:

Anyone who has had a sonogram during
pregnancy knows perfectly well that
the four-month-old fetus responds to

---

[381] Ariel Levy, "Thanksgiving in Mongolia," *The New Yorker* (November 18, 2013).
[382] *Id.*

> outside stimulus. "Let's get him to
> look this way," the technician will say,
> poking gently at the belly of a
> delighted mother-to-be. The **Well
> Baby Book**, the kind of wholegrain,
> holistic guide to pregnancy and
> childbirth that would find its audience
> among the very demographic that is
> most solidly pro-choice, reminds us:
> "Increasing knowledge is increasing the
> awe and respect we have for the
> unborn baby and is causing us to regard
> the unborn baby as a real person long
> before birth..."[383]

This discrimination strikes Wolf as simple bigotry. When we want the baby, it's "Mozart for your belly" and "framed sonogram photos." When we don't want the baby, it's "uterine material." She is right to call this a "bizarre bifurcation." But since Naomi Wolfe is pro-choice, she misses the cause of all this irrational discrimination: *Roe v. Wade*.

The unborn child was defined as a non-person so that our equal protection clause would not apply. This is why we can be bigots against the unborn. We can dislike them, hate them, and abort them. We can be as irrational as we want to be. We can call them babies or fetuses, love them or kill them. The baby's reality shifts with our emotions, with our bigotry, with our knowledge and with our ignorance.

It is quite dangerous to attempt to "resolve" the abortion debate by defining the baby as a non-person whose life is irrelevant. After all, a denial of humanity has often preceded atrocities. And aside from any confusion about how to interpret our equal protection clause, it's quite clear from all the slavery amendments

---

[383] *Supra* note 100.

190

that any dehumanization of people is illegal.[384] You are simply
not allowed to define live human beings as sub-human, as
property.[385]

Preventing atrocities is one of the main purposes of equal
protection. After all, we passed our equal protection clause in
response to all the atrocities of slavery. Our equal protection
clause was an attempt to outlaw state dehumanization of a class of
people. That's what caused all the atrocities.

In footnote 53 of **Roe v. Wade**, the Supreme Court writes, "We
are not aware that in the taking of any census under this clause, a
fetus has ever been counted."[386] Was the failure to fully count the
slaves as people in our census a reliable indicator of the humanity
of the slave, Justice Blackmun?[387]

It's as if the Supreme Court is oblivious to our own past. You're
kicking human beings out of humanity! And we have historical

---

[384] Some conservatives have argued that the equal protection clause only
applies to racial discrimination, because that was the context in which the 14th
Amendment was adopted. *See* Justice Antonin Scalia, "The Originalist,"
California Lawyer (January 2011). And yet the text of 14th Amendment is
much broader than that. "No state...shall deny to any person...the equal
protection of the laws." Broadly speaking, we are not allowed to discriminate
in malign fashion against any people at all. On the other hand, a state has wide
powers to discriminate against conduct. A state can discriminate against
killers, rapists, prostitutes and jaywalkers, because this is discrimination
against an action, not a person. Any human being can avoid this behavior. Are
you free to avoid the class? Then equal protection is satisfied.
[385] A primary motivation for **Dred Scott** was economic. The humanity of the
slave was denied because the Supreme Court was thinking about money. It
would cost too much to recognize the humanity of human beings. And can we
not say the same thing about **Roe v. Wade**? Perhaps the humanity of the
unborn is denied because of money, too. *See* note 334.
[386] *Supra* note 1.
[387] The original Constitution divides our country into "free Persons" and "three
fifths of all other Persons." **Roe v. Wade** actually cites this language as the
Supreme Court strips the unborn baby of her humanity. You are not a person
until the state counts you as one. That's what **Roe v Wade** is saying. Did we
not fight a war over this?

examples of authorities defining classes of people as sub-human. Needless to say, it's a dangerous and risky thing to do. You have to be absolutely right on the life-or-death question. And deconstructing the equal protection clause in order to avoid thinking about the issue is a rather astounding approach to take.

Defining the unborn as sub-human is only defensible if life begins at birth. If life begins at birth, then abortion is not a homicide. Under this rule, if you abort a pregnancy, you are terminating pre-life or future life or "potential life." That might be bad, but it's not the same thing as a homicide.

If, on the other hand, life begins before birth, then **Roe v. Wade** is a baby-killing opinion.

You have to assume that nobody on the Court wanted to kill a baby. Certainly Justice Blackmun's rather emotional opinions in **Webster** and **Casey** suggest that he wanted no such thing.[388] And yet his opinion in **Roe** claims that the life-or-death question is irrelevant. And that suggests a certain lack of care.

Of course we know it's possible that abortion kills a baby. After all, the unborn is a human being. She's not a frog or a chimp or a rock. We also know that a baby can die in the womb, what's often called a miscarriage or a stillbirth. Doctors have no trouble recognizing the difference between a live baby in the womb and a dead one. Why wouldn't it be a homicide for a doctor to turn a live baby in the womb into a dead one?[389]

---

[388] "I fear for the darkness as four justices anxiously await the single vote necessary to extinguish the light." **Planned Parenthood v. Casey**, 505 U.S. 833 (1992) (Blackmun, J., concurring).

[389] Suppose that one day our society recognizes the humanity of the unborn. Could we prosecute an abortion doctor for killing a baby in 1992? No. Our Constitution forbids ex post facto (after the fact) laws. We cannot apply a criminal statute retroactively. Similarly, we did not punish people for atrocities committed under slavery. If your actions are legal when you do them, new authorities cannot punish you after the fact.

Under the common law, there was a "born alive" rule. Murder statutes did not apply to the killing of an unborn infant, unless the baby was born after the attack, took a breath of air, and then died.[390] On the other hand, the common law was also quite clear that abortion was often a homicide. For instance, the classic legal scholar Bracton wrote, "If there be anyone who strikes a pregnant woman or gives her a poison whereby he causes an abortion, if the fetus be already formed or animated, and especially if it be animated, he commits homicide."[391]

The word "animated" is a reference to any voluntary movement from the child. As *Roe v. Wade* admits, the states that were ratifying the equal protection clause were also writing criminal statutes making abortion a very serious felony, equivalent to manslaughter. And dating back to the common law, people who were outlawing abortions were talking about homicides of children.[392]

At oral argument in *Roe*, and in the opinion itself, the Supreme Court made comment of the fact that Texas was not defining abortion as murder. Instead Texas was defining abortion as a crime similar to manslaughter, a lesser punishment.

It's a fair criticism of Texas, and the common law. Why are you not defining abortion as murder? If you think that the baby's life

---

[390] "To kill a child in its mother's womb, though a felony, is no murder, but if the child be born alive, and die by reason of the poison or bruises it received in the womb, it may be murder in the wrongdoer." William Blackstone, *Commentaries on the Laws of England* (1778). Note this common law rule is highly controversial; many states are now defining forced abortions as murder, regardless if the baby is born alive or not. *See* note 398. And note too that many abortionists would be subject to a murder prosecution under the common law rule. *See* notes 295-296, and note 298.
[391] Henry de Bracton, *On The Laws and Customs of England* (1260).
[392] *See* note 192.

begins at conception, or at some other point during the pregnancy, you ought to define abortion as murder, right?

That's the question that Justice Stewart had at oral argument. "There is no state, is there, that equates abortion with murder? Or is there?"[393] In footnote 54 of **Roe,** Justice Blackmun writes, "the penalty for criminal abortion…is significantly less than the maximum penalty for murder…If the fetus is a person, may the penalties be different?"[394]

Of course, the failure to define abortion as murder does not mean that an unborn baby is sub-human. The Supreme Court seems to think that not defining abortion as murder "proves" that these babies are not people. Actually all it proves is that we are discriminating against them. What it might prove is simple bigotry. Maybe we don't give the unborn the same right to life that newborns have because we can't see them.

Why do we have to be certain, anyway? Perhaps Texas had the not unreasonable belief that they could outlaw a procedure that might be a homicide. They weren't sure if it was or was not. But

---

[393] **Supra** note 281. The answer is yes and no. At the time of **Roe v. Wade**, in California you could be charged with murder for killing an unborn baby. **Supra** note 398. But the other rule in California was that a woman had a "health" right to an abortion. **Supra** note 207. Whether it was murder or not depended upon whether mom approved. If she did not want an abortion, it was murder. If she wanted an abortion, it was not. After the passage of the **Unborn Victims of Violence** Act of 2004, this is now the federal rule as well.

[394] **Supra** note 1. Consider the cavalier way the Supreme Court talks about "quickening," which is a common law reference to a baby kicking inside a woman's uterus. The issue came up in murder trials, as men were charged with attacking pregnant women, kicking them in the abdomen, and causing a miscarriage. **Supra** note 192. The issue for the judges was whether these men should be hanged for murder, or whether their crime was less-than-murder. The discussion of whether killing an unborn child is murder or not is of course important. But a finding that it was not murder does not mean there was a common law right to kick a pregnant woman in the abdomen and abort her baby.

it might be. And they wanted to outlaw the procedure out of an awareness of the possibility.

The most infamous line in **Roe v. Wade** is this one: "We need not resolve the difficult question of when life begins."[395] Why isn't Texas allowed to make the same argument? Why can't Texas admit that it doesn't know when life begins either, but it wants to outlaw abortion out of caution and respect for human life? Why do we have to be certain abortion is a homicide before we can outlaw it? Attempted murder isn't a homicide, and we outlaw that. Even if abortion is not a homicide, we might object to the mindset it gives people.

Maybe Texas had a nuanced view of abortion. It's kind of like murder and it's kind of like birth control. Certainly that's more nuanced than the Supreme Court's view, that abortion does not implicate murder at all, and it's just like birth control. In effect Texas is splitting the difference between birth control and murder. So the state is defining abortion as a crime worthy of five years in jail, or ten years if the woman did not consent to the abortion. And there was no punishment for the woman, only for the doctor (or non-doctor).

The Supreme Court took this nuance and used it to dehumanize the child altogether. A better response might have asked Texas to clarify the homicide issue and resolve whether or when abortion kills a baby.

The classic "born alive" rule seems to correlate to the idea that you have to be breathing air in order to be alive.[396] Yet Texas, and many other states, and the common law, also seem to think that abortion is infanticide. So before you take the momentous

---

[395] *Id.*
[396] *Supra* note 390.

step of finding an unenumerated right to abort pregnancies, maybe you ought to ask Texas to straighten out its homicide laws.

Why not recognize the unborn infant's humanity? Equal protection does not forbid abortion. Equal protection says nothing about when human life begins, or when people die. It's a procedural guide. It might help us reason through these issues. For instance, we can take the infanticide issue off the table by applying the same death statutes to the unborn that we apply to you or me.

We actually have laws on the books that answer the life-or-death question.[397] At the time of *Roe v. Wade*, the rule in Texas in regard to when people die was absence of heart and lung function. A death statute like this tells us when people die. So a death statute answers the question of when abortion qualifies as a homicide.

Why is Texas forbidding abortion? The state wants to protect the life of the unborn child. And it claims that life begins when the zygote implants into the walls of the uterus. And yet the Texas death statute suggests that life begins when the baby has heart and lung function. These are different points. And we're talking about whether we are killing a baby, so it's important for these rules to agree.

Maybe the first thing the Court should have done was ask the state of Texas to bring its homicide, abortion, and death statutes into alignment. Overturning the law on procedural grounds would give Texas the opportunity to revisit its death statutes, and to change its criteria in regard to when people die if it wants to. That would respect our right to life, and yet also give the people

---

[397] And we now have unanimous agreement in all 50 states in regard to when people die. *See* notes 405-406 and text.

of the state democratic control over the important life-or-death issue.

Why does the Supreme Court need to overturn the abortion statute at all? One issue in *Roe v. Wade* is that we don't actually know if the state can prosecute a doctor for murder if he aborts an unborn child. From the statute, and the State's defense of the statute at oral argument in *Roe*, it isn't clear whether Texas considers abortion to be infanticide (since it defines life as beginning at implantation) or not infanticide (since abortion has a separate section in the criminal code).

The state of Texas is arguing in *Roe v. Wade* that an unborn baby is a person. If an unborn baby is a person, then somebody who kills her might be punished under the ordinary murder statutes.[398] Does the abortion statute in Texas preclude a murder prosecution? Is the abortionist guilty of abortion, or the murder of a baby? This murkiness in the law creates a notice issue with the citizenry, hence a due process issue.

A far more subtle opinion than *Roe v. Wade* might have voided the abortion statute for vagueness, and asked the state to bring its abortion, murder, and death statutes into alignment. If Texas is really interested in protecting the baby's life, as it's claiming, then it should welcome this opportunity to clarify what it is doing.

---

[398] This happened in California. In 1969, a man named Keeler discovered that a man named Vogt had impregnated Mrs. Keeler. Mr. Keeler viciously attacked his wife, who was in the ninth month of pregnancy. "I'm going to stomp it out of you," he said. He beat her until she was unconscious. Mrs. Keeler was taken to the hospital and a C-section was performed. Her 5-pound baby had died from a skull fracture. Mr. Keeler was charged with assault on his wife and the murder of her baby. The judges in California ruled that the baby was not a person and no murder had taken place. The people of California, outraged by this, insisted that an unborn child be recognized as a human being. California amended its murder statute to include the unborn. All of this happened prior to *Roe v. Wade*. And Justice Blackmun does an odd thing. He cites *Keeler v. Superior Court* in his opinion, denying the baby's humanity. And he ignores the popular response, and the new murder statute.

Chapter 11

The pro-life movement often says that life begins at conception. Implicit from this is the idea that every abortion is a homicide. It's not true. At least, under the death statutes we apply to you and me, it's not true.

Obviously our death statutes might be wrong. A state's death statute is simply our best guess in regard to when human beings die. But what we can't deny is that our society defines--with precision--when people die. We know exactly when people die as a legal matter. All you have to do is look it up.

Yet this is not the question the Supreme Court asks in *Roe v. Wade*. The question the Supreme Court asks is something quite different. When does life begin?

"Conception," say the pro-lifers.

"Birth," says the pro-choice side. And our two opposing sides keep arguing back and forth. It's conception or birth, conception or birth. Either all abortions are homicides or none of them are. There is no middle ground, apparently. Or is there?

In the opinion itself Justice Blackmun writes this: "It should be sufficient to note briefly the wide divergence of thinking on this most sensitive and difficult question. There has always been strong support for the view that life does not begin until live birth. This was the belief of the Stoics."[399]

Here the Court is citing Ludwig Edelstein's book, *The Hippocratic Oath*. Blackmun relies heavily on Edelstein, a

---

[399] *Supra* note 1.

classical scholar, when he dismantles the Oath and argues there is
no need for physicians to follow it, since most of the ancient
pagans did not follow the Oath. That's a rather preposterous bit
of moral reasoning. But here Blackmun is not just reasoning
badly. He's making factually incorrect statements.

He is arguing the ancient Greeks of Athens ("the Stoics") thought
that life began at birth. They did not. The pagans thought
newborns were not rational people and could be abandoned to die.
Blackmun acknowledges as much in footnote 22, when he
discusses Aristotle's abortion theories. "The vegetable stage was
reached at conception, the animal at 'animation,' and the rational
soon after live birth."[400] Soon after live birth is not the same
thing as live birth.

After saying the Stoics thought that life began at birth, Justice
Blackmun writes that birth "appears to be the predominant,
though not the unanimous, attitude of the Jewish faith."[401] The
Supreme Court has just conflated the ancient pagans with the
Jews. The pagans were baby-killers. The Jews were not baby-
killers. The Jews believed in love and marriage and required their
adherents to be married before they had sex. Because sex leads to
babies, and there was no birth control 2000 years ago, and
infanticide is evil.

This is really basic stuff. Indeed, one of the remarkable victories
of Christianity was the worldwide abandonment of infanticide.[402]
Christianity was so successful in making infanticide unthinkable,
our Supreme Court can't even bring up the issue in ***Roe v. Wade***.

Infanticide is unacceptable, and the Supreme Court knows it. But
it wasn't always unacceptable. And Blackmun's sloppy and

---

[400] ***Id***.
[401] ***Id***.
[402] Professor Dellapenna argues the practice was driven underground. ***Supra*** note 192.

wrong characterization of pagan thought in regard to protecting newborns is inexcusable.

This reluctance to discuss the possibility of infanticide is one of the two fundamental flaws of *Roe v. Wade*. (The failure to discuss rape is the other).

The Supreme Court wanted to avoid the appearance of arrogance. So they strike a pose of humility in regard to the baby's life. "(T)he judiciary, at this point in the development of man's knowledge, is not in a position to speculate as to the answer."[403] That's a good sentence if you're denying a right to abortion, because you are scared that it might be a homicide. You don't want to speculate or guess wrong.

But it's a horrible sentence when you are finding a right to abort an unborn infant. Our society needs to know that abortion is not a homicide. Particularly the girls and women who are having these abortions need reassurance that it's not a homicide. Is the Supreme Court shrugging its shoulders and saying that maybe you killed your baby?

Consider, for instance, the bizarre way the Supreme Court frames the life or death question as implicating the beginning of life, while refusing to discuss infanticide at all. Can we divorce the two concepts like that? Most of us assume that life and death are connected. We connect them in our speech all the time. "It's a life or death issue." If you are dead, you are not alive. If you are alive, you are not dead.

Yet the Supreme Court is clearly talking about the beginning of life without any regard to the end of life. This has the effect of unmooring the Court's discussion from factual reality, from our material world. Not surprisingly, this framing makes the Court

---

[403] *Supra* note 1.

talk about the beginning of life as an abstract question, involving philosophers and theologians. The Court talks about Jewish thought, Protestant thought, Catholic thought. As if the beginning of life is merely a spiritual question, and does not really involve us mortals.

What would our response be if the Court said it could not answer the infanticide question? What would we say if the Court said there was massive confusion in regard to when people die, and we "need not resolve the difficult question"? It would result in utter chaos in our society. The cadavers would pile up in the hospitals, because doctors would be terrified to pronounce anybody dead, because they could go to prison, or get sued for being wrong.

Death affects all of us. So of course we have rules in place in regard to when people die.

Maybe we're wrong. Maybe we're arrogant people, filled with hubris, and we think we can answer big questions like that. Nonetheless, we do answer the question. We have to, and so we do. We do the best we can.

By framing the question as the beginning of life, the Supreme Court is asking the question in such a way as to single out the unborn child. Maybe you're alive, maybe you're not alive, it doesn't really matter. That's the startling conceit of *Roe v. Wade*, that the baby's life is irrelevant. And the pro-life movement responds, as is imminently predictable, by talking about the killing of babies.

The Supreme Court's avoidance of the infanticide question was a horrible mistake. And not just because it makes the Court seem as if they have a callous disregard for a baby's life. It was a mistake to avoid the question because the law gives us an answer. The question of when people die is a question that has been resolved by doctors, by philosophers, by theologians, and most importantly--if you want to stay out of prison--by lawyers.

The Supreme Court is ignoring the death issue while it talks about the beginning of life. The Court is framing the issue in a way that singles out the unborn baby, and keeps the issue abstract and spiritual. It's a nice, friendly way to put it. When does life begin? It's a happy question.

When do people die, on the other hand, is a mean question. That's a serious question, and you better answer it. You better think about it and you better be right. That's a question that applies to all of us. We're all going to die. When do we die? And of course we don't want to think about death. Clearly *Roe v. Wade* doesn't want to think about death.

The Court is doing several things here. It is framing the question in such a way as to implicate only the unborn infant, who is defined as sub-human and outside our law. It is defining the life question without regard to the death question, as if death is irrelevant. And it is saying the beginning of life is a question that is spiritual or religious, and one that cannot be resolved by us mere mortals.

What if we flip all this around? What if we recognize the humanity of the unborn? Now they are people like you and I are people. Now they are entitled to the same sort of rules that you and I receive. You can't kill or murder them. They're human beings.[404]

---

[404] *See* Tamar Lewin, "When the Death of a Fetus Is Murder," *The New York Times* (May 20.1994). Prosecutors had brought a murder charge against an armed robber who shot a pregnant woman and killed her unborn child. The defense argument was that the baby was non-viable. The California Supreme Court ruled that the murder charge could go forward "as long as the state can show the fetus has progressed beyond the embryonic state of seven to eight weeks." *People v. Davis*, 872 P.2d 591 (Cal. 1994).

Once we recognize the humanity of the unborn, we want to focus on whether this is a homicide. Because we all know that killing a baby is wrong. The Supreme Court knows it's wrong. That's why they don't want to talk about infanticide or think about infanticide.

If we recognize the baby's humanity--if we treat her as if she is born--immediately we are worried about infanticide. Infanticide focuses our thinking. It makes us careful. We have to be right on this.

Can we answer the death question? Yes. We have answered it. Indeed, all 50 states have the same rules in place.[405] We have widespread agreement in our society in regard to when people die. We die when we have zero activity in our brain stem and cerebral cortex. Thus if a baby has any activity in her brain stem or cerebral cortex, she is alive. If a doctor causes the baby's brain to cease function, he has killed her.

Of course, a state is free to change its death statutes. But under current rules in all 50 states, brain activity is the life-or-death point for human beings.[406]

---

[405] *See* Gary Greenberg, "Lights Out: A New Reckoning For Brain Death," **The New Yorker** (January 15, 2014). "Today, in every state, if your brain, including the brain stem, has been irreversibly and completely destroyed, you are dead."

[406] Some states confuse the issue by keeping heart-and-lung function on the books, in addition to brain activity. In these states a doctor can declare that a person is dead when he or she has no heart and lung function. But that should be read as a proxy for lack of brain activity. When there is a life-or-death controversy, brain activity is the key issue. This is why doctors can do heart transplants in all 50 states--there is no brain activity in the donor. As Greenberg writes, "the reason that cardiac arrest constituted death was that, when the blood stopped flowing, the brain eventually died. Brain death had always been the true death, we just didn't know it." *Id.*

What about conception as the beginning of life? That idea might work if we consider life in isolation. But it starts to fall apart when we think about life and death together.

Suppose a state is defining the beginning of human life at conception. What is that standard measuring? It measures whether you are human (in the class homo sapiens) and whether you are in a state of existence. If you are human and you exist, you're alive. Okay. What would a corresponding death statute look like that matched up with conception?

It would say that we die when our last atom disappears. It's ashes to ashes, and microscopic organism to microscopic organism.

In this scenario, our life begins when our body first makes its appearance, at the molecular level. We grow and get bigger and bigger and bigger. And then, at the end of our life, all our functions begin to stop. Our heart stops, our brain stops, we stop breathing. It's the reverse of the beginning of life. Our body decomposes. We get smaller and smaller. And finally our last atom disappears, and we are gone.

Of course, that would be a rather absurd standard for when people die! You could shoot somebody in the head, and argue they are still alive, because their body is still there. They're not breathing, their heart is not beating, their brain has ceased all function, and their body is going through rigor mortis. Yet, under this crazy rule, people are still alive until their last atom disappears.

So we don't do that. We don't wait for pure nothingness. We announce that a person is dead. We draw our line and say life is over. And we are able to do this because we have biological markers that we adopt in order to measure whether people are alive.

At some times and in some places our life is measured by our
beating heart, or whether we are breathing, or whether we have
voluntary movement. So perhaps our modern rule is wrong, and
will once again change. We do the best we can. But there is no
debate in regard to what our law actually says. In our society we
now have widespread agreement in regard to the life or death
point. Brain activity is the critical issue. If we have any activity
in our brain stem or cerebral cortex, we are alive.

This is not to say that it is crazy to argue that life begins at
conception. It's just that we are conflating other important
concepts, like the zygote's future life, for instance.[407] The
argument here is that life and death are interconnected. It's
illogical to divorce life from death, as if the two concepts are
unrelated and have nothing to do with each other.

What is conception? It is when our body starts to come into being
at the microscopic level. Once human creation has started, are we
alive? Is conception when our life begins? Remember, human
life is about more than a human body. You need a spirit. You
need to be, in some sense, animated. A dead person, for instance,
has a body. We can see it. The body is right there in front of us.
But despite her existence in corporal form, she's not alive.

Is a dead person a human being? Yes, of course. She's in the
class homo sapiens. But she's not a live human being. Or, more
specifically, she's not alive under the biological criteria we use to
mark whether a person is alive. The brain death statute answers

---

[407] Imagine your mother is in a coma. And the children are discussing what
they should do. It would be an intense and private conversation, and there will
be crying. The discussion is in regard to whether you are going to cut off life
support. Maybe somebody will use the word "vegetable." You can see how
siblings would be upset. "That's not Mom anymore. Mom is gone." Now
imagine it is highly likely Mom will be out of the coma in nine months. She
will be healthy and happy and alive. Would it be right to take her off life
support?

the death question, but it also answers the question of what doctors need to look for to mark whether you are alive.

Conception and birth are similar in one respect--both points reference when our body makes an appearance. Conception is when our body first appears inside the uterus, at the microscopic level. And birth is when our body first appears outside the uterus. But the important question is not when our body appears. For instance, a baby can be born dead.

The important question is whether this human body is animated with life. The death statute that answers the homicide question for doctors also answers the question of when life begins. We know the relevant biological criteria a human body needs to be animated with life, and our rule is brain activity.

At the time of **Roe v. Wade**, the death rule in Texas was absence of heart-and-lung function. Over the years, as medical technology advanced and we started doing heart transplants into people, our views adapted. We started to view the heart as more like a pump rather than the basis of human life. And so the old standard of human death gave way to our new one.

This new concept of when people die came up quite often in criminal murder trials, as well as in civil litigation. Criminal defendants, who had made the victim brain dead, would try to argue that they didn't kill anybody; the doctors killed him when they took out his heart.

In a Virginia case in 1972, transplant surgeons were charged in a wrongful death action.[408] The claim was that by removing the patient's heart and kidneys for transplant, they had killed him. The doctors successfully lobbied for a brain-death jury

---

[408] **Tucker v. Lower**, No. 2381 Richmond, Virginia Law & Equity Court, May 23, 1972.

instruction. The jury was told that as a substitute for the traditional rule in regard to human death, they might consider instead "the time of complete and irreversible loss of all function of the brain."

In a famous case in California, ***People v. Lyons***, a victim had received a gunshot wound to the head.[409] He was pronounced dead at the hospital and, with the consent of the family, his heart was removed for transplant. The defendant pleaded not guilty to murder, claiming that the doctors had killed the patient when they took out his heart, not when he shot him in the head. The judge instructed the jury as a matter of law that the victim died when his brain ceased function, and not with the removal of artificial support.

The Supreme Court can perhaps be excused for not being able to answer the life or death question in ***Roe v. Wade***. After all, in many states the standard of death in 1973 was still loss of heart-and-lung function. Typically, when a person dies, your lungs stop breathing and your heart stops beating and your brain ceases function around the same point in time. If you're not breathing, your heart is going to stop, too, and your brain. Or if your heart stops, your lungs will also stop working, and your brain will die. All these events will coincide within minutes.

In the case of the unborn, however, this proximity is out the window. Your heart is beating for eight months before you take your first breath of air. So right away we see the possibility for a big argument. We have a baby with a beating heart who has liquid in her lungs. Is she alive? Not alive? Half-alive?

Perhaps one of the reasons that some people like birth is that this is when we take our first breath of air into the lungs.[410] Yet it's

---

[409] 15 Criminal Law Report 2240, California Superior Court (1974).
[410] ***Supra*** note 390.

entirely wrong to say that the unborn are not breathing in the womb. Rather, they are breathing a liquid instead of a gas. Liquid breathing is a form of respiration in which an organism is breathing an oxygen-rich liquid.[411] And it's not just the unborn who can do this. In the movie, *The Abyss*, we see the technique. It is based on actual science. The rat in the movie is breathing liquid oxygen. A study from the 1960's found that cats can breathe liquid oxygen for weeks at a time.[412] Are we to say that a deep-sea diver loses his humanity when he starts breathing oxygen in liquid form?

Why did total brain death replace heart-and-lung function? Because machines can keep our hearts beating. Machines can keep our lungs breathing. When we discuss a neonatal intensive care unit, we are discussing a machine. An artificial heart can beat and beat and beat. Is that how we want to measure human life?

The rise of the machines that help us breathe and keep our blood circulating caused our medical and legal authorities to lose faith in heart and lungs as a measure of whether a human being is alive. It's not just the dehumanizing aspect of machines doing this work. It's also the fact that total brain death can happen weeks or even months before these other points stop. When the points no longer coincide, we have to pick the important one. And we have. Total and irreversible brain death is our society's rule.

Can we answer the legal question in regard to whether abortion kills a baby? Yes. All 50 states are in agreement in regard to when people die, and the federal rule is the same. We know with specificity when abortion kills a child, under our death statutes.

---

[411] *See* Andrew Tarantola, "Can Humans Breathe Liquid?" *Gizmodo* (August 27, 2013).
[412] *Id*.

Six weeks after conception, the baby starts to have blips of activity in her brain. And that is the critical life or death point.

Philosopher Baruch Brody figured out the importance of brain activity to the abortion debate quite early. He wrote *Abortion and the Sanctity of Human Life: A Philosophical View* for M.I.T. Press in 1975. And the physician John M. Goldenring published a paper in the Journal of Medical Ethics in 1985, *The Brain-Life Theory: Towards a Consistent Biological Definition of Humanness*. Both of these scholars argued that the start of activity in the brain stem was the critical point for when life begins, since the stopping of all brain activity is the critical point for when human beings die.[413]

Of course, we can't expect the Supreme Court to be aware of every book or research paper. But surely we can expect them to be aware of the law? By 1992 total brain death was the standard for when people die across our land.[414] And yet, in *Planned Parenthood v. Casey*, the Supreme Court affirmed *Roe v. Wade* without recognizing this massive change in our law.

The Court writes, "No evolution of legal principle has left *Roe*'s doctrinal footings weaker than they were in 1973. No development of constitutional law since the case was decided has implicitly or explicitly left *Roe* behind as a mere survivor of obsolete constitutional thinking."[415] And yet American law had

---

[413] "The concept that brain death (i.e. total cessation of integrated brain function, especially that of the brain stem) constitutes a person's death has been accepted legally and culturally in most of the world." www.merckmanuals.com

[414] Fans of *Roe v. Wade* try to argue that higher brain activity, or sentience, should be the law. *See* Jed Rubenfeld, "On the Legal Status of the Proposition That Life Begins at Conception," 43 Stanford Law Review 599 (1991). And of course any state is free to change their definition in regard to when people die. But as to what our laws say today? There is no doubt that a person is alive if they have any brain activity at all. *Id*.

[415] *Supra* note 7. The Supreme Court is overlooking a major flaw in *Roe v. Wade*: the opinion is oblivious to the fact that California is recognizing the

undergone a radical change exactly during this time period. We have re-defined when human beings die!

Note too that this radical evolution in legal thinking was not done in regard to the abortion debate. It was done in regard to organ transplants. So this was not a political maneuver to overturn *Roe v. Wade*, designed by people who are hostile to abortion. No, our brain death rules were an organic change in the law, widely accepted by all our states, conservative or liberal.

The Supreme Court in *Casey* is apparently oblivious to this. They are unaware that there has been a massive change in our laws in regard to when people die. And the baby's life or death is a critical issue in the abortion controversy, yes?

The first spark of activity in an unborn baby's brain happens approximately 6 weeks after conception.[416] Many obstetricians measure pregnancy from the last menstrual period, or LMP. Under that calendar, brain activity usually begins 8 weeks after the mother's last period. An abortion after brain activity has begun constitutes a homicide under state and federal law.

What about terminating an embryo without any brain activity? That might be bad, it might be something a state wants to outlaw. But you can't say it's a homicide, at least not under the death statutes in all 50 states. It's too early in the pregnancy to qualify as a homicide. You'd have to change your death statutes before you can say it's a homicide. And of course your new death

humanity of the unborn child, and that people can be prosecuted for murder for killing her. *See* note 398. Pro-lifers have pushed hard to prosecute non-doctors for murder for killing the unborn. *See* note 393. It is possible that unlicensed doctors can and will be prosecuted for murder for performing abortions. *See* note 659.

[416] *See* John Goldenring, "The Brain-Life Theory: Towards a Consistent Biological Definition of Humanness," *Journal of Medical Ethics* (1985).

statute has to apply to all people. That's how equal protection works.

If you abort a tiny infant who has no brain activity, then under our death statutes the doctor did not kill a live human being. And of course our death statutes are designed for precisely this issue. Not for the abortion issue per se, but for the issue of the doctor's criminal liability. Can you charge him with murder? Can you charge him with a homicide? No and no. We have laws on the books in regard to when people die, and aborting an embryo without any brain activity would not qualify.

Once the baby starts to have any activity in her brain stem, on the other hand, to abort her is to kill a baby. This is not a special rule for the unborn, but rather the same rule that we use for all of humanity.

This is not to insist that our death statutes are right. Perhaps they are wrong. After all, even if we define zygotes and early embryos as pre-life, they're not actually dead. Embryos are alive. Zygotes are alive. Indeed, sperm is alive. Doctors can tell the difference between live human sperm and dead human sperm. Perhaps these other forms of life are important, too.

The Catholic Church, for instance, wants to protect all forms of human life. The argument that life begins at conception is an attempt to protect even microscopic human life. And, notably, the Catholic Church also argues that contraception is immoral, and we should respect and revere male sperm and female eggs.

But this reverence for life should not sidetrack us away from the vital issue of whether we are killing a baby. That is an incredibly important issue. And perhaps the Catholic reverence for all forms of human life has made the infanticide charge not as sharp as it should be. Can a homicide happen at the microscopic level? For many people that idea seems rather silly. And it certainly does not correspond with any legal definition of death we have ever adopted.

In 2000, Pope John Paul II was invited to give the views of the Catholic Church in regard to the medical ethics of removing a patient's heart for transplant into another human being. Are we killing the patient when we take out his heart? When do people die? In the context of this discussion, the Pope spoke on the significance of the brain death standard. Here is what he said.[417]

> It must first be emphasized, as I observed on another occasion, that every organ transplant has its source in a decision of great ethical value: "the decision to offer without reward a part of one's own body for the health and well-being of another person." Here precisely lies the nobility of the gesture, a gesture which is a genuine act of love. It is not just a matter of giving away something that belongs to us but of giving something of ourselves, for "by virtue of its substantial union with a spiritual soul, the human body cannot be considered as a mere complex of tissues, organs and functions...rather it is a constitutive part of the person who manifests and expresses himself through it."
>
> Accordingly, any procedure which tends to commercialize human organs or to consider them as items of exchange or trade must be considered morally unacceptable, because to use the body as an "object" is to violate the dignity of the human person.

---

[417] "Address of the Holy Father John Paul II to the International Congress of the Transplantation Society," www.vatican.va (August 29, 2000).

This first point has an immediate consequence of great ethical import: the need for informed consent. The human "authenticity" of such a decisive gesture requires that individuals be properly informed about the processes involved, in order to be in a position to consent or decline in a free and conscientious manner. The consent of relatives has its own ethical validity in the absence of a decision on the part of the donor. Naturally, an analogous consent should be given by the recipients of donated organs.

Acknowledgement of the unique dignity of the human person has a further underlying consequence: vital organs which occur singly in the body can be removed only after death, that is from the body of someone who is certainly dead. This requirement is self-evident, since to act otherwise would mean intentionally to cause the death of the donor in disposing of his organs. This gives rise to one of the most debated issues in contemporary bioethics; as well as to serious concerns in the minds of ordinary people. I refer to the problem of ascertaining the facts of death. When can a person be considered dead with complete certainty?

In this regard, it is helpful to recall that the death of the person is a single event, consisting in the total disintegration of that unitary and integrated whole that is the personal self. It results from the separation of the life-principle (or soul) from the corporal reality of the person. The death of the person, understood in this primary sense, is an event which no scientific technique or empirical method can identify directly.

Yet human experience shows that once death occurs certain biological signs inevitably follow, which medicine has learnt to recognize with increasing precision. In this sense, the "criteria" for ascertaining death used by medicine today should not be understood as the technical-scientific determination of the exact moment of a person's death, but as a scientifically secure means of identifying the biological signs that a person has indeed died.

It is a well-known fact that for some time certain scientific approaches to ascertaining death have shifted the emphasis from the traditional cardio-respiratory signs to the so-called "neurological" criterion. Specifically, this consists in establishing, according to clearly determined parameters commonly held by the international scientific community, the complete and irreversible cessation of all activity (in the cerebrum, cerebellum and brain stem). This is then considered the sign that the individual organism has lost its integrative capacity.

With regard to the parameters used today for ascertaining death--whether the encephalic signs or the more traditional cardio-respiratory signs--the Church does not make technical decisions. She limits herself to the Gospel duty of comparing the data offered by medical science with the Christian understanding of the unity of the person, bringing out the similarities and the possible conflicts capable of endangering respect for human dignity.

Here it can be said that the criterion adopted in more recent times for ascertaining the fact of death, namely the complete and irreversible cessation of all brain activity, if rigorously applied, does not seem to conflict with the essential elements of a sound anthropology. Therefore a health-worker professionally responsible for ascertaining death can use these criteria in each individual case as the basis for arriving at that degree of assurance in ethical judgment which moral teaching describes as "moral certainty." This moral certainty is considered the necessary and sufficient basis for an ethically correct course of action. Only where such certainty exists, and where informed consent has already been given by the donor or the donor's legitimate representatives, is it morally right to initiate the technical procedures required for the removal of organs for transplant.

Chapter 12

If the Catholic Church says that lack of brain activity is vital in the context of organ transplants, why is lack of brain activity irrelevant in the context of early abortions? Isn't the question of life or death of primary importance? One would think the infanticide question is fundamental, and intrinsic. It should be talked about without regard to anything else. If we're killing babies, we need to know this.

After all, we have a biological criterion, a marker that doctors can use to tell whether a person is alive. And doctors aren't just winging it. Our society actually has laws in place that define for us what a person needs to be alive. At different times and at different places we identify different criteria. You need to be breathing. You need voluntary movement. You need a heartbeat. You need brain activity.

We might be right or wrong on any of these points. We do the best we can. But there actually are laws in place in regard to our important life-or-death questions. We should be focusing on infanticide and thinking about our rules in regard to when people die. The way our legal and religious authorities have framed the question ("when does life begin?") distracts us from our primary concern ("is this a homicide?").

For instance, a Republican running for the United States Senate, Richard Mourdock, made a comment about abortion and rape. "I struggled with it myself for a long time, but I came to realize life is that gift from God. And I think even when life begins in that horrible situation of rape, that it is something that God intended to happen."[418]

Richard Mourdock is not a bad person. He believes that life begins at conception, and he's trying to wrap his head around that idea, and what a rape victim should do. And so Mourdock relies on his religious faith and tries to see the miracle of life.

But of course people are appalled, as he would apparently deny emergency contraception to a rape victim.

Religious people often try to find the grace to accept atrocities, and respond with love and forgiveness.[419] Christianity, after all, celebrates the day Jesus of Nazareth was nailed to a cross, suffered horrible pains, and died in a brutal state execution. Christians refer to this day as Good Friday. The Christian emphasis on love and forgiveness can seem paradoxical to people, yet it can also be quite powerful.

Christian theology, properly understood, is about love. The Pope makes that clear in his remarks about heart transplants. But of course the state cannot mandate love. Christians are required to love our enemies. Imagine a Christian theocracy that required us to love our rapist, forgive our rapist, or accept our rape as a reality that we cannot resist. Such a theocracy would be a nightmare for our society, inspiring hate and anger in all of us.

This is why we have an establishment clause. The Christian instruction to love our enemies is beautiful and beguiling and amazing. But we have to be free. If Christian love is mandated by the state, it is not Christian love. "Render unto Caesar the

---

[418] Lucy Madison, "Richard Mourdock: Even Pregnancy From Rape Something 'God Intended.'" *CBS News* (October 24, 2012).
[419] *See* Kevin D. Williamson, "Mother Courage," *National Review* (June 8, 2014).

things that are Caesar's, and unto God the things that are God's."[420]

Mourdock's comment has a deeply theological component, but he is also making some factual, scientific assumptions that religious people might question. Does a baby's life begin at conception? Or is it more accurate to say that the human body starts to come into being at conception?

This is not to deny the miracle of pregnancy, or how amazing the human zygote is. It's merely to deny that it's a homicide to terminate one. It's not actually killing a baby, under any of our death statutes in all 50 states.

So we don't actually have to reach the hard question of whether a rape victim has a right to kill her unborn child. Very early abortions do not qualify as a homicide at all. Indeed, rape victims can take emergency contraception and avoid an abortion, since pregnancy is not simultaneous with ejaculation. Conception does not happen right away. It can happen hours after ejaculation, or five days later.

Consider again what the Pope said in regard to moral certainty. He's referencing doctors who are removing the heart from a brain-dead patient and putting it into another patient. "(A) health-worker professionally responsible for ascertaining death can use these criteria in each individual case as the basis for arriving at that degree of assurance in ethical judgment which moral teaching describes as 'moral certainty.'"[421]

---

[420] Mark 12:17.
[421] *Supra* note 417.

The moral certainty in regard to giving rape victims emergency contraception is so high that even Catholic hospitals will do it.[422]

We have no way of knowing if a woman is pregnant until implantation, a week after conception.[423] No Christian should shy away from administering emergency contraception to a rape victim. If a doctor is doing a good thing--for instance, doing a heart transplant, or treating a rape victim--he might take assurance in our society's rule in regard to the important life or death issue. It is simply not true that a birth control pill or an IUD kills a baby, any more than it is true that taking a beating heart out of a brain-dead patient kills him.

As Mourdock himself said, rape is a horrible crime, a hateful crime. Doctors can and should treat rape victims. That is a holy calling, and a blessed thing to do. Is it not?

We have been mocking the *Casey* Court for writing that "in some critical respects the abortion decision is of the same character as the decision to use contraception."[424] It's such a fantastic disregard for the infanticide issue. And really it shows a disregard for the facts. For instance, nobody in the *Carhart* opinions would be silly enough to analogize how killing a baby outside the birth canal is just like using a condom.

Here, however, the analogy actually makes sense! Emergency contraception is remarkably similar to artificial contraception. In both cases we are using artificial birth control devices, the IUD or

---

[422] In 2001, the U.S. Conference of Catholic Bishops revised the Ethical and Religious Directives for Catholic Health Care Services. Under Directive 36, a woman "who has been raped should be able to defend herself against a potential conception from the sexual assault. If after appropriate testing, there is no evidence that conception has occurred already, she may be treated with medications that would prevent ovulation, sperm capacitation, or fertilization." www.usccb.org.

[423] *See* note 171.

[424] *Supra* note 7.

a type of birth control pill. ***Griswold*** does not identify any of the forms of artificial birth control it is protecting. It's a rather fact-free opinion. Nor does it talk about emergency contraception or the tricky issue of whether or when a birth control device might actually terminate a pregnancy. It's quite obvious in retrospect that ***Roe*** should have focused on rape victims, and emergency contraception.

Note that the arguments against emergency contraception are also similar to the arguments against regular birth control. For instance, Mourdock references God's plan in regard to the creation of a zygote. The implication is that it's bad for humanity to control this. It's for God to control, not us.

And we see the same arguments in Catholic opposition to birth control. Catholics are talking about the sanctity of human reproduction and the miracle of reproduction. And the implication is that it's bad for humanity to control this. Indeed, one might even see from our increased rates of breast cancer--and all the studies that have linked the estrogen-based birth control pill to the rise in breast cancer--that these religious people have a point. Our authorities had a lot of hubris about the safety of birth control pills.

One might say that the Supreme Court (like the Catholic Church!) needs to be careful when it wanders into fields like biology or science. When doing so, it's outside its field of expertise, and is more likely to be wrong. The opinion in ***Griswold*** seems to say that all forms of birth control are protected. But some forms of birth control, particularly emergency birth control, might destroy a zygote. Is that birth control? Or is that an abortion?

Many doctors define pregnancy as starting at implantation rather than conception, since so many zygotes fail to implant into the walls of the uterus.[425] Also there is the theoretical problem of the identical twin. As Laurence Tribe has argued, an identical twin comes into being shortly after conception, when the zygote splits into two zygotes.[426] Thus we can point to human beings who quite obviously did not come into existence at conception.

For most of us, conception is when we come into being. But the existence of identical twins reminds us that conception is not when all of us are created. The point when an identical twin comes into being is not when a sperm fertilizes an egg, but rather the moment the zygote splits into two individual beings.

It's true a zygote has the DNA for a human being. But it might actually have the DNA for two human beings. It has a blueprint for a future person or persons. So we might say that the microscopic zygote is God's design for a life that will come into being in the future.

Of course, we might say the same thing about a sperm or an egg, since God knows which sperm is going to fertilize which egg. If we want to protect the sanctity of future people, should we not protect male sperm and female eggs? Indeed, the Catholic Church says that artificial contraception is wrong.

The pro-life movement is often accused of not just being a religious movement, but a Catholic movement. Thus we have the pro-choice chant, "Keep your rosaries off my ovaries." And many pro-lifers are Catholic. They see all abortions as a violation of the miracle of pregnancy, as something obscene and evil.

---

[425] And also because conception is an utter mystery. We don't know when it happens. All we can do is speculate and guess. *See* notes 170-171 and text.
[426] Laurence Tribe, *Abortion: The Clash of Absolutes* (1990). This issue of identical twins was also mentioned in the Texas appellate brief in *Roe v. Wade*. *See* note 170.

The Supreme Court was aware that the Catholic Church defined conception as the beginning of life. They said so in **Roe v. Wade**. Placing the beginning of life at conception "is now, of course, the official belief of the Catholic Church."[427]

Having the Catholic Church front and center in the pro-life movement is both a blessing and a curse for the pro-life movement. It's a blessing in that Catholics are strong and passionate pro-lifers, who have responded to **Roe v. Wade** with both outrage and a determination to love our enemies. But it's a curse, too, because the Catholic Church wants us all to focus on conception. And conception is far more a microscopic point than it is a homicidal one.

The Catholic Church used to know this. Saint Thomas Aquinas, for instance, talked about early abortions as a sin. "This sin, although grave and to be reckoned among misdeeds and against nature…is something less than a homicide…"[428] Aquinas tried to distinguish between homicidal abortions and non-homicidal abortions. He asked when the unborn became endowed with a soul. And while the specific points Aquinas suggested are not at all helpful, he was right to focus on the human spirit, and not get caught up on the creation of a human body.

It's rather remarkable that Aquinas, who had less scientific knowledge than we have today, was nonetheless right about conception being a bad point. Consider again the identical twin. These babies look exactly alike, because both individuals are created from the same zygote, a zygote that splits into two distinct zygotes. This is rather like how an amoeba reproduces, by splitting. When a zygote splits, two independent humans are formed.

---

[427] **Supra** note 1.
[428] **See** Frank Flinn, **Encyclopedia of Catholicism** (2007); Katherine Brind'Amour, "St. Thomas Aquinas," **The Embryo Project Encyclopedia**.

Do you know any twins? Have you seen any twins? Look at them. Monozygotic twins are quite identical, all the way down to their DNA. Each twin has the same genetic code, the same biological structure. They are biologically identical (with the exception of fingerprints).

And yet, these two identical people are obviously distinct human beings, unique people, apart from one another. Regardless of how identical their bodies might seem, they do not have identical souls. Religious people should be the first to understand this point.

If one identical twin commits a murder or a rape, is the other twin guilty too? Should we lock them both up, since they both have the same DNA, and DNA is now said to define humanity? No. Each twin has free will, a human spirit that is not the same. Their bodies may be identical, but they are unique individuals. This is why it's a mistake for the Catholic Church to talk about human DNA as a marker for a live human baby.

When a zygote is destroyed, are we destroying one baby or two? We do not know. We are too early in the process of creation to know for sure. Thus it may be sinful or bad, but Aquinas is quite right--it is not a homicide. DNA has nothing to do with human death, and so a focus on DNA distracts us from the vital issue of homicide. And while DNA is fascinating and cool--one might even say miraculous--a microscopic organism is not actually a baby yet.

Defining conception as the point when human life begins is a mistake in several ways. It ignores our death statutes in regard to when people die, thus ignores the critical life-or-death point we have adopted as a matter of secular law. Are we to prosecute a doctor for murder for killing a microscopic organism with a birth control pill? And, most damning of all, this argument hits rape victims the hardest. It is rape victims who will be using emergency contraception, and possibly destroying a zygote.

Why is conception important in Catholic theology? Conception is the beginning of human existence. Conception is the moment a human body is conceived by God. And by "conceived" we are very much talking about an idea, a plan. We might think of human DNA as God's design for a human being. It's God's blueprint. Thus, it is a sin to tear up God's blueprint and replace the Lord's will with our own will.

For much the same reason, the Catholic Church objects to birth control. Sex is God's plan for human reproduction, for creating babies.

Of course we might voice religious objections anytime man is willful. After all, human beings are constantly imposing our will on the universe. Did God design human beings with the ability to fly? No. And yet we crave the ability to fly. We have a will to fly. And so we impose our will on the universe and create tools that enable us to fly in the air. Something that we were obviously not designed to do.

Is flying a sin? No. We should take joy in our discoveries and our accomplishments. Like a child, we might brag to God, "Look what we can do!" The sin is not flying, or using birth control. The sin is pride. What makes us dangerous is our vanity. We have faith in our airplanes, in our birth control, in our ability to control the universe.

Consider how we have so easily accepted the idea that sex is now divorced from reproduction. In our culture, sex no longer leads to babies, unless we want it to. We control when we will reproduce. And when our controls fail--as they often do--we are surprised and annoyed. Our technology is not working like it's supposed to. And so we turn to doctors like they are a form of tech support. My birth control is not working right. Can you fix it?

This is, of course, dehumanizing. Much of our technology might make us feel this way, as if we are crowding out the spiritual and the divine. Yet, for the very same reason, one might criticize the Catholic Church for its focus on our DNA blueprint. Yes, God has designed us. But we are not machines. Are we?

Human DNA is obviously important to biological development. But a plan or blueprint for humanity is not the same thing as a life-or-death point. So the Catholic focus on DNA ("God's plan") strikes many people as theological in nature, as opposed to an honest attempt to focus on the life or death of an unborn infant.

Thus many people are convinced that Roman Catholic opposition to abortion is motivated by Roman Catholic opposition to birth control. Are pro-lifers motivated by a desire to protect human reproduction? Indeed, sometimes the Catholic Church conflates birth control and abortion as two activities that are similar. As Pope John Paul II writes, "contraception and abortion are often closely connected, as fruits of the same tree."[429]

The Pope is talking about lust, of course. It's a spiritual argument that human beings like and enjoy sex for our own pleasure. And this leads to unwanted babies. And this leads to infanticide. And of course one might argue--and the Pope is arguing--that birth control gives people the false illusion that we can have all the selfish pleasure we want now with sex, because of our birth control technology.

On the other hand, the Pope is not doing the pro-life movement any favors by conflating birth control and abortion as twin evils.

---

[429] *Supra* note 88.

As the Catholic Church is well aware, many Protestants like birth control and use it all the time. Instead of waking these Christians up to the possibility that abortion is infanticide, the Pope would rather tell them how right the Catholic Church has been about birth control.[430]

Of course the Pope does identify abortion as the killing of a child. Yet supporters of **Roe v. Wade** often dismiss anything the Catholic Church has to say on the subject of abortion, precisely because the Catholic Church's hostility to birth control is so well known.

It is simply wrong to say that the opposition to abortion is just like the opposition to birth control. Indeed, it's a bit of an oversimplification to say that Roman Catholics are opposed to all forms of birth control. They are opposed to artificial contraception. But the Catholic Church approves of celibacy, and also approves of natural family planning.

As Pope John Paul II writes, "the natural regulation of fertility can be correctly understood and lived as the proper expression of a real and mutual communion of love and life."[431] Natural family planning, or NFP, involves women seeking knowledge in regard to the days they are ovulating, and avoiding sex on those days. Studies have shown the symptoms-based version of NFP to be over 99% effective when used as birth control.[432]

---

[430] This is perhaps unfair. The Christian focus is always on spiritual matters. For instance Jesus said very little about infanticide or slavery, two common practices in ancient Rome. This is why we have had slave-owning Christians and aborting Christians. Indeed, there is a big dispute in Christianity about how much we should involve ourselves with the sins of the world. Some Christians think we should speak out against slavery or infanticide, since we have been ordered to love all people. Other Christians believe these fights will lead to anger and hatred and take us away from God.

[431] *See* Pope John Paul II, "Why Natural Family Planning Differs From Contraception," (letter to Dr. Anna Cappella), www.usccb.org.

[432] *See* Petra Frank-Herrmann, et al, "The Effectiveness of a Fertility Awareness Based Method To Avoid Pregnancy In Relation to a Couple's

This suggests that it is acceptable in Roman Catholicism for married couples to plan and organize their reproductive lives. Indeed, marriage is already a planning and organizational mechanism for our reproductive lives. The point of marriage is to constrain human sexuality so that a baby will have two parents. Marriage is an attempt to regulate sex, to constrain our sexual desires so that people will be happy and babies will be loved.

Obviously the Catholic Church approves of marriage, so it approves of human beings who plan parenthood. The Christian focus has always been on love and marriage, so that we might plan for our babies. The Planned Parenthood organization, on the other hand, focuses on artificial controls: birth control pills, birth control devices, and abortion. Yet, from a theoretical perspective, both groups agree that people should have a plan for having a baby. You should know what you are doing.

The sharp conflict is in regard to unplanned parenthood. What do we do about an unexpected child, an accident, a surprise?

It really should not be a surprise. For almost all of human history, sex resulted in babies. Judeo-Christianity teaches that sex ought to be love-making because sex is so often baby-making. This is why, after Christianity defeated the pagans, they began defining sex crimes. Prostitution was now a crime. Fornication was now a crime. This was done to protect babies.

So what happens when we develop reliable birth control? We rely on it. We have faith that we control nature. Even when we don't use any birth control at all, we have this weird faith that we are not going to make a baby. Our society has severed the

---

Sexual Behavior During the Fertile Time," *Oxford Journal of Human Reproduction* (2007). This form of birth control is not to be confused with the rhythm method, which is unreliable.

connection between sex and making a baby in our minds. And so now we are often surprised by our babies. We ask really dumb questions. How did you get pregnant?

Birth control, if you think about it, is rather amazing. We are now controlling our own reproduction as a species. What other animal does that? And maybe there's a vanity in thinking we have this ability, this power. Because the truth is, we have birth control failures all the time.

In the USA we average 1.4 million abortions a year, plus a similar number of single moms who choose to keep their baby. Over 3 million unplanned pregnancies happen every year in the USA.[433] Every 10 seconds we have another unplanned pregnancy.

Mistakes are so common, one wonders if these pregnancies are mistakes at all. Maybe an unintended pregnancy is like a Freudian slip. Your subconscious wants a baby. Maybe, deep within humanity, we have an innate biological drive to reproduce.

We might theorize that our sex drive is actually a reproductive drive. Nature wants us to have children. And perhaps our biological nature, our subconscious drive to have offspring, is at war with our conscious desire to stop reproduction.

Why do we use birth control, anyway? Perhaps Roman Catholics are right, and it is for selfish reasons. We want to enjoy sex without creating a human baby who will impose obligations on us.

Our modern conceit is that we do not need marriage any more. We can have sex without love or marriage. We are free to enjoy sex without any fear of making a baby. And that is modern, too,

---

[433] *See* "Section A: Unplanned Pregnancy in the United States Among All Women," www.thenationalcampaign.org

this idea that we should be afraid of having a baby. The classic view was to be afraid for the baby. We were afraid of the parents and what the parents would do to the baby. And now our modern, selfish mind is afraid of the baby and how the baby will ruin us.

In *Roe v. Wade*, Justice Blackmun writes, "Maternity, or additional offspring, may force upon the woman a distressful life and future."[434] John Hart Ely, in his otherwise very fine critique of *Roe v. Wade*, frames his own pro-choice beliefs in terms of the woman's unhappy future. "Having an unwanted child can go a long way toward ruining a woman's life."[435]

Why are we afraid of a baby? After all, babies are cute and innocent. So why are we distressed? What is this possible ruin?

One suspects that what drives a lot of this fear of the baby is money. We have to feed the baby. We have to shelter the baby. A baby means we're going to have to work. It is often a financial burden to have a child, is it not? And so we are afraid of this baby, this future criminal, this future welfare recipient, who is going to take money from us. Not just take our money, but take our dreams, too.

Pro-lifers talk about babies as a joy, and they see a happy future for people who have children. Yes, you will have to get a job. Yes, you will have to work. But you're going to have to do that anyway. A baby is a gift from God. A baby gives you someone to love.

One might see *Roe v. Wade* as an attack on the sanctity of human life.[436] It's an attempt to seize all control over human

---

[434] *Supra* note 1.
[435] *Supra* note 2.
[436] Ronald Dworkin makes this argument explicit, arguing that it is unconstitutional for a society to respect the sanctity of human life. Ronald Dworkin, *Life's Dominion* (1993). And there's no doubt that many pro-lifers

reproduction. Under **Roe**, it is up to us to decide if we're going to have a child, not God. We decide how many children we're going to have, not God. We decide if we're going to have a boy or a girl, not God. All of this is to be planned by us and controlled by us.

What of the idea that pregnancy is a miracle, a gift from God? The Supreme Court rejects that idea. Human beings create babies. They belong to us. And since the baby is our creation, we can destroy it if we want to.

Over a hundred years ago, the Supreme Court said that corporations are people. In **Pembina Silver Mining v. Pennsylvania**, the Court writes, "Under the designation of 'person' there is no doubt that a private corporation is included."[437]

And over forty years ago, the Supreme Court said that unborn babies are not people.[438] It's rather amazing how we grant humanity to corporations while we deny humanity to unborn children. It's as if we are usurping God's authority. We want to play God.

After all, God did not create any corporations. We did that. We are the omnipotent people who have made corporations. And apparently we are so proud of our creation that we have an urge to

---

see their mission as a holy calling. **Roe v. Wade** itself says that the Hippocratic Oath was adopted in our culture because Christians like it. **Supra** note 1. The abolitionist movement was largely a Christian movement, and the equal protection clause is rooted in the religious idea that we are all children of God. While all of this is true, it's also irrelevant. There are obvious secular justifications for all of these things, including the pro-life movement. One merely has to read Nat Hentoff to understand that. **See** Nat Hentoff, "Beyond the Rehearsed Response," **The Village Voice** (January 30, 1996).

[437] 125 U.S. 181 (1888).

[438] **Supra** note 1.

call it human. "Corporations are people," we say, even as we know this is absurd.[439]

Meanwhile, we find that we cannot design a human zygote. Indeed, we can barely grasp the mystery of human DNA. We are reproducing the same way monkeys and dogs reproduce, through sex and pregnancy.

Perhaps it's out of spite, then, that we deny the humanity of an unborn child. We deny any miracle. We say it's nothing.

Or maybe it's not spite, but greed. After all, our corporations make money for us. So we are proud and happy about our creation. A pregnancy, on the other hand, costs us money. So we are not proud. We are not happy. We deny your humanity, you expensive little child.

---

[439] It's not absurd to say that corporations have legal rights. For instance the First Amendment is broader than a free speech right for individual people. The First Amendment strips Congress of any authority to censor anybody. That's why a corporation like *The New York Times* has a right to print a newspaper. Not because we are pretending corporations are people! Indeed, it's hard to imagine any of the Framers saying corporations are people. That's rather like opening our Constitution with the words, "We the Corporations." And would such a document have been ratified by popular majorities?

Chapter 13

In 1992 the Supreme Court decided ***Planned Parenthood v. Casey***. This is a very important case. The Supreme Court is deciding whether to overrule ***Roe v. Wade***, or to keep going forward.

One of the Justices in the Court's opinion, Anthony Kennedy, is a Roman Catholic. While there is no assigned author in the plurality opinion, and we cannot be sure who wrote what, it is possible that Kennedy is the writer of this line: "Some of us as individuals find abortion offensive to our most basic principles of morality, but that cannot control our decision. Our obligation is to define the liberty of all, not to mandate our own moral code."[440]

There was much speculation at the time that Kennedy had switched his vote.[441] He had originally voted to overturn ***Roe***, and Harry Blackmun changed his mind with a highly emotional appeal. This is perhaps surprising, since Justice Kennedy is a Roman Catholic, and Catholics are taught that abortion is a homicide.

Does Kennedy think abortion kills a baby? He does not say. What the author does say is that abortion violates "our most basic principles of morality." So abortion is like infanticide, or rape, or lying. It's a bad act. But apparently it's a bad act that the state does not have the authority to outlaw.

---

[440] ***Supra*** note 7.
[441] ***See*** Terry Eastland, "The Tempting of Justice Kennedy," ***The American Spectator*** (February, 1993).

What this jurist might be saying is that abortion upsets Catholics, but it doesn't upset other people. So when he says, "our most basic principles of morality," perhaps he's talking about the Catholic Church. But in his job he has to speak for all people. So his Catholic morality "cannot control our decision."

No doubt Kennedy wants to be a good Roman Catholic. But he is also a Supreme Court Justice, and so he feels that he must uphold *Roe v. Wade*.

Kennedy is attempting to do several things with his opinion, vis-à-vis "the Catholic question." He is attempting to uphold a tradition, dating back to John Kennedy, of prominent Roman Catholics who declare their independence from Rome.[442]

He is simultaneously defending a form of jurisprudence ("natural law") that relies upon unwritten rules, as opposed to positive law that everybody can see and read.[443] For instance, nowhere in the Constitution does it say anything about stare decisis. That's an unwritten rule that the Supreme Court has added along the way. In his opinion Kennedy will be arguing not from our Constitution, nor from statutes, but from natural law sources that nobody else can see. He will be using the (unwritten) stare decisis doctrine to defend the (unwritten) "substantive" due process doctrine that was used to find the (unwritten) right for a woman to abort a pregnancy up until the (unwritten) point of viability.

---

[442] "I believe in an America where the separation of church and state is absolute, where no Catholic prelate would tell the president (should he be Catholic) how to act, and no Protestant minister would tell his parishioners for whom to vote...and where no man is denied public office merely because his religion differs from the president who might appoint him or the people who might elect him." -- Transcript, J.F.K.'s Speech on His Religion, *NPR.org*.

[443] The great liberal Hugo Black hated "natural law" because he felt it was too easy for unelected judges to impose their own sense of right on the world. "I fear to see the consequences of the Court's practice of substituting its own concepts of decency and fundamental justice for the language of the Bill of Rights..." *Adamson v. California* 332 U.S. 46 (1947) (Black, J., dissenting).

Natural law is, ironically, a very Catholic sort of jurisprudence.[444] As Sanford Levinson has argued, the natural law doctrine is a Catholic doctrine, a method of finding unwritten laws and adding them to the source material.[445] For instance, the Bible says we cannot kill, but it does not say much at all in regard to birth control. So Catholics and Protestants agree that the Bible forbids killing, but do not agree on birth control. The Roman Catholic Church has discovered an unwritten law about birth control, as well as an unwritten law that says life begins at conception.

Over the centuries, Roman Catholics have discovered many rules in regard to Christianity, rules which they argue are implicit from the Bible. Justice Kennedy is refusing to impose these Catholic rules into our Constitution. Thus we cannot say that life begins at conception. We cannot say that birth control is forbidden.

And yet Kennedy is using a process of "Catholic" reasoning to discover a whole host of new unwritten rules from our Constitution. You have a right to abort a pregnancy up until viability. It does not matter if the Supreme Court is right, the

---

[444] As Andrew Napolitano writes, "Natural law teaches that our rights come from our humanity. Since we are created by God in His image and likeness, and since He is perfectly free--or, if you prefer, since we are creatures of nature born biologically dependent but morally free--freedom is our birthright." *See* Andrew Napolitano, "Dred Scott's Revenge," *Reason* (May 14, 2009). While this sounds wonderful--you can see why revolutionaries like natural law--it's also true that **Dred Scott** and **Roe v. Wade** each argued that they were simply following natural law. The Supreme Court found a natural right to own slaves and a natural right to abort pregnancies. The open-ended nature of natural law is why many of us believe that our unelected jurists should simply follow our positive law, as written. Indeed, Frederick Douglass made a fantastic argument that **Dred Scott** was bad law precisely because the Supreme Court had failed to follow the Constitution. *See* Frederick Douglass, "The Constitution of the United States: Is It Pro-Slavery or Anti-Slavery?" (March 26, 1860).
[445] Sanford Levinson, *Constitutional Faith* (1988).

Supreme Court must be obeyed. It's a new form of natural law that does not agree with what the Catholic Church has to say.[446]

Simultaneously, Kennedy will argue that he is a good Catholic who finds abortion appalling and wrong. He will argue that abortion is "offensive" and violates "our most basic principles of morality." And yet, in a sort of judicial boast, he will say that he must "define the liberty for all." So, despite his own dislike of the practice, Justice Kennedy is telling us that he will not be swayed by his own feelings or religious beliefs.

The main *Casey* dissent is from Justice Scalia, who like Kennedy is a Roman Catholic. Scalia is a serious Roman Catholic.[447]

On January 21, 2013--the day before the 40-year anniversary of *Roe v. Wade*--the *Washington Post* ran an article about Justice Scalia's hat.[448] Scalia wore this hat in a very public way, at the State of the Union address. It was a replica of the hat worn by Saint Thomas Moore, who was executed by the state in 1535 because he was a good Roman Catholic (i.e. he refused to say that it was acceptable for the king to divorce his wife).[449]

"Was Scalia, a Catholic who often speaks about how his faith frames his worldview, subtly stating his defiance of political

---

[446] Imagine a man dressed in black robes who announces, "At the heart of liberty is the right to define one's own concept of existence, of meaning, of the universe..." *Supra* note 7. Now imagine the man is stabbing a baby as he says this. Why is this man dressed in black robes? What religion is this? And why does our society have to allow this sort of barbaric sacrifice? *See* note 506.

[447] When asked his thoughts on the liberal Pope Francis, Scalia said, "He's the Vicar of Christ. He's the chief. I don't run down the pope. I think he's absolutely right." David Savage, "Does Justice Antonin Scalia Believe in the Devil? You Bet." *The Los Angeles Times* (October 10, 2013).

[448] *See* Helena Andrews and Emily Heil, "Surprising Inauguration Fashion," *The Washington Post* (January 21, 2013); *See also* Ann Althouse, "Justice Scalia Was Wearing His Sir Thomas More Hat," *Althouse* (January 22, 2013).

[449] This story is recounted in the movie, *A Man For All Seasons* (1966).

authority, making an argument about religious freedom today, or was his head just really cold?"[450]

It is possible, in fact likely, that Scalia meant the hat as a subtle dig at President Obama, who is attempting to mandate that Catholic hospitals issue birth control pills to anybody who wants them.[451] Scalia and his wife do not use any birth control, which we can deduce because the Scalia family has nine kids.

The last words of Saint Thomas More: "I am the king's good servant, but God's first."[452]

In his *Casey* dissent, Scalia will make abortion arguments that are made by Catholics all the time. It is clear with his dissent that Scalia wants to give voice to the pro-lifers who, up until now, have had no voice in Supreme Court opinions. "The whole argument of abortion opponents is that what the Court calls the fetus and what others call the unborn child *is a human life*."[453] Scalia will also compare *Roe* to the *Dred Scott* decision, and implicitly suggest that abortion is like slavery.

And yet, simultaneously, Scalia is well aware of his oath of office, and how he cannot mandate Catholic teachings to the country. So he will compare abortion to bigamy--an argument that no pro-lifer has ever made--and implicitly affirm the idea that an unborn child is a legal non-person who has no right to life. "The Constitution says absolutely nothing about it."[454]

---

[450] Elizabeth Tenety, "Justice Scalia's Inauguration Headgear: More Than a Hat?" www.faithstreet.com.

[451] *See* Richard Wolf and Cathy Lynn Grossman, "Obama Mandate on Birth Control Coverage Stirs Controversy," *USA Today* (February 9, 2012).

[452] www.thomasmoresociety.org. In the movie, the line is more dramatic: "I die his Majesty's good servant, but God's first."

[453] *Supra* note 283.

[454] *Id*.

Justice Scalia wants to make clear that he will not be recognizing the humanity of the unborn, or striking down any pro-abortion statutes. "Some societies have considered newborn children not yet human, or the incompetent elderly no longer so."[455] Scalia is so determined not to impose his strong Catholic views on our country, he is suggesting states can kill newborns if they want to, or the incompetent elderly.

Do what you want, Oregon!

Readings these opinions, one might suspect that somebody has accused Justice Kennedy of being a bad Catholic, and somebody has accused Justice Scalia of trying to impose his Catholicism on the country. So in his opinion, Justice Kennedy wants to make clear that he is not a bad Catholic. And Justice Scalia wants to make clear that he is not trying to impose his Catholicism on the country.

Abortion causes a particular stress in state officials who are Roman Catholic, since the Pope defines abortion as a homicide. And of course the Republican response to *Roe v. Wade* has been to flood the Supreme Court with Roman Catholics. Scalia and Kennedy are just two of the Supreme Court's Catholics, both nominated by Ronald Reagan. The two Bush Presidents will nominate three more Roman Catholics: Clarence Thomas, John Roberts and Samuel Alito.

At the time of *Roe v. Wade*, there were eight Protestants on the Court, and one Catholic (who was pro-choice), and no Jews. 40 years later, there are six Catholics on the Court, three Jews, and no Protestants.[456]

---

[455] *Id*.
[456] *See* Ann Althouse, "When (If) Sotomayor is Confirmed, There Will Be Six Catholics On the Supreme Court," *Althouse* (June 1, 2009).

That's a remarkable shift!

Roe v. Wade discusses the theological views of the various denominations. According to the Supreme Court, birth "appears to be the predominant, though not the unanimous, attitude of the Jewish faith."[457] While the "moment of conception…is now, of course, the official belief of the Catholic Church."[458]

This might explain why all the Protestants have disappeared from the Supreme Court, to be replaced with Catholics and Jews. If your point is conception, or birth, you might want to play the odds and nominate a Catholic, or a Jew, to the Supreme Court in the hopes that they will agree with you.

In a way this is a rather silly. We don't know what a human being's real spiritual values are, and we don't know how they will respond once given incredible power. Religion is a strong influence on many people. But we all have free will. There are pro-choice Catholics, as well as pro-life Jews.

And yet, unmistakably, the Supreme Court has gone from an institution dominated by Protestants to one that is dominated by Catholics and Jews. Why is this?

One reason is that nominees to the Supreme Court often refuse to talk about abortion at all. We all want to avoid "politicizing" the Supreme Court. And so we talk about jurisprudence and legal process and how you go about resolving cases. And yet Republicans very much want to overturn ***Roe v. Wade***, and Democrats very much want to keep the opinion in place. So maybe religion has become a proxy for how a nominee might vote on the subject.

---

[457] ***Supra*** note 1.
[458] ***Id***.

For instance, we might suspect that Antonin Scalia, in his secret heart, is a pro-lifer. We might deduce this because he's a Roman Catholic, his religion is very important to him, and he and his wife have nine kids. So he's not just a pro-lifer, he's a Catholic pro-lifer. As a Catholic pro-lifer, he believes that every abortion is a homicide. But he cannot impose this Catholic view on our people, and Scalia knows it. To do so is to dictate a specifically Catholic rule. It's to import Scalia's own theology into our Constitution. And he must avoid doing that; the First Amendment forbids it.

So Scalia's argument is simple: *Roe v. Wade* should be overruled. Abortion needs to be resolved by our people and the democratic process. Since Scalia is a Catholic, and he wants to avoid dictating his Catholic pro-life view, his only option is to insist that abortion should be sent back to the political branches. "We should get out of this area, where we have no right to be, and where we do neither ourselves nor the country any good by remaining."[459]

Of course this argument might violate our Constitution in another way. After all, *Roe v. Wade* dehumanized the unborn infant as a matter of law, and stripped her of any possible right to life. And yet our Constitution has specific rules about how we are to treat people. "No State shall…deprive any person of life, liberty, or property, without due process of law; nor deny to any person within its jurisdiction the equal protection of the laws."[460]

Scalia's Catholic view is that life begins at conception. It follows that the unborn is a person at conception. And our Constitution has specific rules about how people should be treated. You

---

[459] *Supra* note 283.

[460] U.S. Constitution, amendment XIV, section 1. The due process clause is concerned with fair procedures when the state takes our life, our liberty, or our property. For an interpretation of our equal protection clause, *see* note 384.

cannot kill them without due process of law, and all people are entitled to the equal protection of the laws.

However, Scalia would admit, maybe he is wrong about when life begins. "There is of course no way to determine that as a legal matter; it is in fact a value judgment."[461] This is when Scalia tells us that some societies "have considered newborn children not yet human, or the incompetent elderly no longer so."[462]

But this argument suggests the state has an awesome power to strip people of their humanity. We can deny humanity to the very old, or the very young. Is this true?

The mind recoils. And Scalia's mind does recoil (from his own argument!) Unhappy with the idea that innocent people can be stripped of their humanity and killed, Justice Scalia starts talking about *Dred Scott*. "In my history book, the Court was covered with dishonor and deprived of legitimacy by *Dred Scott v. Sandford*."[463]

This is out of the blue, as nobody in the *Casey* opinion mentions *Dred Scott*. Why is Scalia comparing abortion to slavery?

Scalia would make the *Dred Scott* comparison once again in his *Carhart* dissent. "I am optimistic enough to believe that, one day, *Stenberg v. Carhart* will be assigned its rightful place in the history of this Court's jurisprudence beside *Korematsu* and *Dred Scott*."[464]

---

[461] *Supra* note 283.

[462] *Id.*

[463] *Id.*

[464] *Stenberg v. Carhart*, 530 U.S. 914 (2000) (Scalia, J., dissenting). Scalia is identifying two infamous cases in the Supreme Court's history, and is drawing analogies between these cases and *Roe v. Wade*. In *Korematsu v. United States*, 323 U.S. 214 (1944), the Supreme Court said it was legal to put innocent Japanese-Americans in internment camps at the start of World War II. And yet the nature of *Korematsu* is quite different from the opinion in *Roe*.

Of course the ***Dred Scott*** opinion is notorious because the Supreme Court dehumanized people from Africa as legal sub-humans who are outside our law. Even free citizens of the United States were defined as non-people. Is Justice Scalia making this comparison because ***Roe v. Wade*** also involves defining the unborn as sub-human, as non-people?[465]

Indeed, the logic of ***Dred Scott*** is eerily similar to an argument that is used in ***Roe v. Wade***. In ***Dred Scott***, Justice Taney writes, "Neither the class of persons who had been imported as slaves, nor their descendants, whether they had become free or not, were then acknowledged as a part of the people."[466] Compare this to the rhetoric of ***Roe***: "All this, together with our observation...that, throughout the major portion of the 19th century, prevailing legal abortion practices were far freer than

---

Imagine if Congress had passed a law protecting the rights of Japanese-Americans, and in ***Korematsu*** the Supreme Court had overturned this law, and dictated that all Japanese-Americans were to be rounded up and put into concentration camps. That would be insane, right? In fact it would be just like ***Dred Scott*** and ***Roe v. Wade***, a shocking usurpation of power by unelected authorities who are denying humanity. But ***Korematsu*** is nothing like that. In ***Korematsu*** the Supreme Court is allowing a war President to do an awful injustice to Japanese-Americans. In other words, the controversy over ***Korematsu*** is not that the Supreme Court has seized power and has dictated something evil. The controversy over ***Korematsu*** is that the Supreme Court failed to do anything. The Court ignored our Constitution and allowed an injustice to happen. Ironically, ***Korematsu*** is most analogous to the abortion dissents (including Justice Scalia's). Scalia is asserting that states have authority to do whatever they want to the unborn child. And he's arguing the Supreme Court should not stand in the way. Scalia's dissent is ***Korematsu*** all over again.

[465] Scalia has argued that the 14th Amendment only applies to racial discrimination. *See* note 384. And while this is a bad reading of equal protection, it's an impossible reading of the 13th Amendment. Does Scalia think we can buy or sell babies, as long as it's race-neutral? Can we set up baby markets? Can we kill off unwanted children? If Scalia's analogy is apt, then our Constitution forbids all this, does it not?

[466] ***Supra*** note 364.

they are today, persuades us that the word 'person,' as used in the Fourteenth Amendment, does not include the unborn."[467]

A victim of dehumanization is defined as a non-person because of the dehumanization, which in turn is used to justify the dehumanization. It's a rather awful use of circular logic.

One can certainly see why a pro-lifer would bring **Dred Scott** into the abortion debate.[468] But why is Justice Scalia? After all, he too is denying the humanity of an unborn child. Justice Scalia is defining the unborn--and apparently the newborns and the incompetent elderly--as sub-human. They are outside the protections of our equal protection clause. "The Constitution says absolutely nothing about it."[469]

Implicitly, Scalia is on board with the dehumanization. Yet Scalia is reminding the Court that it has created a controversy. And lots of people are not on board. Lots of people are defining themselves as pro-lifers, and are quite hostile to a Supreme Court that is defining babies as sub-human and issuing rules about killing them.

Indeed, one gets a sense of this popular response from the Supreme Court's opinion in **Casey**. The vibe is one of an institution under siege. And of course they are. Every January 22nd, on the anniversary of **Roe v. Wade**, hundreds of thousands

---

[467] **Supra** note 1. Professor Dellapenna has sharply criticized Blackmun's history. **See** note 192.

[468] One scholar has written an entire book on the similarities of abortion and slavery. **See** Justin Dyer, **Slavery, Abortion, and the Politics of Constitutional Meaning** (2013).

[469] **Supra** note 283. Of course it's true that the Constitution says nothing about abortion. And the Constitution says nothing about when people die, or when life begins. But what the Constitution does say is that whatever our rules are, they must apply to all people.

of pro-lifers show up at the doors of the Supreme Court to protest its abortion opinion.[470] And pro-choice people show up, too.

This is perhaps why the Supreme Court's opinion in *Casey* spends so much time talking about the Supreme Court. Not only is *Roe v. Wade* under attack, the Court itself is under attack. "(T)o overrule under fire in the absence of the most compelling reason to reexamine a watershed decision would subvert the Court's legitimacy beyond any serious question."[471]

The Court adopts war-like imagery. They are "under fire." And while they are under attack, they will not admit to any mistakes, or reverse course. We will not retreat!

In his dissent, Scalia mocks the joint opinion for its finding that abortion has been resolved once and for all: "Its length, and what might be called its epic tone, suggest that its authors believe they are bringing to an end a troublesome era in the history of our Nation and of our Court."[472]

And then Scalia again compares the writers of the majority opinion to the Supreme Court Justice who wrote *Dred Scott*:

"There comes vividly to mind a portrait by Emanuel Leutze that hangs in the Harvard Law School: Roger Brooke Taney, painted in 1859, the 82nd year of his life, the 24th of his Chief Justiceship, the second after his opinion in *Dred Scott*. He is all in black, sitting in a shadowed red armchair, left hand resting upon a pad of paper in his lap, right hand hanging limply, almost lifelessly, beside the inner arm of the chair. He sits facing the viewer, and staring straight out. There seems to be on his face, and in his deep set eyes, an expression of profound sadness and

---

[470] *Supra* note 155.
[471] *Supra* note 7.
[472] *Supra* note 283.

disillusionment. Perhaps he always looked that way, even when dwelling upon the happiest of thoughts. But those of us who know how the lustre of his great Chief Justiceship came to be eclipsed by *Dred Scott* cannot help believing that he had that case--its already apparent consequences for the Nation--burning on his mind. I expect that two years earlier he, too, had thought himself 'call(ing) the contending sides of national controversy to end their national division by accepting a common mandate rooted in the Constitution.'"[473]

What's striking about this passage is how Justice Scalia sees the slavery issue through the prism of how it affects the Supreme Court. For most of us, slavery brings to mind images of kidnapping people. We think about rape, murder, torture, buying and selling children, breaking up families. We think about racism and dehumanization.

Scalia skips all that. He wants us all to focus on Justice Taney and his sad portrait. Oh, poor, poor Justice Taney! Look what slavery did to you!

Apparently Scalia's purpose in bringing up slavery is not to get us thinking about the humanity of the unborn child. His purpose in bringing up *Dred Scott* is merely to remind the Court of the folly of trying to resolve a divisive issue. And what about the clauses in the Constitution that were adopted in the wake of the Civil War? If abortion is similar to slavery, wouldn't these clauses help resolve this modern crisis?

Scalia says nothing about that. His focus is on the Supreme Court, and how this fight over abortion is hurting the Supreme Court. In this respect Scalia's dissent is quite similar to what the plurality is saying. Much of the *Casey* opinion is focused on the

---

[473] *Id.*

Supreme Court. The Court is talking about itself and how important it is.

"If the Court's legitimacy should be undermined, then, so would the country be in its very ability to see itself through its constitutional ideals."[474] Whoever is responsible for these words is writing like a true autocrat. "It is necessary to understand the source of this Court's authority."[475] Our mystery author is writing in regard to the importance of the Supreme Court's sovereignty. His focus is an authoritarian focus. He is talking about power, his Court's power and his own power, and how best to keep it. "(O)verruling *Roe*…would seriously weaken the Court's capacity to exercise the judicial power…"[476]

Admitting error would make the Court look bad, so no error will be admitted. "A decision to overrule *Roe*'s essential holding under the existing circumstances would address error, if error there was, at the cost of both profound and unnecessary damage to the Court."[477]

Apparently the Supreme Court's authority is more important than right or wrong, or the rule of law. It's more important than the baby's life or the woman's right to choose. How can the Supreme Court best keep its authority, its power, and its status? That is the question that *Casey* asks. And to answer this question, the Court cites the doctrine of stare decisis. It's Latin, of course, the language of Rome, the language of power: "It has been decided."

The authorities have spoken. No more need to be said. Of course, *Casey* is actually one of the longest opinions in the history of the U.S. Reports (*Dred Scott* still holds the record). So despite the authoritative declaration that all is well and abortion has been

---

[474] ***Supra*** note 7.
[475] *Id*.
[476] *Id*.
[477] *Id*.

resolved, there seems to be some rambling insecurity, punctuated by bizarre claims of omnipotence.

Our anonymous Justice goes on to talk about "a Nation of people who aspire to live according to the rule of law. Their belief in themselves as such a people is not readily separable from their understanding of the Court invested with the authority to decide their constitutional cases and speak before all others for their constitutional ideals."[478]

Or, as Louis XIV put it, "I am the state."

The hubris in *Casey* is really astounding. "The Court is not asked to do this very often, having thus addressed the Nation only twice in our lifetime, in the decisions of *Brown* and *Roe*."[479] This is simply false. In neither *Brown* nor *Roe* does the Supreme Court "address the Nation" in this self-conscious, politicized manner, as if you are giving a state of the union. Both cases, while politically important, at least act as if this is Constitutional law and nothing more.

In *Casey* the Supreme Court drops any pretense. At least somebody in the unelected branch is now ready to "address the nation" as a ruler!

While our mystery jurist takes time out from his legal work to command the nation to follow him, Justice Scalia takes the opportunity in his dissent to complain about the American people. "I am distressed as the Court is…about…the marches, the mail, the protests aimed at inducing us to change our opinions."[480] Is

---

[478] *Id*.

[479] *Id*. Some commentators believe that Justice Souter--who drafted the stare decisis part of the opinion--was actually the autocrat. *See* Laura Ray, "Circumstance and Strategy: Jointly Authored Supreme Court Opinions," *Nevada Law Journal* 12 (2012).

[480] *Supra* note 283.

this Constitutional law? Which is worse, the plurality's autocratic demands for obedience, or Scalia's "distress," not about infanticide, but about all the complainers?

Justice Scalia, why make a comparison to slavery, the most vile period in our history, if you are unserious? If you don't think the baby is a baby, shut up about slavery. If you do think the baby is a baby, then you should be fighting tooth and nail for her right to life. Not only should you do that as a moral matter, but as a legal one. Or have you not noticed that our Constitution outlaws slavery, and forbids the dehumanization of human beings?

Eight years later, in his **Carhart** dissent, Scalia would compare abortion to murder. "The method of killing a human child--one cannot even accurately say an entirely unborn human child--proscribed by this statute is so horrible that the most clinical description of it evokes a shudder of revulsion."[481]

Is it not illegal to kill a child? Yet Scalia does not apply the murder statutes, or even bother to discuss the murder statutes. After noting the baby's killing, and how revolting it is--which is a step up in honesty compared to Justice Rehnquist's repression in **Catholic League**--Scalia goes on to deny what he just said.

Six paragraphs after describing his revulsion at a child's murder, Scalia writes, "While I am in an I-told-you-so-mood, I must recall my bemusement, in **Casey**, at the joint opinion's expressed belief that **Roe v. Wade** 'call(ed) the contending sides of a national controversy to end their national division by accepting a common mandate rooted in the Constitution.'"[482]

To a pro-lifer, Scalia's attempt at humor is quite jarring. It's an odd emotion for a man who was just talking about the killing of a

---

[481] **Supra** note 464.
[482] **Id**.

baby.[483] And of course, as a matter of law, Scalia does not recognize the humanity of the baby. She is not a person, so she is not entitled to the equal protection of the laws. Scalia, the *Roe* dissenter, has nonetheless joined this part of the Court's opinion. He agrees with the rest of the Court: the baby has no right to life.

In his *Casey* dissent, Scalia compares *Roe v. Wade* to the *Dred Scott* opinion. *Dred Scott* involves a human being who has been stripped of his humanity by the state. This is why pro-lifers compare *Roe v. Wade* to *Dred Scott*. And yet Scalia also compares abortion to bigamy.[484] There's no violence in bigamy. If abortion is like bigamy, then the Supreme Court has not dehumanized anybody.

So did *Roe v. Wade* dehumanize a baby, or not? Scalia can't decide, or feels no need to decide. This is why he compares abortion to bigamy and to slavery in *Casey*. This is why he's both horrified and bemused in *Carhart*. He's detached himself emotionally and intellectually from considering the humanity of the unborn child.

One of the smartest legal minds of our generation has nothing to say about infanticide, nothing to add in regard to rape, no insights in regard to the abortion issue at all. He has arguments to make about democracy and federalism, but refuses to see the unborn child as a human being with a right to life.[485]

---

[483] The context of the sentence suggests that Scalia is using the word "bemusement" in the colloquial sense, to mean "wry amusement."
[484] *Supra* note 283.
[485] Pro-lifers should credit Scalia for his refusal to adopt the Court's dehumanizing language. Over and over Scalia uses the words "child" or "baby" or "infant" to describe the unborn. In and of itself this is a major and important step towards recognizing a baby's right to life. But we should ask Justice Scalia if his actions comport with his words and ideas. After all, a baby is a person. "No State…shall deny to any person…the equal protection of the laws." *See* note 384.

Right before the *Casey* opinion was announced, Anthony
Kennedy did an interview with a journalist from *California
Lawyer* magazine.[486] The reporter describes how the Catholic
jurist "stands at the window of his high-ceiling chambers, waiting
to go on the bench." Justice Kennedy is staring down through the
glass at all the protesters, hundreds of thousands of them, many of
them waving signs about infanticide and freedom. And Kennedy
says an odd thing.

"Sometimes you don't know if you're Caesar about to cross the
Rubicon, or Captain Queeg cutting your own tow line."[487]

In *Casey*, Scalia accuses the Court of an "almost czarist
arrogance." Yes, that is right. There is certainly a tone in the
opinion that brings to mind the czars, or Louis XIV, or a Roman
emperor. And what's really shocking is that this is apparently the
tone of voice that Justice Kennedy wants his opinion to have. He
is striving to sound like Caesar. And he's adopting this
authoritative style, this dictatorial rhetoric, to mask his fear that
he is actually Captain Queeg.

Who is Captain Quegg? In the movie *The Caine Mutiny*, we see
Humphrey Bogart play Queeg as a sweaty and nervous man.
He's the captain of a ship in World War II who feels his authority
is under attack. Captain Quegg is under great stress, and is
becoming mentally unbalanced. He is playing with his metal
balls and obsessing about strawberries.

Why is Justice Kennedy talking about Captain Queeg?

In the movie, Captain Queeg is obsessed with his authority and
the people who are undermining his authority. And we do see, in

---

[486] *See* Terry Carter, "Crossing the Rubicon," *California Lawyer* (October,
1992). *See also* note 441.
[487] *Id*.

Casey, a Supreme Court opinion that is apparently obsessed with its own authority. There's plenty of dictatorial rhetoric, to be sure, but there is also a great insecurity throughout the opinion, as if the Court is under siege.

Who else in our political history has been accused of acting like a dictator, while he seemed neurotic and insecure? The political analogy that leaps to mind is Richard Milhous Nixon.[488] Nixon was a powerful official who was under attack, and he was sweaty and nervous and combative.[489] Ultimately President Nixon was threatened with impeachment, and forced to resign. He was hounded from office because of a number of scandals, known collectively as Watergate.

The President's press secretary referred to the bugging of the Democratic National Committee as a "third-rate burglary."[490] Nixon claimed that he had no idea what his men had done. But he covered up for them, and was ultimately driven from office.

And Watergate is nothing compared to the scandal the pro-lifers are alleging.

---

[488] *Roe v. Wade* was decided in the midst of the Watergate scandal, which might explain the willingness of the Justices to be so nakedly partisan. *See* note 156. Instead of seeing the Court as bound with a duty to follow the law, they perhaps saw their job as standing in opposition to a President they deemed malign.

[489] While Nixon criticized the opinion in *Roe*, he was actually quite ambivalent about abortion. "(I)t breaks the family," he said. And yet Nixon also had a racist desire to abort interracial pregnancies. "There are times when an abortion is necessary. I know that. When you have a black and a white." *See* Charlie Savage, "On Nixon Tapes, Ambivalence Over Abortion, Not Watergate," *The New York Times* (June 23, 2009).

[490] It's an attempt to minimize the crime. Scalia does a similar thing when he analogizes *Roe v. Wade* to a right to bigamy. He's trying to convince the Court that they can overrule *Roe* without recognizing the humanity of the unborn child. In fact none of the *Roe* dissenters have ever said that an unborn child is a person with a right to life. They are trying to overrule *Roe* without damaging the Court's reputation.

"I am not a crook," said President Nixon. And ***Planned Parenthood v. Casey*** is also in denial mode. None of the Justices actually say, "I am not a baby-killer," but they might as well have said it. Why else is the Supreme Court talking so passionately about their institution? That's the exact same thought that Nixon had when he was under attack. He was worried about the institution of the Presidency. And O'Connor, Kennedy, and Souter are worried about the institution of the Supreme Court.

The institution is under attack, by pro-lifers, who are alleging that babies have died under ***Roe v. Wade***. This charge is so severe, and so damning, that the Justices refuse to discuss the matter. It cannot be true. It's unthinkable.[491]

What is the Supreme Court going to say about Justice Blackmun and his arbitrary memo?[492] One of the journalists who undermined President Nixon, Bob Woodward, is now running articles in the Washington Post about a secret memo and the "arbitrary" word.[493] If a President can be hounded from office, maybe that can happen to a Supreme Court Justice, too.

Is this arbitrary memo a scandal? And if it is a scandal, how should the Supreme Court respond?

Maybe this is why the ***Casey*** opinion writes this sentence: "Any judicial act of line drawing may seem somewhat arbitrary, but ***Roe*** was a reasoned statement, elaborated with great care."[494]

---

[491] A few months after the Supreme Court announced that they had resolved the abortion controversy once and for all in ***Casey***, Dr. Martin Haskell would deliver a paper to the National Abortion Federation about a new surgical technique he had developed--killing the baby outside the birth canal. ***See*** notes 623-626 and text.

[492] ***See*** note 189 and text.

[493] ***Id***.

[494] ***Supra*** note 7.

The use of the word "arbitrary" corresponds to what is most shocking in Blackmun's secret memo, that the points drawn up by the authors of *Roe v. Wade*--the critical life or death points--were actually drawn up without any justification whatsoever.[495] *Casey* is attempting to defuse any potential scandal, so the Court tries to refute the idea that the *Roe* Court was careless or callous.

And *Casey* is doing this because the Supreme Court has scandal on its mind. And it's a momentous scandal. Innocent babies might have died. And rather than addressing this charge openly and honestly, the Court is telling us why they cannot do so.

---

[495] Justice Blackmun's memo describes the end of the first trimester as "arbitrary" and viability as "perhaps…equally arbitrary." *Supra* note 189. And some of the Justices have suggested that protecting babies in the middle of birth is "irrational" too. *Stenberg v. Carhart*, 530 U.S. 914 (2000) (Stevens, J., concurring).

Chapter 14

Of course, not everybody on the Supreme Court thinks of *Roe v. Wade* as a scandal. Only pro-lifers think it's a scandal. Pro-choice people think it's a wonderful opinion and an important advance in the cause of women's liberty.

Sandra Day O'Connor, for instance, likes *Roe v. Wade*. Or, more specifically, she likes autonomy and reproductive choice for women. O'Connor does not like the actual rules of *Roe v. Wade*. Specifically O'Connor was hostile to the idea that the legal rules should track the three trimesters of pregnancy. That was obviously an arbitrary idea.

O'Connor does not believe there is any sort of infanticide scandal the Supreme Court needs to worry about. She is not Catholic; she is not Kennedy. But O'Connor is quite aware that there are other scandals implicated by Justice Blackmun's opinion. The way *Roe v. Wade* was drafted is an acute embarrassment to the judicial branch.

And it's not just the sloppy and haphazard way these abortion rules were conceived.[496] O'Connor is worried about the health and safety of women who are receiving abortions.[497]

---

[496] *See* note 189 and text.

[497] The year after *Casey*, Dr. David Benjamin performed an abortion on Guadalupe Negron, who was 19 weeks pregnant. During the surgery Benjamin lacerated her cervix and punctured her uterus, and then left her alone for an hour. She began to hemorrhage, went into shock, and ultimately had a cardiac arrest. Paramedics would not be called for over two hours. When they arrived, the found the victim naked and bloody, with a breathing tube jammed into her stomach (instead of her trachea), causing stomach fluids to go into her lungs. She was already dead when the paramedics examined her. Dr. Benjamin was charged with depraved indifference to human life and convicted of murder in the 2nd degree. He was sentenced to 25-to-life. *See* Lynette Holloway, "Abortion Doctor Guilty of Murder," *The New York Times* (August 9, 1995).

Why can't we protect the health of women? What's wrong with doing a health inspection of an abortion clinic, or licensing the staff? Why are we excluding abortion from all the safety protocols of the liberal welfare state?

It's a rewriting of history to say that ***Roe v. Wade*** was a feminist opinion protecting the rights of women. None of the Justices--not Blackmun, not Brennan, not Marshall--are ideological feminists at the time ***Roe*** was written. They perhaps have an agenda, but it is not a feminist one.

Actual feminists would show up on the Supreme Court, of course. Sandra Day O'Connor--the first woman to sit on the Supreme Court--is a feminist, and her opinion in ***Casey*** is feminist. In fact it's an ode to women. Ruth Bader Ginsburg is a feminist pioneer. As women arrive on the Supreme Court, we see a shift in focus away from abortion doctors and towards the rights of women. It's a subtle but important distinction.

In her dissent in ***Akron v. Akron Center for Reproductive Health***, O'Connor attacks the Court's arbitrary first trimester rule. "The fallacy inherent in the ***Roe*** framework is apparent: just because the State has a compelling interest in ensuring maternal safety once an abortion may be more dangerous than childbirth, it simply does not follow that the State has no interest (in ensuring) that first trimester abortions are performed as safely as possible."[498]

What many pro-choice people fail to recognize is that abortion clinics are bringing all the abortion litigation after ***Roe***, not women. It's Planned Parenthood that is suing Danforth, and Planned Parenthood that is suing Casey. Planned Parenthood is a

---

[498] ***Supra*** note 190. O'Connor's fears are warranted. For instance, the abortion pill has killed several women in the first trimester. *See* note 152.

billion-dollar-a-year "non-profit" who is always suing to strike down state health regulations that affect its business model.

Safety regulations cost money. No industry likes them.

The interests of an abortion clinic and the interests of a pregnant woman seeking an abortion are not the same thing. That's O'Connor's point. As she put it in her *Akron* dissent, "A health regulation, such as the hospitalization requirement, simply does not rise to the level of 'official interference' with the abortion decision."[499]

Note how O'Connor is focused on women. She is protecting "the abortion decision." Who makes that decision? The pregnant woman makes that decision. That is where the right lies, with the individual woman. It's not a right of abortion clinics to be free of health regulations. O'Connor has no interest in protecting the right of an abortion clinic to perform cheap and unsafe abortions.

O'Connor is implicitly recognizing the idea that a pregnant woman likely has no idea of the health risks involved in her surgery. This is why we need state oversight. We are all free to contract, but many of us do not have the knowledge to contract effectively, particularly when it comes to our medical care. We have to trust that our doctors know what they are doing.

But if there is no state oversight, how can we trust that?

O'Connor's question is very basic. Why are we forbidding oversight of abortion clinics and abortion doctors? Isn't the health and safety of women an important concern? We have this oversight in all other forms of medical practice. This is actually a damning criticism of *Roe*, and O'Connor is not afraid to make it.

---

[499] *Id.*

In *Planned Parenthood v. Casey*, Justice O'Connor finally gets her way. Harry Blackmun's arbitrary first trimester rule is discarded. From now on, state health authorities can pass any and all health regulations to protect the safety of women, as long as these laws are not an "undue burden" on the right to abortion itself.

Of course, the *Casey* opinion is also relying upon stare decisis to uphold *Roe*. And yet the Supreme Court is simultaneously overturning one of the major rules in *Roe v. Wade*. This duality undercuts the argument that the Supreme Court cannot change its mind or fix its mistake. Scalia makes exactly this point in his blistering dissent. "It seems to me that stare decisis ought to be applied even to the doctrine of stare decisis, and I confess never to have heard of this new, keep what you want and throw away the rest version."[500]

The Supreme Court is overturning part of the opinion while they simultaneously claim they have no authority to overturn the opinion! Without a doubt, this logical flaw weakens the Court's argument. Nonetheless, O'Connor feels this strong need to fix *Roe*. Why?

She wants to turn it from a pro-abortion opinion that is focused on population control and doing abortions on the poor, the young, and the single, to a more liberal doctrine that is focused on the individual woman. She wants to focus on the pregnant woman and her right to make the choice. And, fundamentally, she wants to protect the health and safety of women who have this surgery.

O'Connor is likely the author of this passage:

> Abortion is a unique act. It is an act
> fraught with consequences for others:

---

[500] *Supra* note 283.

256

for the woman who must live with the implications of her decision; for the persons who perform and assist in the procedure; for the spouse, family, and society which must confront the knowledge that these procedures exist, procedures some deem nothing short of an act of violence against innocent human life; and, depending on one's beliefs, for the life or potential life that is aborted. Though abortion is conduct, it does not follow that the State is entitled to proscribe it in all instances. That is because the liberty of the woman is at stake in a sense unique to the human condition and so unique to the law. The mother who carries a child to full term is subject to anxieties, to physical constraints, to pain that only she must bear. That these sacrifices have from the beginning of the human race been endured by woman with a pride that ennobles her in the eyes of others and gives to the infant a bond of love cannot alone be grounds for the State to insist that she make the sacrifice. Her suffering is too intimate and personal for the State to insist, without more, upon its own vision of the woman's role, however dominant that vision has been in the course of history and our culture. The destiny of the woman must be shaped to a large extent on her own conception of her spiritual imperatives and her place in society.[501]

That is a very strong passage. It's a feminist speech that is pro-woman, without being shrill or combative. O'Connor was the

---

[501] **Supra** note 7. Some commentators suggest this passage was written by Anthony Kennedy. *See* note 479.

first woman to sit on the United States Supreme Court. Not surprisingly, her vision is far more feminist than anything Harry Blackmun said in *Roe v. Wade*. Justice Blackmun's opinion sees the abortion doctor as the hero. The pregnant woman is in distress and somebody needs to save her. *Roe* talks about the "stigma of unwed motherhood," and casts the single pregnant woman as a rather pathetic figure. The abortion doctor is the hero who will rescue her.

In his confirmation hearing before the United States Senate, Harry Blackmun talks about "the treatment of little people, what I hope is a sensitivity to their problems."[502] Yes, he is sympathetic and empathetic, a good liberal. But Blackmun is also looking down, seeing the poor as beneath him. He sees the young, poor, single Jane Roe as a "little person," while an actual little person--the unborn baby--he will define as an object, as property. Blackmun is defining humanity down. Adults are defined as little people, while actual helpless babies are defined out of existence.

Casey is trying to revamp this idea. The abortion doctor is not the focus. Now the pregnant woman is the hero. She is pregnant; she is dignified; she is autonomous. And whatever she chooses, that choice is up to her. It is certainly not up to the abortion doctor, or the state, to manipulate her.

Contrast the way O'Connor talks about a pregnancy to the way Blackmun talks about a pregnancy. O'Connor sees no stigma at all. She is talking about "pride" and "love" and "sacrifice." She is talking about a pregnant woman with respect. O'Connor sees her as an equal. She does not talk about her like she is pathetic. O'Connor is not trying for pity. O'Connor has been pregnant, she

---

[502] *See* Tinsley Yarbrough, *Harry Blackmun: The Outsider Justice* (2008). *See also* Mary Meehan, "Justice Blackmun and the Little People," www.meehanreports.com (2004).

knows what it feels like, and she can easily imagine herself as a pregnant woman who does not want to be pregnant.

One way we might think about this part of **Casey** is that the author is rewriting **Roe**, trying to make it sound more noble and of higher purpose.

Note also how inclusive O'Connor's rhetoric is. Is she dismissing the concerns of the pro-life movement? She is not. She references the reality that many people see abortion as "an act of violence against innocent human life."[503] O'Connor is not some pro-abortion socialist who wants to use abortion as population control to remove the cancer of poverty from our society. She rejects that, unequivocally. She wants to talk about the autonomy of women.

So we might applaud Justice O'Connor for seeing women as individuals, and framing the right as a woman's right to choose. Her opinion is not pro-abortion; it is pro-choice. She is aware of the danger, to women, of the Court's pro-abortion policies. She is seeking to moderate **Roe**, to find a middle ground. And she believes she can do this by focusing on the liberty of women, as well as their health and safety.

On the other hand, there are still problems with O'Connor's approach. Most notably she is still dehumanizing the unborn baby, and won't allow any state to recognize the baby's life, or protect the child. This attitude would cause the **Casey** three to split in noisy acrimony eight years later. Justice Kennedy would feel so betrayed by O'Connor and Souter, any worry he has about a possible scandal would go out the window. In the two **Carhart**

---

[503] It would be ironic if Anthony Kennedy was the author of all the feminist passages and Sandra Day O'Connor was the autocrat! It's a joint opinion, and one cannot know for certain who wrote what. But based on her prior dissents, it seems quite likely that O'Connor was the force pushing to protect the safety of women in abortion clinics.

opinions, Kennedy would talk about abortion with such baby-killing detail that many law students become pro-lifers just by reading those cases.[504]

Planned Parenthood v. Casey, on the other hand, is a celebration of women, liberty, autonomy, choice, dignity and freedom. Abortion sounds really good when you talk about it in these terms. ***Casey*** talks about abortion in a very abstract way, as "reproductive choice."

O'Connor is focused on choice because she wants to move the Supreme Court away from a pro-abortion bias. She wants us to focus on women, and so she makes the pregnant woman and her choice the center of our attention.

Yet one might also see a lot of this rhetoric in ***Casey*** as an attempt to hide from the reality of abortion. What do we make of this passage, for instance? "These matters, involving the most intimate and personal choices a person may make in a lifetime, choices central to personal dignity and autonomy, are central to the liberty protected by the Fourteenth Amendment."[505]

Is it true that abortion is "central to personal dignity"? What's dignified about an abortion? It's a very invasive and undignified surgical procedure. Indeed, going to an obstetrician is often undignified. One might add that pregnancy can be undignified, too, with vomiting and bladder control issues. Is sex dignified? Is a miscarriage dignified? When you take an RU-486 pill, for instance, you can't be sure when the miscarriage will happen. It could happen on the bus, it could happen on the street, it could happen at work. Does any of this sound dignified?

---

[504] *See* notes 647-649 and text.
[505] *Supra* note 7.

We have a marriage ceremony to add dignity (and love) to human sex and reproduction. We feel the need to add dignity to sex and reproduction because these processes are biological, and can be very messy and undignified.

How did you get pregnant? We had sex like a couple of animals.

You know who is extremely dignified? Supreme Court Justices are dignified. In their sexless black robes, they are dressed like priests.[506] They have titles like "Your Honor" and "Justice." They want to be dignified and, as *Casey* makes clear, they are worried about their own high office. This concern with dignity, and their own status, might corrupt their opinions. *Casey* is rampant with this self-regard.

We must preserve our dignity!

Is it true that American women had no dignity before *Roe v. Wade*? Even if you want to say that sexual liberty is fun, or important, is it credible to say that a sexually conservative society is undignified? Do the Amish have dignity?

For that matter, did Susan B. Anthony have dignity?[507] All the early feminists were opposed to abortion.[508] One might say these women--who were radicals in their day--are old-fashioned and

---

[506] Justice Hugo Black thought the Supreme Court should wear suits, just like the people in the other branches of the federal government. *See* Roger Newman, *Hugo Black: A Biography* (1994). Justice Black perhaps suspected that people dressed like priests might be more likely to use "natural law" and to decide cases by reference to the universe.

[507] A prominent pro-life organization has named itself after Susan B. Anthony. *See* www.sba-list.org

[508] *See* www.feministsforlife.org. Even the founder of Planned Parenthood, Margaret Sanger, was hostile to abortion. Many pro-lifers dislike Sanger, because of her racism and her support for eugenics. *See* note 11. But Sanger actually made many pro-life comments. For instance she described abortion as "vicious" and "dangerous" in 1932. *See* www.sangerpapers.wordpress.com.

wrong.[509] But is it fair to say they are undignified or vulgar people?

Is it undignified to protect women from medical harms? Imagine a surgical abortion in 1789, without any anesthesia.[510] What's dignified about surgery without anesthesia?

After all, the abortion right that the Supreme Court is protecting has to be safe for women. That's why O'Connor is shifting us away from the argument that states cannot protect the health and safety of women. We might say it's disrespecting the autonomy of women ("paternalistic") for a society to say that abortion is bad for women. But what if abortion really is bad for women?[511]

Suppose we find out some medical information that the Supreme Court does not know in 1992. For instance, medical researchers are starting to agree that abortion increases a woman's risk for future premature births.[512] Or science might prove that elective

---

[509] "Guilty? Yes. No matter what the motive, love of ease, or a desire to save from suffering the unborn innocent, the woman is awfully guilty who commits the deed. It will burden her conscience in life, it will burden her soul in death; but oh thrice guilty is he who…drove her to the desperation which impelled her to the crime!" Susan B. Anthony, *The Revolution*, July 8, 1869.

[510] Anesthesia (specifically, ether) was discovered in the middle of the 19th century. The idea of "elective" surgery before anesthesia is ridiculous. In fact surgical abortion wasn't much of an option at all until the discovery of penicillin after World War II. And even then it would be a couple of decades before the introduction of a flexible curette. *See* note 223. When Professor Dellapenna calls abortion-on-demand in the 17th century a "myth," he's being polite. *Supra* note 192.

[511] One danger in seeking an abortion is that many of our best obstetricians avoid abortion practice. What this means is a significant number of abortion doctors went to dubious medical schools, and many of them seem to be in trouble with medical authorities. A pro-life organization keeps a database of abortion doctors on-line. *See* www.abortiondocs.org. Andrew Rosenthal of *The New York Times* says this website is an "intimidation effort." A more neutral observer might say that it's a very helpful resource in sorting out the abortion doctors who are more likely to damage women. It's an on-line database that keeps track of lawsuits, criminal complaints, and license issues for doctors in the abortion industry.

[512] *See* notes 65-66 and text.

abortion is responsible for our society's dramatic, six-fold increase in dangerous ectopic pregnancies.[513] Would it be "undignified" to protect women from these medical harms?

O'Connor's opinion seeks to normalize abortion, so that it is treated like all other surgeries. She obviously wants to de-politicize abortion, so that we do not have all these street protests.

Roe v. Wade was a radical opinion. It ushered in a set of abortion rules that were imposed on our country by unelected rulers. And by the time of *Casey*, the Supreme Court is clearly under attack. There is a popular revolt, people are unhappy, and many feel like they have no voice in our own society.

The Supreme Court is trying to respond. It is a joint opinion. And there is a dichotomy in *Casey*, a deep division. Somebody on the Court is responding in autocratic fashion and is talking about the institution of the Supreme Court. This person is more domineering and dictatorial, not less.

But somebody else on the Court is responding in a smarter way. They are focusing on the liberty of the individual, and trying to get Americans to see *Roe* as respectful of human dignity and autonomy. It is not an autocratic opinion. It is not dictatorial. This person wants us to focus on liberty and freedom.

And yet, despite this focus on the pregnant woman in *Casey*, one might still criticize the opinion--and the Supreme Court in general--for its lack of regard for individual people. Yes, the Court is talking about autonomy and the dignity of the individual. But what if abortion is not actually a dignified experience? What if the surgery is not necessary for human dignity? Then the Supreme Court's rhetoric is divorced from factual reality. It's an

---

[513] *See* notes 68-69.

abstract idea, an ideological proposition as opposed to what really happens in an abortion clinic.

What you abort a pregnancy, what happens to you? What happens to your life?

On November 10th, 2013, the magazine *New York* published 26 stories of women talking about their abortions.[514] This is unusual in our media. Abortions are done in secret, and we don't have a lot of good journalism in regard to the subject.

In this article we see an incredible variety of circumstances, and emotional reactions, in regard to abortion. These are rather like the stories women share on afterabortion.com.[515] When the Supreme Court talks about "dignity" and "autonomy," we might compare these words to the reality of what abortion is often like for women.

Here is a woman, Nicole, 19, from Kentucky, talking about her abortion.

> It was this past spring. The due date's coming up--I'm dreading it. I wanted to keep it. My boyfriend always had football practice, so he couldn't go to the doctor appointments with me. If he'd gone, he would've felt differently. But he said, "No way." I wanted to show him that I loved him enough to do it for him. When I was thirteen weeks, we made an appointment at the closest clinic in Kentucky, four hours away, but the night before, we decided not to go. At two in the morning, he called and said, "Get dressed." I said, "I don't want to

[514] Meaghan Winter, "My Abortion," *New York* (November 10, 2013).
[515] *Supra* note 99 and text.

go." We both cried the whole way there. I don't think abortion is killing, but I'd always been against it. When I told him the credit-card scanner at the clinic wasn't working, he asked if I was making it up. We went to get $1,000 from a gas-station ATM. I was hysterical, and he said, "Okay, you don't have to go back." I was so happy. Then he said, "We drove all this way. Stop crying, act like a woman." I was angry, but I was so sleepy and tired of fighting. When I had the ultrasound, I asked for the picture and a nurse said, "Seriously?" A month later, he said he regretted it too. When I cry about it, I cry alone. He thinks it would make me sad to talk about, but I don't want our baby to think we forgot. I've never heard of anybody else having an abortion here.[516]

This story is radically different from O'Connor's discussion of autonomy and dignity. O'Connor casts the pregnant woman as the decider. *Casey* is actually more inclusive than *Roe*, which relegates the father to footnote 67.[517] There is no father in *Roe*, and no baby. Instead we have a pregnant woman, who is considered in isolation. The father is irrelevant, and the baby is defined out of existence.

And yet in real life, every pregnancy has a father. And every pregnancy has a baby.

By reducing the pregnant woman to an autonomous individual, feminism is destroying her relationships. Feminism and *Roe v.*

---

[516] *Supra* note 514.
[517] "Neither in this opinion nor in *Doe v. Bolton*...do we discuss the father's rights, if any exist in the constitutional context, in the abortion decision." *Supra* note 1. In *Danforth* the Supreme Court would make it official--the father (like the baby) has no rights. *Supra* note 104.

Wade dismisses the father as irrelevant. "It's my body, it's my choice." And how does this power grab over human reproduction affect men? Perhaps they too will deny fatherhood. They will start to see sex in autonomous fashion, as something individuals do. There is no relationship.

"I wanted to show him that I loved him enough to do it for him." And she wants to remember and mourn her lost baby.

We see, in Nicole's story, a tragedy. She is trying to love her boyfriend and make him happy. Meanwhile, her boyfriend, who comes across as a jerk, is denying his fatherhood and his obligations as a father. *Roe* makes this easy for him to do.

He tells her to "act like a woman," by which he means, "induce a miscarriage."

Is *Roe v. Wade* helping Nicole?

She is being pressured by her boyfriend to have an abortion. "I wanted to keep it." She's not interested in feminist politics, in winning a fight. She wants a loving, healthy, happy relationship with her boyfriend. And she wants her baby. And she can't have those things.

One might imagine a society where Nicole's desire to keep her baby is protected. And, in this society, the pressure is now on her boyfriend to step up and be a man. Do you love Nicole? Do you love the baby you created? Marry her. Be a father to her child. Kiss her belly and tell her that you love her.

This attempt by the Supreme Court to give women all control over human reproduction has been a quiet disaster for many women. Fathers have disappeared. And women are left with two unhappy choices: abort or be a single mom.[518]

Nicole's boyfriend is not a father to her baby. He denies his fatherhood, rejects it, in the same way that **Roe v. Wade** rejects it, and feminism rejects it. And so Nicole has an abortion in order to make him happy. And he's not happy. And she's not happy.

She has to cry in secret.

Here's another woman, Abby, 28, who is describing her two abortions.[519]

> The first time I was 25, in New York. From the time I was a teenager, the idea of having an abortion if pregnant was a no-brainer. I had this idea you can't let life get in the way of your plans. My friend drove me. The procedure was in a tiny, bright white room—it was like a nightmare, but it was over really, really quickly. They moved me into this communal healing room. Women were reclining on big, pillowy chairs. I remember feeling comforted, warm—we'd all been through the same experience. Two years ago, I was in Oklahoma. I wasn't given a choice in method—I got the pill. My boyfriend worked in Idaho—I was alone. They gave me all this paperwork that said, "This is serious. You could die," and an antibiotic, painkiller, and a latex glove and a pill to shove up my vagina. At home, the antibiotic made me vomit and shit everywhere. I thought, *Fuck the latex glove! Fuck them for thinking I can't*

---

[518] The focus on "choice" distracts us from how awful these new choices are.
[519] *Supra* note 514.

> *touch myself!* After the contractions started, my hands turned into claws. I was dehydrated. I had this underlying feeling that I was being made to suffer, to repent for my situation. I called my boss. He took me to the ER. It cost $2,000. When I stood up, the bed was covered in blood. I felt ashamed, but the way he reacted with kindness, I saw that I could choose not to feel ashamed. When I went home, I got up to pee, and this gray golf-ball thing came out. I thought, *So I just flush the toilet?*

Abby is pro-choice. She says abortion is a "no-brainer." She's had two abortions. And yet, do we get a sense from Abby's story that she feels dignified or autonomous? She describes her first abortion as a "nightmare," and only feels comfort afterwards, when she has a sense of unity with other women who have been through the same experience. Her use of the word "nightmare" suggests a certain trauma. One might imagine a soldier fighting in a war describing a "nightmare," and then talking about the camaraderie he felt afterwards, when he was safe.

Many women cannot talk about their abortions. Many men cannot talk about their war experiences. If we make this comparison, if we see abortion as possible trauma in the same way we see war as possible trauma, we might start to despise **Planned Parenthood v. Casey**. O'Connor is talking about the dignity of a pregnant woman in the same way that we might talk about the dignity of an American soldier. We might agree that soldiers, and pregnant women, are dignified. And yet death is not dignified, so war and miscarriages are not dignified, either.

Abby is cursing her doctors like she's a U.S. Marine. "Fuck the latex glove. Fuck them…"[520] She describes blood and vomit and shit and contractions and pee and shoving a pill up her vagina.

O'Connor is like a leader who is giving a patriotic speech about why it is necessary to go to war. You would expect such a speech to talk about dignity and sacrifice. She even mentions "an act of violence against innocent human life." But for the most part, O'Connor is trying to give us an uplifting speech.

Abby is like a soldier who is keeping it real. She is brutally honest about her experiences.

The powerful ruler is giving us her ideology about the necessity for this particular war. She has a speech about how dignified all the soldiers are who are going to have to go through this ugliness. She herself is not going to inform us what war is like.

If you want the truth, you need to talk to individuals who are dealing with the reality of it. You need journalism and you need photographs. You want to see an abortion? Look at photographs of abortion. You want to know what war is? Look at photographs of war.

Of course, when you send people off to war, you do not want to focus on death and killing. You might want to hide this information from people. Your ideology requires suppression of the truth and hiding of facts. There is a tremendous amount of repression and denial in *Planned Parenthood v. Casey*. There is a willful desire not to discuss the reality of abortion. That's because abortion, like war, is an ugly thing.

---

[520] *Id.*

Chapter 15

Planned Parenthood v. Casey righted one of the awful ideas in *Roe v. Wade*, that we had no interest in the health or safety of pregnant women in the first trimester. Of course we need health regulations of surgeries and pharmaceuticals. The health and safety of women is a vital issue.

Indeed, as pro-choice people argue, sometimes pregnancy itself is a dangerous medical condition. We might need to do an abortion because of a medical emergency. What constitutes a medical emergency? One obvious answer is when the pregnant woman's life is in danger.

For instance, one of the most life-threatening situations to a pregnant woman is when she suffers an ectopic pregnancy. In this situation, the zygote has not attached to the walls of the uterus. Instead the organism has attached inside the fallopian tubes, or some other area of a woman's reproductive system. If the mother does not spontaneously abort, a tubal pregnancy will almost always be fatal to both mother and child. As such, it is clearly a medical emergency.

As Justice Blackmun writes in *Roe v. Wade*, "Neither in Texas nor in any other State are all abortions prohibited. Despite broad proscription, an exception always exists."[521] And that exception is "for an abortion procured or attempted by medical advice for the purpose of saving the life of the mother."[522]

Justice Blackmun goes on to argue that allowing doctors to kill babies in this fashion suggests that the baby is not a human being,

---

[521] *Supra* note 1.
[522] *Id*.

not a person who is entitled to the equal protection of the laws. The rejoinder would be that we have always had a right to kill in self-defense, or in defense of the lives of others.[523] When a baby is a mortal threat to her mother--as in an ectopic pregnancy--of course doctors have a legal right to kill the child. This was true before *Roe v. Wade* was ever decided.

And *Roe* went a lot farther than finding a right for doctors to do an abortion in a medical emergency. In a medical emergency, the doctor really is protecting the woman's health and safety. And yet in *Roe v. Wade*, the Supreme Court said there was a constitutional right to do an elective abortion, which is an abortion for no medical purpose at all.[524]

After the Supreme Court said abortion was a right thing to do, the number of women undergoing this procedure skyrocketed in our society. Tens of millions of American women have had abortions. Along with this radical shift in our culture, we have also seen increases in breast cancer, increases in premature births, a recent increase in fatalities in pregnant women, and a dramatic, 6-fold increase in life-threatening ectopic pregnancies.[525]

Is the Supreme Court responsible for any of this? Perhaps *Roe v. Wade* has actually caused this rise in medical emergencies involving women and their unborn children.

It is truly shocking that the Supreme Court mandated in *Roe* that a pregnant woman's health was an illegitimate concern in the first trimester. And in cases like *Danforth* and *Akron*, the Supreme

---

[523] *See* Eugene Volokh, "Medical Self-Defense, Prohibited Experimental Therapies, and Payment for Organs," *Harvard Law Review* 120 (2007).
[524] The Supreme Court offers a very broad definition of "health" abortions in *Roe v. Wade* and *Doe v. Bolton. See* note 205. But the opinion assumes that doctors will be performing surgeries even if there is no medical benefit. Under the rules of *Roe*, you can have a "health" abortion until birth, and an abortion for any reason whatsoever until viability.
[525] *See* Chapter 2.

Court overturned health regulations in the second and third trimester, too. And the Supreme Court did all this without any discussion of medical risks or the medical realities of how abortion actually works.

After *Casey* overruled this part of *Roe v. Wade*, state health officials once again had the authority to protect the health and safety of women. For instance, after the Supreme Court issued *Casey* in 1992, many state health officials started requiring abortion clinics to use ultrasounds, and to share these ultrasounds with their patients. This regulation is designed both to protect the health and safety of patients, and also to inform the woman's choice with factual information.

Why are state officials mandating an ultrasound? It's dangerous for a doctor to be ignorant. After all, abortion is a blind procedure. A doctor needs to see what is going on inside the mother's uterus. He needs to confirm the age of the baby, determine how many babies there are, and make sure he's not leaving behind any baby parts inside the woman after he performs an abortion.[526]

Here is what the Guttmacher Institute has to say about the practice of using ultrasounds in abortion clinics. "Since the mid-1990's, several states have moved to make ultrasound part of abortion service provision. Since routine ultrasound is not considered medically necessary as a component of first-trimester abortion, the requirements appear to be a veiled attempt to personify the fetus and dissuade a woman from obtaining an abortion.

---

[526] An estimate of a baby's age from an ultrasound can be off by two weeks in either direction. If you fail to do an ultrasound? The estimate might be off by two months. A mistake like this has dramatic consequences for the woman who is undergoing an abortion. *See* note 538 and text.

Moreover, an ultrasound can add significantly to the cost of the procedure."[527]

Of course pro-lifers would like women to see their baby before they abort it. Pro-lifers are confident that science and technology will confirm what pro-lifers believe--that the unborn is a human baby. The abortion industry seems to concede this argument as they fight and litigate over the ultrasound. They don't want pregnant women to see an ultrasound of their child. They want to hide information from women and keep them in the dark.

Is an ultrasound medically necessary? If the doctor fails to do one, he might find himself being sued for medical malpractice.

Consider the case of a Yugoslav immigrant named J.B., who received an abortion in a Planned Parenthood clinic in San Francisco in 1997.[528] The doctor did not bother using an ultrasound, and thus he had no idea that his patient was actually pregnant with twins. So when he operated on the patient, he successfully aborted only one of her babies. The other child was left alive inside her womb.

A couple of months later, J.B. returned to the abortion clinic, complaining of a swollen stomach and morning sickness. At her request, a nurse performed a urine test. She was surprised to discover that the patient was indeed still pregnant.

This clinic did not perform abortions after 20 weeks, so the doctors referred J.B. to another clinic that did. There she had her first sonogram, which revealed the second twin, alive, and missing an arm and a leg.

---

[527] "Requirements for Ultrasound," www.guttmacher.org. How can a doctor (or nurse!) be certain it is a first trimester abortion if you do not do an ultrasound?

[528] *See* Cheryl Wetzstein, "Planned Parenthood Told To Pay $672,610 for Botched Abortion," *The Washington Times* (March 1, 2001).

J.B. had been considering keeping her remaining baby before the ultrasound, but felt she had no choice but to have another abortion now, after seeing what had happened to her child.

She filed a medical malpractice suit against Planned Parenthood Golden Gate, a non-profit who oversees nine abortion facilities in the San Francisco Bay area. In a trial before Superior Court Judge Douglas Munson, the jury awarded J.B. $650,000 for mental anguish, $1,875 in past medical costs, $14,500 for future psychiatric expenses and $6,240 in lost earnings.[529]

Her testimony was so horrifying that three jurors later said they wanted to give her over $1 million dollars.

According to her attorney, Christopher Dolan, J.B. still has severe emotional distress. She cries uncontrollably when she sees babies, especially twins. And she is unable to function in a romantic relationship. "She testified on the stand that she hallucinated and saw blood all over her lower legs and pelvic area," said Mr. Dolan.[530]

Despite what the Guttmacher Institute has to say about ultrasounds, they are obviously an important part of the health and welfare of pregnant women. Indeed, after this lawsuit, over 99% of the abortions now done in Planned Parenthood clinics involve the use of ultrasounds.[531] It's a shame that a medical malpractice suit first had to be filed before this obvious safeguard was put into place.

In fact, it's hard to see why pro-choice people would object to ultrasounds, or want to keep them from women. It's hardly "pro-

---

[529] *Id.*

[530] *Id.*

[531] *See* Steven Ertelt, "Pro-Abortion Rape Myth Debunked, 99% of Abortion Clinics Do Ultrasounds," *LifeNews* (February 22, 2012).

choice" to hide information from the patient (not to mention the doctor!) A 3-D ultrasound, for instance, allows a pregnant woman to see inside her own uterus. It informs her choice with specific facts about the unborn. How human does it look? Is it a baby? An ultrasound makes a pregnant woman a smarter, more educated person. It gives her knowledge about what is happening inside her uterus.

Yes, this information might make the woman decide to keep her baby. On the other hand, it might give her relief that the unborn doesn't look like a baby at all.

It's strange that Guttmacher says an ultrasound is an "attempt to personify the fetus." How does an ultrasound do that, exactly? After all, we are told by our Supreme Court that an unborn infant is not a human being, not a person, and abortion is not a homicide. Surely a 3-D ultrasound would serve as factual confirmation in regard to what our authorities are telling us?

Yet the response is quite the opposite. Apparently information is to be censored and hidden from women. We can't look at an ultrasound, because then we might not have an abortion. Do we think women will only have abortions if they are kept in the dark?

In North Carolina, a federal judge struck down an ultrasound requirement, arguing that it violated the First Amendment.[532] Does an ultrasound offend the free speech clause? As usual, it's

---

[532] Contrast this legal argument with the media campaign. *Supra* note 160. The media was filled with stories about the possibility that women would be raped with ultrasounds. A *New York Times* columnist used the word "rape" four times when talking about ultrasounds. *See* Nicholas Kristof, "When States Abuse Women," *The New York Times* (March 3, 2012). Doonesbury ran a cartoon about doctors raping their patients with ultrasounds. *See* Ewen MacAskill, "Doonesbury Strip on Texas Abortion Law Dropped By Some US Newspapers," *The Guardian* (March 11, 2012). Not surprisingly, when the abortion clinics sued in federal court, they did not try to argue that their doctors would be raping women with ultrasounds.

abortion doctors who are bringing all the litigation over the ultrasound, not women. Abortion doctors do not want to share their ultrasounds with their patients. And, they argue, it violates the free speech rights of a doctor to make him share this information.

Abortion is based on an ideology, an idea that there is no baby in the uterus. The free speech argument is that we cannot force the doctor, or his patient, to recognize the humanity of the baby. And an ultrasound is perceived as a danger to this pro-choice ideology. It might upset our prejudices if we actually see what is inside our uterus.

Here is the Supreme Court describing the right to choose in **Planned Parenthood v. Casey**. "At the heart of liberty is the right to define one's own concept of existence, of meaning, of the universe, and of the mystery of human life."[533]

The Supreme Court is talking about abortion the same way it might talk about free speech. We have a right to whatever ideas we want to have. But of course pregnancy is not an idea. Pregnancy is a reality. And none of us are entitled to our own set of facts.

And yet here is the Supreme Court, in an abortion case, talking about "one's own concept of existence." Pregnancy is reduced to a concept, to an idea, and we are all free to think whatever we want to think about it. And for this idea to prevail, we have to hide the factual reality of pregnancy from ourselves. If we see an ultrasound, we see what is inside our uterus. And the "mystery of human life" is not a mystery anymore.

It's very odd to analogize abortion to a concept or an idea about life. *Casey* is talking about pregnancy as if this is free speech.

---

[533] *Supra* note 7.

The pregnant mom is an author, or a creator. But in human reproduction, we are not creating a book or a play or a movie. We had sex and we created a baby.

According to the Supreme Court, as the creator of a human life, apparently we have a right to define what it is. We get to say, "it's a baby," and it's a baby. We get to say, "it's nothing," and it's nothing. Like any writer, we can kill off characters we don't like. "No, no, I don't think Jane should be pregnant in the third act. Let's erase that."

The Supreme Court is describing the heart of liberty as a right to play God. You get to decide if somebody else is human or not, alive or not alive, a baby or not. There is no reality, no universe, outside of your own will. Your will is all, and you can remake the universe according to your will. Our Supreme Court is granting to a pregnant woman an awe-inspiring power to determine what the universe is to be.

This overblown rhetoric is quite dangerous. After all, human beings are not God. We do not have a power to redefine babies out of existence. An abortion does not turn back any clock. An abortion is not undoing a pregnancy; it is stopping one. If this baby is alive, we are killing our child.

This is why ultrasounds are routinely hidden from patients in abortion clinics. It is why our media does not run photographs of aborted infants. We have to hide from the reality of what we are doing. We have to hide it, suppress it, and deny it.

Perhaps we censor and hide ultrasounds, and abortion photographs, because we recognize the possibility for a tremendous amount of guilt. We are denying, hiding, and repressing any knowledge that we have created a baby. And we deny our own responsibility for what we are doing.

Judith Jarvis Thomson once compared pregnancy to a kidnapping. Here is her famous hypothetical: "You wake up in the morning and find yourself back to back in bed with an unconscious violinist. A famous unconscious violinist. He has been found to have a fatal kidney ailment, and the Society of Music Lovers has canvassed all the available medical records and found that you alone have the right blood type to help. They have therefore kidnapped you, and last night the violinist's circulatory system was plugged into yours, so that your kidneys can be used to extract poisons from his blood as well as your own."[534]

It is quite odd to compare pregnancy to a kidnapping. And what about this utter failure to talk about sex from the people who say abortion is a right? Where is sex in Judith Jarvis Thomson's famous hypothetical? It's not there. And **Roe v. Wade** itself is sexless. The father is relegated to footnote 67. If you didn't know how babies are created, you might think Jane Roe had been mugged by a stork.

The Supreme Court is denying a woman's sexual agency, and denying her responsibility. It's as if pregnancy just happens to women and we don't know how. You wake up and you are pregnant. You wake up and you are strapped to a violinist.

Thomson's argument is that most of us would free ourselves from the violinist, even if this action would cause the violinist to die. We don't have any duty to this person. We are a victim of force and violence, and we can free ourselves from this situation without any guilt. We would do this even if our actions cause the violinist to die. Thus, in the case of a woman who is raped, she has a right to free herself, even if doing so would kill a baby.[535]

---

[534] Judith Jarvis Thomson, *Philosophy & Public Affairs* 1 (1971).
[535] Most of us would free ourselves from the violinist right away, not wait months and months. If you have a non-homicidal solution (emergency birth

But of course Thomson's argument does not work for a woman who is engaging in reproductive sex. Reproductive sex means there is a possibility that you will be reproducing. When you consent to sex, you are consenting to the possibility that you might make a baby.

And we know this. We know that we are responsible for our sexual lives, and thus we are responsible for any babies that we create.

After all, our society still holds men responsible for any babies we have fathered. It does not matter under the law if we use a condom, or some other form of birth control. If we engage in reproductive sex, we are responsible for reproduction. Morally, legally, and ethically, men are responsible for our reproductive sex lives. And men are responsible for any babies we create.[536]

Isn't it fair to say that women are also responsible for sex and reproduction?

Indeed, this knowledge of our responsibility is why there is so much repression over abortion. We cannot look at ultrasounds. We cannot look at abortion photographs. We have to hide from the reality of what we are doing. The baby's reality upsets our ideas and our ideologies.

It's ironic that abortion is portrayed as a freedom or a liberty, because so much of our aborting society relies upon sexual

---

control) that allows you to escape this fiendish plot, why wouldn't you choose that option?

[536] *See* Ann Althouse, "Do We Pity the Man Who Is, Against His Will, Forced Into Fatherhood?" *Althouse* (August 1, 2013). Althouse refers to an unhappy father as a "splooge stooge." Her point is that men are adults, and smart, and in control of our bodies, and so we are deemed responsible when we create a baby. (Althouse does not apply this adult standard to women).

repression, denial, and censorship. Why are we hiding from ultrasounds, from scientific knowledge?

Perhaps we should teach people about abortion before we have sex and before we have a pregnancy. How awful to find out the truth of what an abortion is, after you have already had the surgery? We should not keep this information from people. We should teach people about sex, and sexual reproduction, so they understand how important it is.

Sex education should include moral questions. Young people need to be challenged to think about what they are doing. It's not enough to show students feminist-approved porn from Sweden, or diagrams of the fallopian tubes. Sex education needs to include discussion about pregnancy, abortion, and babies. Look at abortion photographs. Talk to aborting women. Go to a hospital and look at a preemie in a NICU. That's how you prepare young people for their sexual lives.

Instead, our very smartest people try to talk about abortion without talking about abortion. They avoid the subject. *Casey* in particular is an awful example of this, with its talk of "the universe" and the "mystery of human life." A focus on facts might have grounded the opinion in reality, what an abortion is, how it works. Instead the opinion is unmoored from sex, reproduction, health issues, even the life-or-death issue.

Our society is deeply repressed over our abortions. We deny, we hide, and we look away.

Consider the case of Jennie Lynn McCormack. The *New Republic* writes about her case in its December 21, 2012 issue.[537]

---

[537] Ada Calhoun, "The Rise of DIY Abortions," *The New Republic* (December 21, 2012).

McCormack is a divorced single mom, unemployed, and had already had one abortion when she got pregnant again. The father of her baby was Buddy Lee, an ex-con who had been paroled out of prison for armed robbery. He was back in prison, as his parole had been revoked for drinking. So McCormack was pregnant without a father in the picture. She was poor, she already had three kids, and she didn't want another one.

McCormack decided to have another abortion. But she couldn't afford to go to a doctor. So she asked her sister to order abortion pills for her on-line. There was no ultrasound, so she was not sure of her baby's age.

"By the time the medication arrived in an unmarked envelope on December 23, she was in her second trimester--at, she thought, week 14. Following the instructions, she took the first pill right away and the others some hours later. That night, she started having cramps."[538]

McCormack had her induced miscarriage on Christmas Eve. She gave birth in her own bathroom. It was painful and she lost a great deal of blood. And the baby was bigger than she had expected. She was not in the 14th week. More like the 19th week or the 23rd week.

The baby was a little girl.

McCormack did not call 911 during her miscarriage. She did not call 911, even after she had lost a lot of blood. Instead she mopped up the bathroom floor. And she wrapped her dead baby in a trash bag, and put the trash bag in a box. And then she hid the box under her bed.

---

[538] *Id.*

That night, Jennie Lynn McCormack went to a Christmas Eve dinner at her father's house. She didn't mention her miscarriage, or the dead baby under her bed. Instead she wrapped presents for her three children and put them under her Christmas tree.

The dead baby stayed under her bed for a week. According to Ada Calhoun, the reporter for the *New Republic*, "It didn't feel right to her to throw it away."[539]

When the baby's cadaver started to smell, McCormack took the box out from under her bed and wrapped it in more trash bags. Now she placed the body outside her house, on her back porch. She hid the body under the cover of her barbecue grill. It stayed there for another week.

Finally Jennie confided to a man she knew. She had had an abortion at home, and she did not know what to do with the body. The man told his sister, and his sister called the police.

On January 9, 2011, two officers arrived at McCormack's house. She led them to her barbecue grill and said, "My baby is in the box."[540]

It's fair to say the police officers were upset by what they saw. "We see dead bodies, daily, weekly, in all different stages," said Detective Brian McClure. "But seeing a recognizable baby in a garbage bag, frozen, outside, in a garbage pile, decomposing..."[541]

His partner, Val Wadsworth, said, "I wouldn't wish anyone to that scene or investigation. We unwrapped it and released it to the

---

[539] *Id*. We might interrupt this narrative to ask Dr. Stotland--the former president of the American Psychiatric Associatieon--if she is still certain abortion trauma is a "myth." *Supra* note 89.
[540] *Id*.
[541] *Id*.

funeral home, and the next day was the autopsy. The funeral director who was there said it was the worst smell he'd smelled in his thirty-five years of the funeral home…I can't imagine what it did to her, to have that baby right underneath you for so long, trying to sleep with it there. When they had it thawed out and laying on the table, it was just sad. Sad feeling. Sad little pathetic face. It was just terrible."[542]

Reading this, it does not sound like a constitutional right. It sounds like a crime. And yet, McCormack was not convicted of any crime. The charges were dismissed.

McCormack filed suit to determine if she had a right to do this. The United States Court of Appeals for the Ninth Circuit said she did, in *McCormack v. Hiedeman*.[543] The Court skipped over most of the facts in the case. So the reader has no idea that McCormack almost died, or that she kept her dead baby under her bed for a week, and then in her barbecue grill for another week.

Obviously these facts are appalling. That's why our unelected judges would prefer to hide them.

When we hear about a dead baby under a bed, or in a barbecue grill, we think, "That's a crime." But our federal judges insist it is not a crime. It is a right thing to do. The Supreme Court says abortion is a right. And so this too is right. Presumably this is why the Supreme Court wants to talk about abortion rights in the abstract, without any facts. We don't like the facts. The facts upset us. But now our federal courts are engaging in their own sort of repression and denial. Let's not talk about the dead baby under the bed. Let's pretend it's not there.

---

[542] *Id*.
[543] 694 F.3d 1004 (2012).

The problem with all this ideology divorced from reality is that we can't avoid reality. We can say abortion is a right thing to do. We can sell abortion pills on-line. But what Jennie McCormack discovered is that when you swallow abortion pills and cause a miscarriage in your bathroom in the 19th week of your pregnancy, you are going to have a dead body in your house.

What is she supposed to do with the dead body in her house, Justice O'Connor? You said the "destiny of the woman must be shaped to a large extent on her own conception of her spiritual imperatives."[544] But this isn't a spiritual issue at all. She has a dead body in her house. She's hiding it under her bed. It's in her barbecue grill. That's an actual dead body. We don't get to imagine she is something else. She is what she is.

The Supreme Court's ideology is from the ivory tower. And yet the actual facts are like something out of a Hitchcock movie. It's like **Rear Window**. We're not talking about spirituality. Our questions are far more down to earth. How do you get rid of a corpse?

And this poor woman can't acknowledge her dead baby. She can't even think about it. She might have kept it under her bed forever and ever, except it started to stink. So now we're in **Psycho**. Norman Bates could not admit that his mother had died. And Jennie McCormack is holding on to her dead baby for weeks. She can't let go. It's horrific and it's very sad.

And what's irritating--if not outrageous--is how our authorities keep insisting this is sane behavior. It's a right thing to do.

Why didn't she call 911? Isn't that the normal thing to do when you're having a miscarriage?

---

[544] Assuming it is Justice O'Connor who drafted this passage. It may, of course, be Souter or Kennedy (or a clerk).

Our authorities--and our media--told Jennie McCormack that she was exercising her right to choose. And yet, on Christmas Eve, she's bleeding on her bathroom floor, with a dead baby at her feet. And she's shocked. She's shocked at what she did. What she did to herself, and what she did to her baby.

She was not expecting a child. And she felt a guilt that was so overwhelming that she couldn't do anything. She couldn't bury her baby in the woods like a proper criminal. And she couldn't call 911 and ask for help. All she can do is hide the body, and pretend as if nothing unusual has happened.

Chapter 16

The repression in *McCormack v. Hiedeman* mirrors the repression in *Planned Parenthood v. Casey*. Our unelected judges are ignoring the facts of abortion. They are ignoring the horror stories.

That is not really surprising. Of course the government wants to spin abortion in the best possible way. The unelected branch of our government has mandated these abortion rules. So, out of self-interest, the judiciary minimizes the atrocities that have occurred under *Roe v. Wade*.

What is surprising is how complicit our media has been in this regard. Abortion journalism is awful in our country.[545] Many of our so-called "mainstream" journalists don't bother to cover the reality of abortion at all. They cover the fight over abortion--they cover the politics--but they have no information about abortion to give to the reader. They don't know anything, apparently, and have no interest in finding out anything.[546]

---

[545] In 1981, Robert Lichter and Stanley Rothman did a survey of 240 journalists at the most influential national media outlets--including *The New York Times*, *The Washington Post*, *The Wall Street Journal*, *Time*, *Newsweek*, *U.S. News & World Report*, *ABC*, *CBS*, *NBC*, and *PBS*. 90% of journalists agreed that a woman has the right to decide for herself whether to have an abortion. 79% agreed strongly with this pro-choice position. In 1995, Stanley Rothman and Amy Black did a follow-up survey. The potential for bias had actually gotten worse. Now 97% of journalists agreed that a woman has a right to decide for herself whether to have an abortion. And 84% agreed strongly with this position. *See* "The Media Elite," and "The Media Elite Revisited," www.mrc.org.

[546] It's rather surprising how many journalists do not understand the rules of *Roe v. Wade*. For instance, many articles claim the opinion only protects first trimester abortions. *See* Ramesh Ponnuru, *The Party of Death* (2006).

The typical abortion article involves blatant ideological bias.[547] Our media never uses the word "baby," for instance, and always uses the word "fetus."[548] Our reporters never use the word "pro-life," and always use the term "anti-abortion."[549] And our

---

[547] Some of the worst examples of ideology run rampant are in regard to the history of abortion. For instance, an abortion advocate, Cyril Means, Jr., invented an entirely false history of abortion rights in order to help the Supreme Court write *Roe v. Wade*. *See* Justin Dyer, "Fictional Abortion History," *National Review* (December 24, 2012). Credulous Supreme Court Justices believe this false history because they want to believe it. And forty years later, pro-choice journalists are repeating this false history, without any clue how silly it is. For instance, Ranana Dine writes, "the Puritans…kept abortion as a part of Puritan family life." *See* Ranana Dine, "Scarlet Letters: Getting the History of Abortion and Contraception Right," *Center for American Progress* (August 8, 2013). And Katha Pollitt insists abortion was a legal right for centuries. *See* Katha Pollitt, "Abortion in American History," *The Atlantic* (May 1, 1997). While Ms. Pollitt says that aborting a 16-week fetus was legal (and safe!) in the 16th century, she might think about concepts like "anesthesia" or "penicillin" or "flexible curette." *See* note 192.

[548] *See* David Shaw, "Abortion Bias Seeps Into News," *The Los Angeles Times* (July 1, 1990). According to Shaw, "some reporters participated in a big abortion rights march in Washington last year." The article quotes Ethan Bronner, a reporter for the *Boston Globe*. "I think when abortion opponents complain about a bias in newsrooms against their cause, they're absolutely right." Bronner had an editor at the *Boston Globe* who demanded that he rewrite his description of an abortion procedure. He quotes his editor: "As far as I'm concerned, until that thing is born, it is really no different from a kidney; it is part of the woman's body." To hear an unborn baby referred to as "that thing" is quite jarring. And what's remarkable is the comment that "it is really no different from a kidney." A charitable observer would say this is an unscientific way to describe an unborn child. And note the editor is repeating what Professor Tribe said in his book. *Supra* note 426, at 102. (Tribe says the unborn infant is "a part of the woman's body" and analogizes the child to "an arm or a kidney").

[549] "In a November-December 1989 memo sent out electronically to its news service subscribers, *The New York Times* informed inquiring editors that the *Times*' policy is to describe abortion opponents not as prolife but as antiabortion." James Kelly, "Seeking a Sociologically Correct Name For Abortion Opponents," *Abortion Politics in the United States and Canada* (1994). Of course the entire basis of the pro-life movement is that an unborn baby has a right to life. By renaming the pro-life movement "anti-abortion," *The New York Times* is describing this movement as opposed to a surgery. And that is how pro-choice people view abortion, as a surgery and nothing more. When *The New York Times* says the pro-life movement is opposed to a surgery, and simultaneously negates any reference to the unborn child, it is announcing its bias to the world.

journalists never, ever, run a photograph of an aborted infant. We hide these images, as if abortion is an atrocity. We censor abortion photographs in the same way we often censor images of homicide or suicide.[550] And yet simultaneously our authorities say that no atrocities are happening.

An unbiased media would ask questions about this. If abortion is not a homicide, our media should show photographs of abortions. On the anniversary of *Roe v. Wade*, our media should show us what an abortion is. We should see abortions at 6 weeks, at 10 weeks, at 14 weeks, at 18 weeks, at 22 weeks. Our people should be educated in regard to what abortion looks like, and what it looks like in the different stages of pregnancy.[551] And yet we are kept in the dark.[552]

What justifies this censorship?

We are told that the most appalling images, representing abortions from the second or third trimester, are a "small percentage" of abortions. The Supreme Court puts that percentage at 10 to 15%; the Guttmacher Institute reports a 11% number.[553] And yet the absolute numbers are quite high.[554] Over the 40 years of *Roe v.*

---

[550] *See* Torie Rose DeGhett, "The War Photo No One Would Publish," *The Atlantic* (August 8, 2014).
[551] It is likely this will upset people. And yet our medical authorities assure us that there is no such thing as post-abortion stress syndrome. *See* note 86. If indeed the unborn is a non-person, and this is non-violence, there should be no problems.
[552] Pro-lifers are divided in regard to photographs of aborted infants. Many pro-lifers hate these images. Other pro-lifers feel that truth is more important than sensitivity. Pro-choice people, on the other hand, are united. They believe that abortion photographs should be ruthlessly censored, and no mention should be made of them. Since our authorities deny that abortion is an atrocity, this attitude is suspicious (particularly among journalists!) Why are you censoring a photograph of a non-atrocity? *Id.*
[553] *Supra* notes 208 and 328.
[554] Using percentages to minimize atrocities is an awful journalist practice. For instance, Julie Rovner of NPR did a story on partial-birth abortion. *Supra* note 258. She cites Guttmacher, and uses their "0.2 percent" statistic. It is

Wade, the abortion clinics report that over 6 million babies have been aborted in the second or third trimester.[555]

So why are we suppressing photographs of these abortions? Not because these abortions are rare, but because they are so appalling and upsetting. We hide the truth because the ideology of choice cannot withstand the reality of what abortion actually is.

There are a handful of journalists who have done fine work in this area. Liz Jeffries and Rick Edmonds ran an article in the *Philadelphia Inquirer* that was so ground-breaking, it was entered into the Congressional Record. The story was in regard to the "dreaded complication" of aborted babies who are born alive.[556]

Perhaps the most famous abortion journalist is Nat Hentoff, a writer for the *Village Voice* and the *Washington Post*. Hentoff is obviously an independent thinker. For instance, he published this article in the *Washington Post* in 1993: "Ana Rosa Rodriguez was born in 1991 without a right arm. Actually, she was not supposed to have been born. Her mother, 19-year-old Rosa

likely this was an undercount in 2000. (Guttmacher is a biased source). And it's certainly an undercount at the time of her story (February 21, 2006). After all, in *Stenberg v. Carhart*, the Supreme Court has announced that partial-birth abortion is the safest of all late-term abortion procedures. Once our authorities say that, it stands to reason the entire abortion industry is going to shift to partial-birth abortion. It might be medical malpractice not to shift! *See* notes 247-248 and text. And partial-birth abortion is not limited to viable babies. As Rovner notes, it was more common for abortion doctors to use the procedure before the 22nd week than after. By 2006 it's entirely possible partial-birth abortion accounted for 1% or 2% or 3% or even 4% of all abortions that year. And since there were 1.2 million abortions in 2006, the number of babies who were killed outside the birth canal in 2006 might have been 12,000, or 24,000, or 36,000, or 48,000. In any event, saying "thousands" or "tens of thousands" would be better journalism than "0.2 percent."

[555] More specifically, the abortion clinics (and Guttmacher) hide this number, preferring to give us a percentage, thus giving us the illusion that these abortions are rare. *Id*.

[556] Liz Jeffries and Rick Edmonds, "Abortion: The Dreaded Complication," *The Philadelphia Inquirer* (August 2, 1981).

Rodriguez, a Dominican immigrant, 7 ½ months pregnant, had gone to Dr. Abu Hayat on New York's Lower East Side for an abortion. It was botched; Ana Rosa was born the day after. But in the course of the doctor's attempts to dismember her the day before, Ana Rosa's right arm had been torn off."[557]

You can see how this journalism might upset people who are pro-choice. Abortion rights involve a lot of denial and repression. We are denying the baby's humanity as a matter of law. Any article or story that reveals the baby's humanity or gets the reader thinking about the baby's humanity is a danger to *Roe v. Wade*. This is why, for instance, we never see a photograph of an aborted baby in our mainstream media.

Hentoff is perhaps the first reporter to really attack this ideology. He wrote a number of pro-life articles in the mainstream press. Hentoff is Jewish, an atheist, an ACLU liberal. His honesty cost him a number of friendships, but he did it anyway.

Not surprisingly, Bob Woodward has done some amazing journalism in this area. Obviously he's no pro-lifer, and has never written or thought much about the possibility that abortion might kill a baby. Yet Woodward is responsible for much of our inside information in regard to abortion politics. He got access to the inside of the Supreme Court and exposed all the maneuvers and shenanigans that resulted in *Roe v. Wade*.[558] Woodward also published Justice Blackmun's "arbitrary" memo, and grasped its significance as a violation of judicial ethics.[559]

One of the most interesting journalists writing today is Mollie Hemingway, who has published many articles in *The Federalist* exposing the abortion industry. In particular Hemingway has

---

[557] Nat Hentoff, "Can a Non-Person Be a Victim?" *The Washington Post* (March 27, 1993).
[558] *Supra* note 156.
[559] *Supra* note 189.

made some brilliant criticisms of institutional media, its bias and its censorship.[560]

Other journalists have strayed from the party line. In 1995, Naomi Wolf published an article in the *New Republic*, "Our Bodies, Our Souls," that discussed the emotional trauma of abortion for a number of women, and criticized the pro-choice movement for avoiding the homicidal implications of abortion.[561]

Emily Bazelon, despite her pro-choice bias, has done some interesting journalism in the *New York Times*. She ran a story on post-abortion stress syndrome and interviewed an abortion counselor.[562] It's rather painful reading Bazelon as she struggles with her ideology. She knows that abortion cannot possibly cause depression, so she's denying the trauma while reporting on it. But at least she's reporting on it!

And of course there is independent media. The internet is filled with pro-life voices who are outside the control of the elites who run newsrooms. The tone and outlook of pro-life media is similar to the abolitionist newspapers that used to campaign against slavery in the 19th century.[563] There is no attempt here for

---

[560] *See* Mollie Hemingway, "Virginia's Blood-Spattered Abortion Clinics and Onerous Hallway Widths," *The Federalist* (October 25, 2013); Mollie Hemingway, "Planned Parenthood's Abortion Theater," *The Federalist* (November 18, 2013). Mollie Hemingway, "Shiny, Empty Uteruses," *National Review* (November 3, 2014).

[561] *Supra* note 100. Camille Paglia used to attack Naomi Wolf as "Little Miss Pravda." But Wolf's abortion article is sharp and insightful. It's possible that going through pregnancy and childbirth freed Wolf from her ideological straitjacket.

[562] *Supra* note 86.

[563] *See* abort73.com; liveaction.org; lifedynamics.com; toomanyaborted.com; lifenews.com; lifesitenews.com; meehanreports.com; abortiondocs.org; clinicquotes.com; kermitgosnellcrimes.wikispaces.com; abortionwiki.org; nrlc.org; sba-list.org. And that's just the tip of the iceberg! Naturally many of these groups cross over into advocacy. On the other hand, advocacy groups often know far more about a subject than ordinary journalists.

"balance." Instead they try to get the facts out into the public consciousness, facts the mainstream media seeks to hide.

Life Dynamics does investigative journalism into the practices of abortion clinics.[564] Their journalism is so good that one of their interviews was submitted in an amicus brief to the Supreme Court in *Stenberg v. Carhart*.[565] Among the fantastic stories done by *Life Dynamics* includes one story of a doctor killing newborns, and another story about abortion clinics helping statutory rapists cover up their crimes.[566]

Christina Dunigan is a pro-life journalist who is tirelessly documenting all the women who have died from abortion. Her research skills are first rate. She shares her knowledge in two blogs, *Cemetary of Choice* and *Real Choice*.[567]

One of the strongest collections of pro-life voices is in the *Human Life Review*.[568] Founded by James P. McFadden in 1975, it's an academic resource that publishes a wide variety of ideas in regard to the moral conflicts of our day, including abortion, euthanasia, and cloning.

Monica Migliorino Miller is one of the most important journalists we have. She estimates that half of the abortion photographs we see on-line are her work. She documents with rigor what abortion looks like. Some of her work was showcased in a *New York*

---

[564] Life Dynamics is a pro-life organization formed by Mark Crutcher. He is the author of *Lime 5* (1996), a shocking account of abortion in our society.
[565] *See* findlawimages.com/efile/supreme/briefs/05-380/05-380.mer.ami.usjf.pdf
[566] *See* Brian Rogers, "Houston Doctor Accused of Illegal Abortions," *Houston Chronicle* (May 17, 2013); Steven Ertelt, "Tapes Show Planned Parenthood Abortion Ctrs Hiding Statutory Rape," *Life News* (April 13, 2011).
[567] www.realchoice.blogspot.com; cemetaryofchoice.wikispaces.com.
[568] The journal published an article by Ronald Reagan, while he was President, on the 10th anniversary of *Roe v. Wade*. *See* Ronald Reagan, "Abortion and the Conscience of a Nation," *The Human Life Review* (February 3, 1983).

Times photography blog.[569] She is the author of ***Abandoned: The Untold Story of the Abortion Wars***.

Bernard Nathanson, a former abortionist, produced ***The Silent Scream*** in 1984.[570] It's the most famous pro-life movie. However, one of the most shocking pro-life movies is very likely a short and brutal 6-minute film called ***Hard Truth***, produced by the Center for Bio-Ethical Reform.[571] Its founder, Gregg Cunningham, a former member of the Pennsylvania House of Representatives, introduces the movie.

One of the most interesting journalists in our country isn't a journalist at all. Ann Althouse, a law professor and blogger, runs the blog ***Althouse***. Her eclectic blog is one of the most popular legal blogs on the internet. Althouse is a pro-choice feminist, yet she has an incredible integrity and an open mind. Above all she has a commitment to free speech. Readers of ***Althouse*** knew all about Dr. Kermit Gosnell, two years before his murder trial.[572] Most of America, on the other hand, was kept in the dark.

In general, the internet has been a disaster for ***Roe v. Wade***. We get information faster now, and more voices are heard. There was a kind of monopoly over news coverage for many years. That monopoly has been upset. Anybody who does an internet search

---

[569] *See* Damien Cave, "Behind the Scenes: Picturing Fetal Remains," *The New York Times* (October 9, 2009). *See also* www.imagesofabortion.com.

[570] Dr. Nathanson became a pro-lifer in the 1970's, after he had performed the surgery 5,000 times (and presided over 61,000 abortions). And an amazing thing happened--he changed his mind. He came to believe that abortion was the killing of a baby. Try to imagine the anguish in admitting that you had killed so many innocent people. Try to imagine the strength, the courage, it takes to be that honest. He is the author of ***Aborting America*** (1979) and ***The Hand of God*** (1996).

[571] "Hard Truth (About Abortion)," www.youtube.com. The haunting music cuts off about two-thirds of the way through the movie. The production values are sub-standard and unsophisticated. And yet, if you see this amateur video, you will never forget it. *See also* note 347.

[572] *See* Ann Althouse, "Pennsylvania Is Not a Third World Country," *Althouse* (January 19, 2011). www.althouse.blogspot.com.

on "abortion" will see photographs of aborted babies.[573] All of Nat Hentoff's pro-life articles are on-line.[574] Harry Blackmun's arbitrary memo is on-line.[575] Professor Miller's photographs are on-line. *Hard Truth* is on youtube. It's hard to repress factual information in the age of the internet.

Yet it still happens. The murder trial of Kermit Gosnell is an obvious example. Here is an abortion doctor who was charged with multiple counts of murder for killing newborns. And yet the media wasn't covering the story.

Recall the William Waddill murder trial. It was a media circus in Los Angeles. And yet the overwhelming majority of people in our country have no idea who William Waddill is. That is very likely intentional. The people who run our networks do not like stories about abortion doctors who are charged with murdering newborns.

Almost four decades later, the media tried to do the same thing with Dr. Kermit Gosnell. Whoever makes these media decisions ruled that it's not a national story. This is why, according to Gallup, only 7% of Americans were following the Gosnell case "very closely," and 18% were following the case "somewhat closely." Meanwhile, Gallup reports that 54% of the people in our country have no idea who Kermit Gosnell is.[576]

---

[573] The most famous abortion photograph is a baby pro-lifers refer to as Malachi. *See* www.priestsforlife.org. Another famous photograph is an unborn infant who reaches out of the womb and grabs the finger of a surgeon. *See* michaelclancy.com. (The medical show *House* did an episode loosely based on this event).

[574] *See* groups.csail.mit.edu/mac/users/rauch/nvp/hentoff.html

[575] www.justfacts.com/abortion.blackmun.asp

[576] "This makes the Gosnell case one of the least followed news stories Gallup has measured." *See* Lydia Saad, "Americans' Abortion Views Steady Amid Gosnell Trial," www.gallup.com (May 7, 2013).

You might think a murder trial involving an abortion doctor charged with multiple counts of murder would be a national story. It implicates abortion rights, and the Supreme Court, and *Stenberg v. Carhart*. It's not just a murder trial. Implicitly there is a political scandal here, too. And yet, if there's no media coverage, the media might be implicated in what amounts to an ideological attempt to hide the news.

Why is the media so uninterested in an abortion doctor who is charged with murdering newborns in Philadelplhia?

Here is Conor Friedersdorf, talking about the media blackout in *The Atlantic*. "Until Thursday, I wasn't aware of this story. It has generated sparse coverage in the national media, and while it's been mentioned in RSS feeds to which I subscribe, I skip past most news items. I still consume a tremendous amount of journalism. Yet had I been asked at a trivia night about the identity of Kermit Gosnell, I would've been stumped and helplessly guessed a green Muppet. Then I saw Kirsten Power's *USA Today* column. She makes a powerful, persuasive case that the Gosnell trial ought to be getting a lot more attention in the national press than it is getting."[577]

Here is a huge story, an abortion doctor who is a serial killer. And yet the media is refusing to cover the story. So that became the story. The murder trial itself was overshadowed by the media's inability to talk about the murder trial. Why wasn't the national media covering the Gosnell case?

Kirsten Powers, a Democrat who served in the Clinton administration, was so embarrassed about this attempt to hide the

---

[577] Conor Friedersdorf, "Why Dr. Kermit Gosnell's Trial Should Be a Front Page Story," *The Atlantic* (April 12, 2013). Friedersdorf's article included the first publication of abortion photographs in a mainstream publication.

news, she wrote a column about the cover-up by our media in *USA Today*.[578]

Once the media itself became part of the story, they had to cover it. Friedersdorf--obviously not a reader of *Althouse*--had no idea that an abortion doctor was being prosecuted for murder for killing babies in his abortion clinic. But since Friedersdorf is an actual journalist who is interested in doing actual journalism, he jumped on the story once he heard about it.

Most reporters had to be dragged, kicking and screaming, to cover a murder trial of an abortion doctor.

The officials who were prosecuting Dr. Gosnell had roped off several rows in the courtroom for the media. They were expecting a media circus. It should have been a "trial of the century." After all, abortion is the most hotly contested political issue in our country, rivaling the fight over slavery from a century before. And here an abortion doctor is being prosecuted for multiple counts of murder for killing newborns. The story practically writes itself. You just had to show up and report.

Nobody showed up. The seats remained empty for most of the trial.[579]

Here is Megan McArdle, writing in *The Daily Beast*. "The evangelicals in my twitter and Facebook feed are asking, justifiably, why these crimes seem to be nowhere in the media. You'd think that a lurid crime touching an issue of major national importance would be covered everywhere. And yet, there's been very little."[580]

---

[578] Kirsten Powers, "Abortion Clinic Horror," *USA Today* (April 11, 2013).
[579] *See* Ed Morrissey, "Photo of the Day: Media Row at the Gosnell Trial," *Hot Air* (April 12, 2013).
[580] Megan McArdle, "Why I Didn't Write About Gosnell's Trial--And Why I Should Have," *The Daily Beast* (April 12, 2013).

McArdle continues: "I'll tell you why I haven't covered it. To start, it makes me ill. I haven't been able to bring myself to read the grand jury inquiry. I am someone who cringes when I hear a description of a sprained ankle. But I understand why my readers suspect me, and other pro-choice mainstream journalists, of being selective--of not wanting to cover the story because it showcased the ugliest possibilities of abortion rights. The truth is that most of us tend to be less interested in sick-making stories--if the sick-making was done by 'our side.' Of course, I'm not saying that I identify with criminal abortionists who kill infants and grievously wound their patients. But I am pro-choice."[581]

Here is Althouse, writing on McArdle's self-censorship: "I think it's a confession that she just didn't want to have to think about it. It was squeamishness and a political commitment to abortion rights that she didn't want rumpled."[582]

This is interesting because McArdle's squeamishness seems to be anti-feminist. Imagine if McArdle was a beat reporter. You couldn't assign her to cover a murder or a rape or any violent crime at all. Your first instinct might be to assign her to a fashion show. She's a woman, maybe she likes clothes.[583] She doesn't like violence. She's squeamish. A sprained ankle upsets her.

Of course, McArdle is just being honest about her fears. And she is afraid. How do we know she's afraid? She does not want to read the grand jury report. She's afraid to read it. She's afraid of what's in it. She's afraid of the brutal truth.

---

[581] *Id*.
[582] Ann Althouse, "But I understand why my readers suspect me, and other pro-choice mainstream journalists, of being selective…" *Althouse* (April 13, 2013).
[583] McArdle is an economist who has a very sharp analytical mind.

Why is somebody like McArdle afraid to read about violence? Perhaps it's because she is afraid of death. It is one of our primal fears, after all. Violence reminds us of death and how we are all going to die. But it's hardly feminist for McArdle to admit to her fears and vulnerabilities. Try to imagine Bob Woodward saying he's not covering a murder story with national implications because blood makes his stomach go all wobbly.

Maybe one of the reasons we are censoring abortion photographs in the media is chivalry. We want to protect women and children from these ugly scenes of violence. Consider, for instance, *St. John's Church v. Scott*.[584] This was a case where pro-lifers were showing photographs of aborted babies outside a church service.

There were about 200 children at the church service, and many of them started to cry.

Why are they crying? They are crying because a photograph of an abortion looks like a baby who has been murdered. And this upsets children. It's a reminder of the vulnerability of children. Yes, you could die, too.

Nor can we explain to our children why these angry people are showing photographs of dead babies. We would have to explain abortion politics, and the woman's right to choose. But now you've just told your child that these babies were actually killed by their parents. This is not actually going to comfort your child. Now they are going to feel even more distress. Infanticide is bad enough, but mom paid for it?

You could try to use the Latin word to get your child to stop crying. "It's not a baby, it's a fetus." But children are

---

[584] *See* Adam Liptak, "In Abortion Protests, Which To Protect, Children or Speech?" *The New York Times* (May 13, 2013); Adam Liptak, "Justices Decline Case on Graphic Abortion Images," *The New York Times* (June 10, 2013).

emotionally honest and they have already seen the photographs. It's not likely the Supreme Court's Latin trick is going to work on them.

Or we could just censor the photographs and make it a crime for citizens to speak.

Our judge out in Colorado decided this was the only way to resolve the case. So he issued an order in the case forbidding the pro-lifers from "displaying large posters or similar displays depicting gruesome images of mutilated fetuses or dead bodies in a manner reasonably likely to be viewed by children under 12."[585]

It's entirely natural to want to protect your child from the brutality of the world. It's a form of patriarchy. Indeed, we might see *St. John's Church* as a fight between two forms of patriarchy. The pro-lifers want to protect children. That's why they are exposing the infanticides. They want the law to recognize the child's humanity and to protect her right to life.

Look at it! Look at what we are doing!

The parents in the church (some of whom might be pro-lifers too) are understandably distressed at what this protest is doing to their own children. They want to protect their children's innocence. And the judge's order is an attempt to protect the innocence of children. We want to hide sex and violence from our children. We want to protect you from the brutality of the world.

Of course this argument only works in regard to children. But Megan McArdle is not a child. She's an adult. Should we be hiding the reality of abortion from adult women? Or is this censorship a form of patriarchy, a protective instinct that reduces women to children?

---

[585] *St. John's Church v. Scott*, 296 P.3d 273 (Colo. App. 2012).

Are we hiding aborted babies from women because women are sensitive people and they might cry?

Another possibility is that we are censoring this reality to protect our romantic illusions about women. We don't like to think of women committing atrocities. Decapitation and dismemberment, that's something men do. That's why we want to keep women out of the war zones, for crying out loud.[586]

Of course, pro-choice people deny that abortion is an atrocity. But you can't simultaneously deny that abortion is an atrocity while you censor the images of abortion because they are atrocities. And if it's not an atrocity, why are we censoring the images?

It's kind of weird to say, "I'm pro-choice," while at the same time you say that abortion is so awful you can't look at one. In other words, you can only support abortion rights as long as you keep yourself in a state of ignorance about what an abortion is?

Ann Althouse makes the argument that we are not censoring abortion to protect our innocence. We are censoring abortion to protect our guilt.

Althouse is pro-choice, but she's fearless and intellectually rigorous on the subject. And she wants to know why our media is not covering the Gosnell case. "Why not shine a bright light on Kermit Gosnell and yell *monster*? Make it clear to everyone that you think he is so different from properly professional abortionists. If you don't, you reveal that you have a nagging

---

[586] *See* Emily Greenhouse, "Women in War Zones," *The New Yorker* (July 30, 2014).

suspicion that he is not. And that's the one thing you don't want anyone to see."[587]

She's charging that our national media is avoiding the Gosnell murder trial because of abortion politics. That is to say, the very reason this murder trial is a national story--infanticide in an abortion clinic--is the same reason why the national media is not covering it. The media has gotten into the habit of hiding abortion from our people, and so the media cannot cover the trial of an abortion doctor who is charged with killing newborns.

More Althouse: "Why did they not jump at the opportunity to display so vividly that health care services to the poor (or to women) are not what they should be and no one cares? They didn't want to risk that. There's a deep fear--true shame--about this other matter that I'm talking about."[588]

It's a dead baby in an abortion clinic. That fact overshadows everything. Pro-choice people simply do not want to associate "dead baby" with "abortion clinic." They had to distance themselves from this crime, and to do that they had to ignore it.

The *New York Times* coverage was particularly bad.[589] The reporter who was assigned to the trial, Jon Hurdle, spent five minutes in the courtroom and then walked out again. We know this because one of the local beat reporters in Philadelphia made fun of the *New York Times* guy for his lack of interest.[590] And this lack of interest showed up in the *New York Times*.

---

[587] *Supra* note 582.
[588] *Id*.
[589] This is a shock because the *New York Times*, while recognizably liberal, has always done fact-based journalism.
[590] J.D. Mullane, "What I Saw At the Gosnell Trial," *PhillyBurbs.com* (April 13, 2013). "An hour into afternoon testimony, Jon Hurdle of the *New York Times* showed up, and a few minutes later was gone." Mullane took the photograph of the empty press section that would go viral on the internet. *See* note 579.

The first paragraph in Hurdle's article read, "In opening statements in court on Monday, prosecutors charged that a doctor who operated a woman's health clinic here killed seven viable fetuses by plunging scissors into their necks and 'snipping' their spinal cords and was also responsible for the death of a pregnant woman in his care."[591]

Dr. Gosnell was being prosecuted for multiple counts of murder. He was charged with killing newborns. The born/unborn distinction is, of course, vital as a matter of criminal law. Unborn babies are dehumanized in our society, and can be aborted. Born infants are citizens, and it's murder to kill them. Yet the *New York Times* was apparently unable to grasp this distinction. Hurdle was so used to covering abortion like a *Pravda* reporter, he kept using the word "fetus" to describe newborns.[592]

One possibility is the *New York Times* was simply being a liberal newspaper, and was automatically taking the side of the defendant. Adopting the prosecution's "baby" language might have prejudiced the case against Dr. Gosnell. However, this explanation was blown out of the water after the verdict was announced. Even after the jury convicted Dr. Gosnell on three counts of murder for killing newborns, the *New York Times* reporter was still saying "fetus" in his article describing the convictions.

---

[591] Jon Hurdle, "Abortion Doctor's Murder Trial Opens," *The New York Times* (March 18, 2013). The other reporter assigned by the *Times*, Trip Gabriel, managed to make the same mistake. "Dr. Kermit Gosnell is charged with killing seven viable fetuses…" *See* Trip Gabriel, "Online Furor Draws Press to Abortion Doctor's Trial," *The New York Times* (April 15, 2013).
[592] It is highly likely that *The New York Times* had an editorial policy insisting that the word "fetus" is always used in any abortion story. After all they have an editorial policy in regard to the word "pro-life." *See* note 549. And when the newspaper reported on the murder conviction of Dr. Raymond Showery in 1984, they also used the word "fetus" (in regard to a baby the doctor had drowned in a bucket). *See* note 252.

As the *Times* put it, the "verdict came after a five-week trial in which the prosecution and the defense battled over whether the fetuses Dr. Gosnell was charged with killing were alive when they were removed from their mothers."[593] It was like watching HAL trying to reboot.

The *New York Times* was roundly mocked for its biased coverage of the Gosnell murders. "Fetus, fetus, fetus, fetus," said the *National Review*.[594] The *Media Research Center* ran a story about the inability of the *New York Times* reporter to use the "baby" word.[595] This unofficial dehumanization by our media is so bad, and so notable, that other journalists started talking about it.

This doctor has been convicted of murder for killing babies and the *New York Times* is still denying the humanity of the victims. It's so ideological. It's like a Marxist who can't comprehend that the wall is actually coming down. And, just like a Marxist, when the chorus of people mocking the *Times* reached a crescendo, they removed the original story from their website and made it disappear.[596]

Another reporter, Trip Gabriel, was assigned to rewrite Hurdle's copy. So now we have a new story, radically different from the previous version. The new story reported it like this: "A doctor

[593] *See* John Jalsevac, "New York Times Reports Gosnell Murdered 'Fetuses,' Not Babies," *Life Site News* (May 13, 2013); Vince Coglianese, "NYT Calles Murdered Babies 'Fetuses' in Article About Gosnell Conviction," *The Daily Caller* (May 13, 2013).
[594] Kathryn Jean Lopez, "Fetus, Fetus, Fetus, Fetus, Fetus, Fetus," *National Review* (May 13, 2013).
[595] Matthew Balan, "New York Times Breaks Gosnell Guilty Verdicts By Labeling Victims 'Fetuses' Six Times," *Media Research Center* (May 13, 2013).
[596] *See* "Media Outlets Still Calling Murdered Babies 'Fetuses,'" *The Washington Free Beacon* (May 13, 2013).

who was responsible for cutting the spines of babies after botched abortions was convicted Monday of three counts of first-degree murder in a case that became a sharp rallying cry for anti-abortion activists."[597]

What happened to the original story? It's vanished. Don't bother using Google, you won't find it. While the *New York Times* does not pretend that they never wrote the story, they certainly did make it disappear.[598]

Why was the *Times* coverage so bad? For the same reason the newspaper did not want to report on the trial in the first place. The pro-lifers were right. Babies had died. And the "newspaper of record" had no interest in reporting on this.

More importantly, Hurdle had no idea how to report on it. Like many reporters he's approaching an abortion story with a pre-formed ideology in his mind. He knows what the story needs to be ("pro-lifers are wrong"), and he's quite willing to ignore any facts that conflict with this narrative.[599]

---

[597] Jon Hurdle and Trip Gabriel, "Philadelphia Abortion Doctor Guilty of Murder in Late-Term Procedures," *The New York Times* (May 13, 2013).

[598] *See also* James Taranto, "All the News That's Fit To Scrub," *The Wall Street Journal* (June 3, 2011). And this is not the only instance of ideology undermining the search for truth at the paper. In 1995 *The New York Times* ran a very sympathetic article about Dr. Brian Finkel, an abortionist who had been sued multiple times by his patients. The *Times* suggested these lawsuits were frivolous and unethical. *Supra* note 62. A few years later, a journalist for the *Phoenix New Times* reported that Dr. Finkel referred to his abortion clinic as a "Vaginal Vault." *See* Amy Silverman, "The Terminator," *Phoenix New Times* (June 17, 1999). A few years after that, Dr. Finkel was convicted of 22 counts of sexually molesting 13 women while they were under anesthesia. *See* Thomas Fields-Meyer, "The Doctor's Secret," *People* (January 26, 2004). And it's not just that *The New York Times* screwed up the original story. They had no follow-up report, no retraction, no apologies to the attorneys (or the women) the newspaper had implicitly maligned.

[599] A couple of days after this wrangling over language in *The New York Times*, Hurdle would write perhaps the best article about the murders in the newspaper. *See* Jon Hurdle, "Doctor Starts His Life Term in Grisly Abortion Clinic Case," *The New York Times* (May 15, 2013).

The *Times* is worthy of our attention because it's a very smart newspaper, and the people who write for it are very smart. But very smart people can also be opinionated, and sometimes our opinions can be so strong that we are actually incapable of doing journalism. Reporters need to be open-minded and inquisitive, not lazy and prejudiced.[600]

The *New York Times* has gotten into trouble for this sort of behavior before. In the 1930's they helped cover up all of Stalin's atrocities.[601] The *Times* reporter, Walter Duranty, won the Pulitzer Prize for his Pravda-like material.[602] 70 years later, the *New York Times* finally got around to trying to set the record straight.

As the *Times* reported: "A Columbia University history professor hired by the *New York Times* to make an independent assessment of the coverage of one of its correspondents in the Soviet Union during the 1930's said yesterday that the Pulitzer Prize the reporter received should be rescinded because of his lack of balance in covering Stalin's government."[603]

---

[600] Perhaps realizing its coverage of the Kermit Gosnell trial was shoddy, the *Times* has made efforts to improve its abortion journalism. *See* Erik Eckholm, "Undercover Video Targets Abortion Doctor," *The New York Times* (May 8, 2013); Erik Eckholm, "Maryland's Path to an Accord in Abortion Fight," *The New York Times* (July 16, 2013); Ruth Padawer, "The Two-Minus-One Pregnancy," *The New York Times* (August 10, 2014).

[601] *See* S.J. Taylor, *Stalin's Apologist* (1990).

[602] *Id.* The newspaper acknowledges that Taylor's book is quite good. *See* Francine Du Plessix Gray, "The Journalist and the Dictator," *The New York Times* (June 24, 1990). Indeed, the *Times* characterizes its journalism from the Soviet Union as "some of the worst reporting to appear in this newspaper." *See* "The Editorial Notebook," *The New York Times* (June 24, 1990).

[603] *See* Jacques Steinberg, "Times Should Lose Pulitzer From 30's, Consultant Says," *The New York Times* (October 23, 2003).

Not surprisingly, people who actually knew the truth--but were not believed--remain quite angry with the *New York Times*, and how it covered up these murders.

"The most vocal demands came from Ukrainian-Americans who contended that Mr. Duranty should be punished for failing to report on a famine that killed millions of Ukrainians in 1932 and 1933."[604] Specifically, the Soviet army took all the food stock out of the Ukraine, closed the border, and waited for the people to starve to death.[605] It's mind-boggling that the *New York Times* managed to miss that story. And yet they did.

A British reporter, Gareth Jones, actually reported on the mass killings at the time, what he called a Holodomor, or "murder by famine" in the Ukraine.[606] But Stalin's man at the *Times*, Walter Duranty, denied the reports, and much of the world was fooled.[607] The Pulitzer Prize was given to a false and dishonest account about the wonders of Communism, while all the atrocities under Stalin were ignored.

In his report to the *Times*, Professor von Hagen concluded that Duranty's reporting was a "dull and largely uncritical recitation of Soviet sources."[608] We see this same sort of error committed over and over in regard to abortion. The ideology of the reporter blinds them in their mission to find out and report on truth.

For instance, consider the shoddy reporting of the modern day atrocities in China. There is the case of a woman named Feng Jianmei. In June, 2012, in a small village in China, police raided this woman's home and arrested her. They didn't just arrest her,

---

[604] *Id*.
[605] www.holodomorct.org
[606] *See* Ray Gamache, *Gareth Jones: Eyewitness to the Holodomor* (2013).
[607] *See* Walter Duranty, "Russians Hungry But Not Starving," *The New York Times* (March 31, 1933).
[608] *Supra* note 603.

they put a pillowcase over her head and shoved her into a police van.[609]

What was her crime? She was seven months pregnant.

China has a notorious "one child" policy. If you have more than one child, you are subject to a criminal fine. Since she was pregnant with a second child, Jianmei and her husband owed the state $6,350. They didn't have the money to pay the authorities. So she was kidnapped instead.

In a police hospital, she was blindfolded, thrown on a bed, and forced to sign a "consent form" that she was not allowed to read. And then she was forcibly aborted with an abortion drug.

This particular abortion became rather infamous because family members took photographs. In one photo, Jianmei is in a hospital bed, in shock, traumatized. Lying next to her is the body of her small child, murdered by the state.[610]

The photographs were uploaded on the internet, and went viral.

Readers of *Althouse* knew about this case very quickly.[611] Althouse is not a journalist. She's a law professor with a Yahoo feed. But she's doing the job of ten reporters, covering the stories that our media should see as a matter of course.

---

[609] "Officials Forcibly Abort the Baby of Feng Jianmei, Who Was 7 Months Pregnant," *All Girls Allowed* (June 12, 2012).

[610] Of course institutional media will not run the photograph. Pro-life media will. *See* Steven Ertelt, "Chinese Woman Seven Months Pregnant Beaten, Forcibly Aborted," *Life News* (June 12, 2012).

[611] Ann Althouse, "Feng Was Not Forced To Abort…A Lot of Us Tried To Educate Her. She Agreed To the Abortion Herself," *Althouse* (June 15, 2012). *See also* Evan Osnos, "Abortion and Politics in China," *The New Yorker* (June 15, 2012). *ABC* and *CBS* also ran stories about Feng Jianmei.

Now contrast *Time Magazine*. This is how our national media reports on forced abortions in a police state. This article was two years before the incident with Feng Jianmei, but indicates just how biased our media was. Laura Fitzpatrick is writing an article dated July 27, 2009, called "A Brief History of China's One Child Policy."[612]

"Is the world's most populous nation about to get more crowded? Reports surfaced in international media last week that in an effort to slow the rapid graying of the workforce, couples in Shanghai-- the country's most populous city--would be encouraged to have two kids if the parents are themselves only children. Shanghai officials have since denied any policy shift, saying this caveat is nothing new, but the contradictory reports are another manifestation of ongoing rumors that Beijing is rethinking the controversial one-child policy that has for the past three decades helped spur economic growth--but extracted a heavy social cost along the way."[613]

Apparently, according to *Time Magazine*, dragging pregnant women out of their houses and forcibly aborting them inspires economic growth.

Of course *Pravda* comparisons are unfair. Our government is not mandating this stupid article. But you don't have to mandate it if people in the media have such authoritarian thoughts on their own, or if they are simply regurgitating what Communist officials are telling them.

"The one-child policy relies on a mix of sticks and carrots. Depending on where they live, couples can be fined thousands of dollars for having a supernumerary child without a permit, and

---

[612] Laura Fitzpatrick, "A Brief History of China's One-Child Policy," *Time* (July 27, 2009).
[613] *Id*.

reports of forced abortions or sterilization are common. Blind rural activist Chen Guangcheng made international headlines in 2005 for exposing just such a campaign by family-planning officials in Eastern China…"[614]

What's worse, reducing a pregnant woman to an animal who is motivated by "sticks and carrots," or referring to police who kidnap pregnant women and kill their babies as "family-planning officials"? *Time Magazine* goes on to inform us about the "carrot" in China's one child policy. "Those who volunteer to have only one child are awarded a 'Certificate of Honor for Single-Child Parents.'"[615]

The article concludes with a positive endorsement of population control in authoritarian states. "Since 1979, the law has prevented some 250 million births, saving China from a population explosion the nation would have difficulty accommodating."[616]

Here is a more honest account of what a forced abortion policy is like in *The New York Times*. It's in the form of an Op-Ed written by Ma Jian, a writer who lives in China.[617] Ma is describing an attack on a woman who was eight months pregnant. It's similar to the Feng Jianmei case. This woman was kidnapped by police officers and taken to a secret hospital. There an abortion drug was injected into her abdomen to force a miscarriage. She was actually tied to an operating table during her ordeal.

"For two days she writhed on the table, her hands and feet still bound with rope, waiting for her body to eject the murdered baby. In the final state of labor, a male doctor yanked the dead fetus out by the foot, then dropped it into a garbage can. She had no

---

[614] *Id.*

[615] *Id.*

[616] *Id.*

[617] *Supra* note 84.

money for a cab. She had to hobble home, blood dripping down her legs and staining her white sandals red."[618]

Two years after suggesting that the one-child policy was "saving China," **Time Magazine** ran an article that criticized the forced abortion of Feng Jianmei.[619] "Just how much is a dead baby worth?" asked the article. "This week, a settlement from China's Shaanxi province put that figure at $11,200." China was paying the money (and firing some officials) in order to try to make all the bad publicity disappear. It seems even the American press was finally noticing.[620]

---

[618] *Id*.

[619] Hannah Beech, "Forced-Abortion Victim Promised $11,200, But Family Fears For Life," **Time Magazine** (July 13, 2012).

[620] Beech's first sentence is notable because it references the humanity of the unborn child ("baby"), the violence of an abortion ("dead"), and the way we have turned our unborn children into commodities with price tags ("worth").

Chapter 17

It took the Supreme Court 27 years to actually describe the abortion surgery. Finally, in 2000, the Court began talking about abortion in graphic detail in ***Stenberg v. Carhart***.[621] Before this case, the Supreme Court had always used grandiose words when talking about the right to choose. For instance, in ***Planned Parenthood v. Casey***, the Court writes, "At the heart of liberty is the right to define one's own concept of existence, of meaning, of the universe, and of the mystery of human life."[622] The unborn baby's life is a mystery, and it's a mystery the Supreme Court has no interest in solving, or even discussing.

All this non-discussion makes the two ***Carhart*** opinions rather remarkable. For the first time, the Supreme Court is writing about the abortion procedure with factual accuracy. But you can't do that without upsetting people. This makes the two ***Carhart*** opinions perhaps the most shocking cases ever to be published in the U.S. Reports.

What is so frightening about the ***Carhart*** opinions? These two cases involve a new form of abortion practice.[623] Abortion doctors started a technique of inducing birth in pregnant

---

[621] ***Supra*** note 202.

[622] ***Supra*** note 7.

[623] Or is it new? ***Roe v. Wade*** actually references partial-birth abortion. The first footnote in ***Roe*** mentions another Texas statute that is not at issue in the case, the crime defined by Article 1195: "Whoever shall during parturition of the mother destroy the vitality or life in a child in a state of being born and before actual birth, which child would otherwise have been born alive, shall be confined in the penitentiary for life or for not less than five years." ***Roe*** specifies that this statute is not involved in the opinion. And yet in ***Stenberg v. Carhart*** the Supreme Court insists that ***Roe*** gives doctors a right to kill a baby in the middle of birth. ***Supra*** note 202.

women.[624] Once the baby is halfway outside the birth canal, the abortion doctor would stab the child and kill her.

Over a 15-year-period, from 1992 to 2007, tens of thousands of babies were murdered outside the birth canal.[625] And yet none of these murders were recognized as murders, because our unelected officials defined these babies as non-people, and the homicides as non-homicides. And, as usual, our media had no questions about this, and did little or no reporting on it.

Pro-lifers began talking about partial-birth abortions in 1992, when they discovered that Dr. Martin Haskell had developed a new abortion method that involved killing the baby in the middle of birth, and was teaching the procedure to other doctors.

In 1995 partial-birth abortion was banned in Nebraska. Many other states quickly followed suit. Abortion doctors filed lawsuits in federal court, claiming this was a right thing to do. Some federal judges said there is a constitutional right to do a partial-birth abortion. Other federal judges said there is no such thing.

Congress began holding hearings on the procedure. In March of 1996, a registered nurse testified under oath before a House subcommittee.[626] Here is what she said:

---

[624] Some abortion doctors would actually induce labor via the use of drugs. Others would use forceps to pull the baby out of the uterus.

[625] In a survey done in the year of the *Carhart* litigation, an abortion rights group estimated that 2,200 partial-birth abortions were performed in 2000. *See* Lawrence Finer and Stanley Henshaw, "Abortion Incidence and Services in the United States in 2000," www.guttmacher.org. Over 15 years this annual rate would result in 33,000 partial-birth abortions. Note that over 700 abortion facilities did not participate in the survey. Also it is highly likely that many doctors shifted procedures once the Supreme Court said partial-birth abortion was a constitutional right (and safer than the D&E). *See* note 554.

[626] *See* www.priestsforlife.org/testimonies/1132-statement-of-brenda-pratt-shafer-rn-before-the-subcommittee-on-the-constitution.

Mr. Chairman and honorable members of the Judiciary Committee, I am Brenda Pratt Shafer. I am here before you, at the request of the Committee, to relate to you my experience as an eyewitness to what is now known as the partial-birth abortion procedure.

I am a registered nurse, licensed in the State of Ohio, with 14 years of experience. In 1993, I was employed by Kimberly Quality Care, a nursing agency in Dayton, Ohio. In September, 1993, Kimberly Quality Care asked me to accept assignment at the Women's Medical Center, which is operated by Dr. Martin Haskell...

I worked as an assistant nurse at Dr. Haskell's clinic for three days-- September 28, 29, and 30, 1993.

On the first day, we assisted in some first-trimester abortions, which is all I'd expected to be involved in. (I remember that one of the patients was a 15-year-old-girl who was having her third abortion).

On the second day, I saw Dr. Haskell do a second-trimester procedure that is called a D & E (dilation and evacuation). He used ultrasound to examine the fetus. Then he used forceps to pull apart the baby inside the uterus, bringing it out piece by piece and piece, throwing the pieces in a pan.

Also on the first two days, we inserted laminaria to dilate the cervixes of women who were being prepared for the partial-birth abortions--those who were past the 20 weeks point, or 4 1/2 months. (Dr. Haskell called this procedure "D & X", for dilation and extraction.) There were six or seven of these women.

On the third day, Dr. Haskell asked me to observe as he performed several of the procedures that are the subject of this hearing. Although I was in that clinic on assignment of the agency, Dr. Haskell was interested in hiring me full time, and I was being given orientation in the entire range of procedures provided at that facility.

I was present for three of these partial-birth procedures. It is the first one that I will describe to you in detail.

The mother was six months pregnant (26½ weeks). A doctor told her that the baby had Down Syndrome and she decided to have an abortion. She came in the first two days to have the laminaria inserted and changed, and she cried the whole time. On the third day she came in to receive the partial-birth procedure.

Dr. Haskell brought the ultrasound in and hooked it up so that he could see the baby. On the ultrasound screen, I could see the heart beating. As Dr. Haskell watched the baby on the ultrasound screen, the baby's heartbeat was clearly visible on the ultrasound screen.

Dr. Haskell went in with forceps and grabbed the baby's legs and pulled them down into the birth canal. Then he delivered the baby's body and the

arms--everything but the head. The
doctor kept the baby's head just inside
the uterus.

The baby's little fingers were clasping
and unclasping, and his feet were
kicking. Then the doctor stuck the
scissors through the back of his head,
and the baby's arms jerked out in a
flinch, a startle reaction, like a baby
does when he thinks that he might fall.

The doctor opened up the scissors,
stuck a high-powered suction tube into
the opening and sucked the baby's
brains out. Now the baby was
completely limp.

The doctors who are killing the child do not dispute this testimony. They just use different words. To them, a baby in the middle of birth is a "fetus," and a partial-birth abortion is a "D&X." And these are the sorts of words abortion proponents always use to minimize the horror of what they are doing. What's unnerving is how they are still using this rhetoric, even when talking about a baby outside the birth canal. Birth does not seem to be changing their minds, or their rhetoric. It's eye-opening to people.

Why are abortion doctors killing babies outside the birth canal? These doctors had formed the medical judgment that killing a baby inside the uterus is dangerous to the mother. This suggests that the abortion industry (and the Supreme Court) had been quite wrong about the safety of late-term abortions. They had been wrong for decades. Birth is safer than abortion at this stage of the pregnancy.

Clearly birth is safer for the mother than the D&E surgery. *Carhart* would confuse this issue by dishonestly suggesting that the baby had to be killed. Even the American College of Obstetrics and Gynecologists (the ACOG) did not say that.

At least, they did not say that until Elena Kagan, who is not a doctor, rewrote their medical findings for them.[627]

At the time, Kagan was serving as counsel for the White House. Bill Clinton was President. According to the *Washington Post*, in 1996 Dr. George Tiller paid $25,000 in order to have coffee with the President.[628] Dr. Tiller was a notorious abortion doctor from Kansas who specialized in partial-birth abortion, and had a website where he advertised his services.[629]

Kathleen Sebellius, who would become Secretary of Health and Human Services in the Obama administration, also had ties to Dr. Tiller. When she was governor of Kansas, she hosted a party for Dr. Tiller and his abortion staff at the governor's mansion in 2007.[630]

How did Dr. Tiller get himself invited to the governor's mansion, and to the White House? He bought that access.[631]

This is important because the ACOG report on this abortion surgery was rewritten by the Clinton administration. The original ACOG report said that their panel "could identify no circumstances under which the (partial-birth) procedure…would

[627] *See* William Saletan, "When Kagan Played Doctor," *Slate* (July 3, 2010).
[628] Lorraine Adams, "Abortion Doctor Thanked Clinton at Coffee," *The Washington Post* (April 1, 1997).
[629] *See* www.drtiller.com. After Dr. Tiller's murder, his website was turned into a solicitation for donations to help fund abortions and other health services for the poor.
[630] *See* Jill Stanek, "Sebelius Hosts Tiller and Staff at Guv's Mansion," www.jillstanek.com (May 29, 2008).
[631] *See* Robert Novak, "A Pro-Choicer's Dream Veep," *The Washington Post* (May 26, 2008); *See also* note 628.

be the only option to save the life or preserve the health of the woman."[632]

The abortion doctors were having a problem: the obstetricians in the ACOG were not on board. They denied that you had to kill the baby. A C-section is always a possibility, and is always as safe as any killing procedure.

This is why Dr. Tiller bought his access, and perhaps why Elena Kagan ultimately rewrote the ACOG report. She herself drafted a new conclusion for the ACOG. According to the new statement, written by Kagan, partial-birth abortion "may be the best or most appropriate procedure in a particular circumstance to save the life or preserve the health of a woman."[633]

And the ACOG signed off on it.

This would be embarrassing for many federal judges, including the five Supreme Court Justices who participated in Justice Breyer's opinion in **Carhart**. Justice Breyer would authoritatively cite Kagan's sentence in his opinion, word for word.[634] He thought he was citing an independent medical authority, the American College of Obstetrics and Gynecology. He had no idea that the ACOG had been told what to say by the Clinton White House, who in turn had heard some suggestions from Dr. Tiller about the necessity of killing babies outside the birth canal.

Of course this is really embarrassing for the ACOG. These medical authorities have been telling us since **Roe v. Wade** that abortion is safer than birth. And then, when abortion doctors start inducing birth because it is safer for the mother than abortion,

---

[632] *Supra* note 627.
[633] *Id*.
[634] *Supra* note 202.

what do they say? They don't know what to say. The Clinton White House has to write their medical opinions for them.

The non-doctor Elena Kagan would join the Supreme Court in 2010.

Dr. Tiller himself would die in a very ugly and violent way. His abortion clinic was fire-bombed in 1986.[635] The doctor was shot in both arms by a pro-life vigilante in 1993.[636] And in 2009, while he was attending a church service, Dr. Tiller was murdered.[637]

Of course this is a legal and medical fiasco. Perhaps one the most embarrassing aspects of this entire murderous circus are the **Carhart** opinions themselves. In **Stenberg v. Carhart**, five Supreme Court Justices say there is a constitutional right to kill a baby outside the birth canal.[638] In **Gonzales v. Carhart**, five Supreme Court Justices reverse themselves and say there is not a constitutional right to kill a baby outside the birth canal.[639]

The **Carhart** opinions shock us for two reasons. One, the reader becomes aware of what a late-term abortion actually is, what is involved in aborting a woman who is five months pregnant or more. The Supreme Court has hinted at this horror before--in **Simopoulos** and in **Catholic League**--but those cases involve the discovery of cadavers. **Carhart** is describing the actual killings.

But it's not just the graphic nature of the opinions that upset us. There's an intellectual upset at the heart of **Carhart**. The baby is in the process of birth, and so her legal status is in doubt. Is this a

---

[635] **See** Joe Stumpe and Monica Davey, "Abortion Doctor Shot To Death in Kansas Church," **The New York Times** (May 31, 2009).
[636] **Id**.
[637] **Id**.
[638] **Supra** note 202.
[639] **Supra** note 208.

fetus or a baby? Is this abortion or murder? We start to wonder about the importance of location. And then we start asking if a murder could happen inside the uterus.

The *Carhart* opinions were a disaster that was several decades in the making. The Court had never focused on the possibility of infanticide in its abortion opinions. *Casey* was particularly glib on the subject. Rather incredibly, the Supreme Court had never discussed the medical procedure of abortion with any detail.

For several decades the Supreme Court has responded to the infanticide charge of the pro-life movement by trying to hide the bodies. They sent Dr. Simopoulos to prison because he embarrassed them with a dead baby in a motel room.[640] Justice Rehnquist made the ridiculous assertion that we do not have a right to bury our dead in a funeral service.[641] Over and over the Supreme Court tried to avoid any baby-killing scandal.

So the *Carhart* opinions are quite shocking. People on the Court are openly discussing the homicide of a baby, and using words like "kill."[642] Even the word "baby" is used.[643] Justice Breyer opens his opinion by apologizing for how much he is about to horrify us. "Because Nebraska law seeks to ban one method of aborting a pregnancy, we must describe and then discuss several different abortion procedures. Considering the fact that these procedures seek to terminate a potential human life, our

---

[640] *Supra* note 242.

[641] *Supra* note 342.

[642] The second sentence in Justice Scalia's dissent in *Carhart*: "The method of killing a human child--one cannot even accurately say an entirely unborn human child--proscribed by this statute is so horrible that the most clinical description of it evokes a shudder of revulsion." *Supra* note 464.

[643] Justice Kennedy quotes nurse Shafer in *Carhart II*: "The baby's little fingers were clasping and unclasping, and his little feet were kicking. Then the doctor stuck the scissors in the back of his head…" *Supra* note 208.

discussion may seem clinically cold or callous to some, perhaps horrifying to others."[644]

And then Justice Breyer goes on to write about "a free-floating fetal head that can be difficult for a physician to grasp and remove…"[645] We also hear, for the first time, about the "possibility of horrible complications arising from retained fetal parts."[646]

In *Carhart II*, Justice Kennedy quotes Brenda Shafer's testimony. "The doctor opened up the scissors, stuck a high-powered suction tube into the opening, and sucked the baby's brains out. Now the baby went completely limp…"[647] Kennedy also writes of a doctor who squeezes the baby's skull after it has been pierced "so that enough brain tissue exudes to allow the head to pass through (the cervix)."[648] Kennedy describes how an abortion doctor would "pull the fetus out of the woman until it disarticulates at the neck, in effect decapitating it."[649]

Justice John Paul Stevens makes a morbid joke about the spilling of ink. "Although much ink is spilled today describing the gruesome nature of late-term abortion procedures, that rhetoric does not provide me a reason to believe that the procedure Nebraska here claims it seeks to ban is more brutal, more gruesome, or less respectful of potential life than the equally gruesome procedure Nebraska claims it still allows."[650]

Of course this is actually aimed at Justice Kennedy, who implicitly upheld the practice of the D&E abortion in *Planned*

---

[644] *Supra* note 202.
[645] *Id.*
[646] *Id.*
[647] *Supra* note 208.
[648] *Id.*
[649] *Id.*
[650] *Supra* note 495.

Parenthood v. Casey, and is now upset by it. Stevens is right that it's quite illogical for Justice Kennedy to say that our Constitution requires the brutal and gruesome D&E while it does not require the brutal and gruesome D&X. Both procedures are equally barbaric, and Justice Kennedy cannot explain why he is opposed to one and is in favor of the other.

Yet Stevens is hardly a paragon of rationality. Once he acknowledges that a D&E abortion is "brutal" and "gruesome," he too should be overruling *Roe* and *Casey*. It's absurd for Stevens to insist that our Constitution requires brutality. Indeed, our Constitution forbids "cruel and unusual punishments," and yet here is Stevens (and Ginsburg) arguing that our Constitution requires "brutal" and "gruesome" medical procedures.

If this brutal and gruesome killing was a method of capital punishment, Stevens would no doubt say that our Constitution forbids it. But since a baby is on the receiving end of the brutality, Stevens says our Constitution requires it. Is that rational?

Dissenting in *Carhart*, Justice Kennedy makes several pro-life comments. "The majority views the procedures from the perspective of the abortionist, rather than from the perspective of a society shocked when confronted with a new method of ending human life."[651] For the first time, Justice Kennedy is referencing infanticide. He's implicitly accusing the majority of voting to kill babies.

The sharp U-turn in Justice Kennedy's rhetoric might surprise some people. And yet, we really should not be surprised. People wake up to pro-life arguments every day. Because of the way the media covers abortion in our society, a lot of people have a default pro-choice position. They are pro-choice because they

---

[651] *Stenberg v. Carhart*, 530 U.S. 914 (2000) (Kennedy, J., dissenting).

haven't seen an abortion, they haven't seen a photograph of an aborted child, and they're simply not aware of what is going on.

And then something happens, an awakening, a shift in perception. For some people it's as simple as going through a pregnancy and loving a baby inside the womb. Their eyes open and they see what they did not see before.

Perhaps this is what happened to Justice Kennedy in **Stenberg v. Carhart**. There is a very obvious, very fundamental shift in the way he is talking about abortion. Once you make this transformation, once you start to think about infanticide in a serious way, it's hard to say this is a right thing to do.

Here is Justice Kennedy in **Carhart**, describing the D&E, an abortion procedure that he implicitly said the Constitution requires in **Planned Parenthood v. Casey**:

> The fetus can be alive at the beginning of the dismemberment process and can survive for a time while its limbs are being torn off. Dr. Carhart agreed that "when you pull out a piece of the fetus, let's say, an arm or a leg and remove that, at the time just prior to removal of the portion of the fetus,...the fetus (is) alive." Dr. Carhart has observed fetal heartbeat via ultrasound with "extensive parts of the fetus removed," and testified that mere dismemberment of a limb does not always cause death because he knows of a physician who removed the arm of a fetus only to have the fetus go on to be born "as a living child with one arm." At the conclusion of a D&E abortion no intact fetus remains. In

Dr. Carhart's words, the abortionist is
left with a "tray full of pieces."[652]

It sounds like Kennedy is appalled by what he is describing, does it not? His rhetoric in regard to abortion is quite different than how he sounded in *Casey*. For one thing, he is now far more specific and detailed about the subject at hand. He's not talking about "the universe." He's talking about the actual abortion surgery. So perhaps that's an important difference, suggesting why the Supreme Court might overrule itself, at least in regard to these ugly D&E abortions. *Casey* was vague and unfocused, perhaps even ignorant. *Carhart* and *Carhart II* are detailed and factual, written by people who now understand with more specificity what they are talking about.

And yet *Carhart II* does not overrule *Casey*. The second *Carhart* opinion overrules the first *Carhart* opinion, and nothing more. Doctors no longer have a constitutional right to induce birth and kill a child halfway outside the birth canal. But what about the dismemberment of babies inside the uterus? What about the D&E?

It is "equally gruesome," and yet our Constitution still requires the D&E, apparently.

So that's quite odd. In *Carhart*, Justice Kennedy, the fifth vote to uphold *Roe* and *Casey*, is writing like a pro-lifer. He's talking about infanticide. He uses terms like "dismemberment" and "tray full of pieces" to describe a D&E abortion. And yet in *Carhart II* he and the rest of the Supreme Court decide to leave *Casey* in place. Apparently there's still a constitutional right to do a D&E abortion. Dismemberment is a good thing. Tray full of pieces is a right thing to do.

---

[652] *Id.*

What's so ironic about the **Carhart** cases is the entire Supreme Court is now on record as disparaging D&E abortions. The pro-choice Justices (Breyer, Ginsburg, Stevens, O'Connor, Souter) have given us all an entire laundry list of awful things that can happen to a woman whose doctor dismembers a 20-week baby while the child is inside her uterus. The doctor has to pull out "sharp bone fragments." He might cause "uterine perforations" with his own instruments. Sometimes there is "infection-causing" baby tissue left behind in the uterus. Indeed, the liberal Justices say that a D&E abortion is "potentially fatal" to the mother.[653]

That's why doctors started the practice of killing babies outside the birth canal, after all. A D&E is dangerous!

On top of this, the pro-choice Justices Stevens and Ginsburg call the D&E "brutal" and "gruesome."[654] Another supporter of **Roe**, Justice Kennedy, writes that the fetus "dies just as a human adult or child would: it bleeds to death as it is torn from limb to limb."[655]

And yet these are the same people who would say, in **Carhart II**, that our Constitution requires the D&E abortion. Apparently, after our little detour into killing tens of thousands of babies outside the birth canal, we are back to "normal," which is to say, we are back to saying that D&E abortion is a constitutional right.

The about-face in **Carhart II** is quite awkward. In **Carhart** the Supreme Court jettisons the D&E abortion as "potentially fatal" and "brutal" and "gruesome." And now, in **Carhart II**, the Court is trying to reinstall this brutal medical procedure as a constitutional right.

---

[653] **Supra** note 202.
[654] **Supra** note 495.
[655] **Supra** note 651.

And what about the stare decisis argument of *Casey*? What about this idea that it would look bad for the Supreme Court to overrule itself, that it must always stay the course? That idea seems to be abandoned in rather embarrassing fashion in *Carhart II*. None of the five Justices in *Carhart II* are convinced that we must kill babies outside the birth canal, just because the Supreme Court said we must in *Carhart*.

Indeed, a cynic might suspect that the difference between *Carhart* and *Carhart II* is that Justice O'Connor retired, and she was replaced by a new Justice, Samuel Alito. If the Supreme Court wants to convince pro-lifers that there is no hope to reverse *Roe*, that we have to give up, *Carhart II* says the opposite. *Carhart II* says keep fighting, keep waiting for Justices to retire and keep replacing them.

Apparently our abortion fight has not been resolved after all!

Indeed, the stare decisis argument in *Casey* was always odd, since the Supreme Court felt the need to fix *Roe*, to rewrite the opinion. And the fix did not work. We are still fighting over abortion. And the biggest fighter for stare decisis in *Casey*--Justice Kennedy--abandons the doctrine when he becomes upset about the death of a baby in *Carhart*.

Why did Justice Kennedy affirm *Roe v. Wade* in *Casey*? What was he trying to do?

The opinion says that *Roe* cannot be overruled "under fire." Okay, who is attacking the Supreme Court, and what are they saying? Pro-lifers are attacking the Court, and they say the Court is responsible for infanticides.

The *Casey* Court has no interest in admitting this, and so five people vote to uphold *Roe v, Wade*.

Now, after the *Carhart* opinions, this justification for upholding *Roe* is gone. It's not just pro-lifers who are talking about abortion killing a baby. Supreme Court Justices have said it themselves in published opinions. Justice Kennedy references infanticide in multiple places in *Carhart* and *Carhart II*.

His hope in *Casey*, that the authority and prestige of the Supreme Court can carry the day, has been shattered. Indeed, his graphic and brutal opinions in *Carhart* and *Carhart II* are a dagger in the heart to any pride we might take in our Supreme Court.

Obviously the five Justices who overruled *Carhart* thought that partial-birth abortion was far more damaging and embarrassing to the Court's prestige than any attempt to correct a mistake. But of course the problem for the Supreme Court, and for *Roe v. Wade*, is that the graphic infanticides of *Carhart* and *Carhart II* undermine *Roe v. Wade* itself.

Indeed, it's not just the infanticides of *Carhart* that put *Roe v. Wade* in danger. Yes, the opinions are very graphic. The D&E is described for the first time, and so we begin to be appalled by the D&E. But even more damning for the Supreme Court, and *Roe v. Wade*, is that the born/unborn distinction has been violated in a very primal way.

Up until *Carhart*, the born/unborn distinction has always been sacrosanct. In his concurrence, Justice Stevens argues it is "irrational" to object to the killing of a child outside the birth canal, while we accept the killing of an unborn child.[656] And yet this irrational distinction has always been at the heart of *Roe v. Wade*. Newborns are citizens; unborn infants are sub-human.

---

[656] *Supra* note 495.

As the baby crosses from one legal category to another, we start to recognize how arbitrary our rules have been. The child is simply moving in space, from inside the uterus to outside the uterus. And yet inside the uterus she is sub-human property, while outside the uterus she is a citizen of the United States, and it is murder to kill her.

Dr. Kermit Gosnell, who would be convicted of multiple counts of murder for killing newborns in his abortion clinic, might justifiably complain that **Carhart** seems to suggest that killing newborns is a right, too.[657] After all, Dr. Haskell and Dr. Carhart are just two of the many doctors who are killing babies outside the birth canal.[658] If these babies are people, the murder statutes would seem to be implicated.[659] And yet nobody on the Supreme

---

[657] *See* Chapter 19.

[658] At least 90 doctors can be identified who are providing abortions after 22 weeks. *See* www.abortiondocs.org. And many of these doctors often serve as a front man for an entire class of anonymous doctors who might be willing to do late-term or partial-birth abortions. For instance, Dr. Steven Brigham is the Ray Kroc of the abortion industry. Under his umbrella, "American Women's Services," he owns and operates 16 abortion clinics in four states. *See* www.americanwomensservices.com. His website says they will provide abortions up to 36 weeks. After he was arrested for murder, the press finally started to investigate. *See* Eyal Press, "A Botched Operation," *The New Yorker* (February 3, 2014).

[659] A surprising number of abortion doctors have been prosecuted for murder. Dr. William Waddill was prosecuted twice for killing a newborn. *See* Chapter 7. Dr. Bruce Steir was charged with 2nd degree murder after his patient died. *See* Julie Marquis, "Abortion's Cause Celebre," *Los Angeles Times* (December 1, 1998). Dr. Raymond Showery was convicted of murder for drowning a newborn. *Supra* note 688. Dr. David Benjamin was convicted of 2nd degree murder for depraved indifference to human life when he killed his patient along with her baby. *Supra* note 497. A non-doctor, Alicia Ruiz Hanna, was convicted of 2nd degree murder for killing her patient in the first trimester. *Supra* note 137. Dr. Gordon Goei was arrested for murder in California, on suspicion that he had murdered a newborn. *See* "Doctor Arrested After Abortion of 26-Week Fetus," *The Los Angeles Times* (May 21, 1998). Dr. Joseph Melnick was prosecuted for murder in Philadelphia for allowing a newborn to die. (He would be convicted of a lesser charge). *See* "Doctor Is Convicted in Death of a Fetus After an Abortion," *The New York Times* (June 13, 1989). Dr. Kermit Gosnell was convicted of multiple counts of murder for stabbing newborns. *See* Chapter 19. (Four other people in his

Court discusses the murder statutes in **Carhart**, not even the dissenters.

Not one Supreme Court Justice wants to revisit the non-definition of "person" offered by **Roe v. Wade**. Nobody in **Carhart** or **Carhart II** argues that a baby outside the birth canal has a right to life. Not one Justice discusses when the murder statutes might apply. Despite how appalled and upset all nine of the Justices seem to be, these same nine Justices repeatedly and continually deny the baby's humanity as a matter of law.

In particular you would think the opponents of **Roe** would use this opportunity to discuss the killing of a baby, and whether it qualifies as murder. And yet they say not a word about murder. This is quite odd, since this abortion procedure is inches away from a murder prosecution. Obviously murder is implicated. When do the murder statutes apply? When does birth happen? When does citizenship attach?

In **Roe v. Wade**, of course, the Supreme Court is talking about unborn infants, so you can see why there is so little discussion of

---

clinic were also convicted of murder). Dr. Douglas Karpen of Houston was prosecuted for murder for strangling newborns. (The grand jury refused to indict). *See* Helen Pow, "Second 'House of Horrors' Abortion Clinic Where Doctor 'Twisted Heads Off Fetus' Necks With His Bare Hands' Is Investigated In Texas," **The Daily Mail** (May 16, 2013). And in 2011, Dr. Steven Brigham and Dr. Nicola Riley were arrested and charged with murder for killing unborn infants. *See* Marie McCullough, "Abortion Provider Steven Brigham Charged With Murder in Maryland," **The Philadelphia Inquirer** (December 31, 2011). The novel theory of the police was that Brigham was a fraud (he was unlicensed in Maryland, and Riley had never performed a late-term abortion before), and since this unlicensed doctor had obtained consent to abort the pregnancy by fraud, it was a non-consensual abortion. In many states you are not allowed to kill an unborn child against the will of the mother. *See* note 398. Maryland is such a state. "A prosecution may be instituted for murder or manslaughter for a viable fetus." The prosecutor elected not to go forward with a murder trial. So it's an open question if an unlicensed doctor can be prosecuted for murder for killing an unborn baby if consent for the abortion is obtained via fraud.

murder. (**Roe** does discuss murder, but only in the context of trying to prove that an unborn baby is not a person).[660] But here, in the two **Carhart** cases, the baby is in the process of birth.

She's half-born, and half-unborn. Part of her is a citizen, and the rest of her is property. She's half a baby and half a fetus. And this is half a murder prosecution, and half a constitutional right. You would think somebody might mention this problem.

Yet the Supreme Court cannot bring itself to discuss the murder part of the equation. All of the Justices are upset and appalled, and none of them will address what is upsetting and appalling them. They are unanimous in their silence.

---

[660] *See* notes 393-394 and text.

Chapter 18

If we are allowed to outlaw abortion, what will this do to the safety of the procedure? It will get more dangerous. When a woman has an illegal abortion, she is more likely to die.[661] Thus feminists charge right-to-lifers with being callous to all the injuries an aborting woman might receive.

Should this argument convince us to support abortion rights?

Imagine a society where there is a legal right for a man to assault a woman. Women are second-class citizens in this society. And a lot of women are attacked, since this violence is deemed a lawful assault. And other people see this violence against women, and they are unhappy about it.

Finally the citizens in this society pass a law. Women are human beings, and it's a crime to assault them.

After this new law is passed, many women who had been victims of assault start buying guns, since they are now people with rights, and in this society a person has a right to buy a gun.

The next year, 1000 rapists are shot while assaulting a woman.

A men's rights group is very unhappy about this. "Look at all the men who are dying! We need a constitutional right to assault a woman, so it will be safer." The men sue in federal court. And in

---

[661] *See* Katha Pollitt, "Abortion in American History," *The Atlantic* (May 1, 1997). On the other hand, legalizing abortion makes a felony seem like a right thing to do. It can give people the illusion that abortion is simple and safe. And in order to keep it legal, we tell lies about the nature of the surgery, we hide the violence of it, and we dismiss or ignore any possible injuries to a woman's reproductive system.

a famous opinion, our Supreme Court rules that a woman is not a person, and has no right-to-life. What you do in privacy is your own business. And so a man has a constitutional right to assault a woman.

After this ruling, women can no longer buy guns. And the number of dying rapists drops dramatically. The men's rights group is very happy about this. "Yea! We're never going back to the bad old days."

And yet these right-to-lifers won't shut up about the violence. And some men are getting very angry. "You don't like men! You're a man-hater! Do you know what it's like to get shot? It's horrible! Why do you want men to get shot? We are going to keep our constitutional right to assault women."[662]

Of course this hypothetical seems ridiculous to feminists who deny the humanity of the unborn. All they see are pregnant women who are dying in illegal abortions. To them it makes a lot of sense that abortion should be legalized and safe (or at least safer). They don't see any assault, because they don't see the humanity of the victim. There is no victim.

And yet can we really deny the humanity of the unborn? Consider how valuable these babies are. For instance, after an abortion, medical researchers want to buy the cadavers so they can do scientific experiments. A dead baby is far more valuable to a scientist than a mouse or a rat. That's because the unborn are a part of our species. They are human beings.

On March 8, 2000, the news show *20/20* did a surreal story about a doctor, Dr. Miles Jones, who sold baby parts to medical

---

[662] One might say this analogy breaks down because babies cannot operate guns, and cannot defend themselves. Is that how we want to define people, by our capacity to commit violence?

researchers.[663] Attorneys filed a transcript of the report as part of an amicus brief to the Supreme Court in ***Stenberg v. Carhart***.[664] Here is that transcript:

CONNIE CHUNG: "Now, a story we guarantee most of you have never heard before. The subject is highly charged and controversial. Behind the scenes of some promising medical research, big money is being made from the sale of fetal body parts. Chief correspondent Chris Wallace has been investigating this story. Chris?"

CHRIS WALLACE: "Connie, our hidden camera investigation has found evidence that some businessmen are trafficking in fetuses. One has even put out a price list. And there are claims that some are selling fetuses that women have not even given for research. Here's what can happen when something that is supposed to be used to spur medical breakthroughs is used instead to make money."

CHRIS WALLACE (V.O.): "It's a moment too painful to imagine--after getting radiation treatments for cancer, Cindy Smith, a mother of five, learned she was pregnant with twins."

CINDY SMITH: "They basically told me that my children were dying inside me, that I was the only thing keeping them living."

CHRIS WALLACE (V.O.): "Cindy decided to end her pregnancy. She says her only comfort came from signing this consent form, giving the fetuses to medical researchers, looking into cures for terrible diseases."

CINDY SMITH: "What I wanted to do was make something positive out of a horrible situation."

CHRIS WALLACE (V.O.): "What she didn't know is that this man would be making money off her twins."

---

[663] The episode broadcast on March 8, 1999.
[664] ***Supra*** note 565.

MILES JONES: "If you have a guy that's desperate for, let's say, a heart, then he'll pay you whatever you ask."

CHRIS WALLACE (V.O.): "His name is Dr. Miles Jones, and he says he can make big bucks selling human fetuses to researchers."

MILES JONES: "Let's say someone needs feet. Feet are real common. They are not hard to get."

CHRIS WALLACE: "A *20/20* hidden camera investigation has found a thriving industry in which aborted fetuses women donate to help medical research are being marketed for hundreds, even thousands of dollars. We showed what we found undercover to Arthur Caplan, director of the University of Pennsylvania Center for Bioethics."

ARTHUR CAPLAN: "That's trading in body parts, there's no doubt about it."

CHRIS WALLACE: "Turning human fetuses into a commodity."

ARTHUR CAPLAN: "Into a product."

CHRIS WALLACE (V.O.): "There's a demand for fetal tissue, because doctors believe it may be the key to medical breakthroughs, cures for Alzheimer's and Parkinson's disease, diabetes and other illnesses. Some researchers use fetal cells, others need whole organs or limbs. But no one on either side of the abortion debate wants fetal research to become an incentive for abortions. So laws have been passed to draw a clear line. A woman must decide to have an abortion before she's approached to donate the fetus. Abortions can't be altered to get better specimens. And above all, tissue can't be sold for profit. Despite all that, some businessmen have slipped in and turned human fetuses into dollars."

DEAN ALBERTY: "This is purely for profit. Everything was about money."

CHRIS WALLACE (V.O.): "Dean Alberty worked for two companies that acted as middle men, getting the fetuses from abortion clinics and shipping tissue to researchers."

DEAN ALBERTY: "When I got the fetus, I'd already have a checklist telling me what specific organs they were looking for."

CHRIS WALLACE (V.O.): "The law allows tissue companies to recover their costs. This government agency charges $100 per shipment. But take a look at what one private company is demanding. Opening Lines put out this price list: $325 for a spinal cord, $550 for a reproductive organ, $999 for a brain. Alberty says he helped put together the price list."

CHRIS WALLACE: "Is there any way to justify these prices?"

DEAN ALBERTY: "No. There is not."

CHRIS WALLACE: "So what does this price represent?"

DEAN ALBERTY: "That represents greed."

CHRIS WALLACE (V.O): "Who runs Opening Lines? Dr. Miles Jones, the Missouri pathologist whose company handled Cindy's fetuses. Last year Jones not only mailed out the price list, but also this brochure."

CHRIS WALLACE: "Fresh fetal tissue harvested and shipped to your specifications where and when you need it."

DEAN ALBERTY: "That's correct."

MILES JONES: "Pleased to meet you."

UNIDENTIFIED WOMAN: "Nice to meet you."

CHRIS WALLACE (V.O.): "We wanted to find out for ourselves how these companies do business. So, posing as a prospective investor, a **20/20** producer met with Dr. Jones, who wanted to talk over dinner."

UNIDENTIFIED WOMAN: "What does a brain go for? What does a kidney or liver go for?"

MILES JONES: "It's market force. It's what you can sell it for."

CHRIS WALLACE (V.O.): "Over lobster bisque and roast duck, Dr. Jones explained the business of selling human fetuses."

MILES JONES: "We had projections of $50,000 a week. And, you know, some weeks you can hit that and some weeks you can't. It's just a matter of being able to match supply and demand."

CHRIS WALLACE (V.O.): "Dr. Jones said the average specimen costs him just $50 plus overhead, but that he charges an average of $250. The law only talks about recovering costs. But on a single fetus, Jones said he can make $2500."

MILES JONES: "That's one fetus--the cost of procuring it is the same whether you get one kidney or you get two kidneys, a lung, a brain, a heart. It's the same cost that you've put into it."

UNIDENTIFIED WOMAN: "But you keep charging?"

MILES JONES: "Each researcher gets charged."

UNIDENTIFIED WOMAN: "And each time that's just money in the bank?"

MILES JONES: "Mm-hmm."

CHRIS WALLACE: "Turning human fetuses into a commodity."

ARTHUR CAPLAN: "It's flat out buying and selling, flat out profiteering. It's flat out saying, 'I'm going to charge you whatever you're going to pay me."

MILES JONES: "You can't kill the golden goose but you can certainly keep it well fed and it will lay lots of eggs for you."

CHRIS WALLACE: "A human fetus as a golden goose. I know you've been studying this business a long time, but does that shock even you?"

ARTHUR CAPLAN: "That's kind of blatant. 'I'm going to get the maximum value of mining a fetus,' is--is--it's shocking."

It's quite foreseeable, actually. Our authorities define the unborn as sub-human, as property. Of course the Supreme Court did not use the word "property" in **Roe v. Wade**. But when you strip babies of their humanity, that's what you are doing. Mom owns the property. Other people want to buy the property.

Defining the unborn as a commodity has other awful implications. For instance, many people can now shop for the baby they want. The Supreme Court has a regime where any unwanted baby can be aborted. But since the baby is now defined as a commodity, people are now able to discriminate with specificity.

For instance, girls are often aborted because they are girls.[665] The handicapped are aborted because they are handicapped.[666] Mothers and fathers are invited to discriminate, to get rid of the babies they don't want.[667] Populations disappear.

---

[665] In the USA the hostility runs the other way, with many parents preferring a baby girl. *See* "Gender Preference in the United States," www.in-gender.com.
[666] A surprising number of people think a baby with a handicap justifies a late-term abortion. Indeed, members of the Supreme Court have suggested as much. *Supra* note 96. And yet federal law says it's illegal to discriminate against the handicapped. *Supra* note 675.
[667] Some parents, unhappy that they are pregnant with twins, have a doctor do a "reduction." They kill one of the twins and keep the other. *See* Ruth Padawer, "The Two-Minus-One Pregnancy," *The New York Times* (August 10, 2014).

A company called 23andMe was recently granted a patent over a process that allows parents to design their baby.[668] This technology allows a person to handpick a sperm or egg donor, unite their DNA with your DNA, and see what characteristics your baby might have. You can shop for sex, height, weight, eye color, hair color, muscle performance, even personality characteristics like warmth or a sense of humor.

The 23andMe patent does not implicate abortion on its own, since this analysis can be done in an IVF lab before any zygotes are created. And of course information itself is not bad or evil. But it's still unsettling to treat human reproduction like you are buying a product. Do you want to order your baby with blonde hair and blue eyes?

Of course we already do a certain amount of shopping when we engage in mating and reproduction. We pick the mate we want. But abortion allows us to destroy unwanted people, or future people. *Roe v. Wade* allows us to terminate unwanted infants. In the future we will be able to terminate on the basis of unwanted genes or biological profile. We're already going down this road.

In her *Carhart II* dissent, Justice Ginsburg writes about aborting the handicapped. "Severe fetal anomalies and health problems confronting the pregnant woman are also causes of second-trimester abortions; many such conditions cannot be diagnosed or do not develop until the second trimester."[669]

---

[668] *See* "The Science and Ethics of Personal Genetic Testing," *The Diane Rehm Show* (October 28, 2013). www.thedianerehmshow.org.

[669] *Supra* note 96. In an interview with *Nightline*, Ron Fitzsimmons, the executive director of the National Coalition of Abortion Providers, said that partial-birth abortion was rare, and these late abortions were done primarily on babies who were severely handicapped. Fitzsimmons later admitted that he had "lied through his teeth." He claims the procedure is done far more often than he had said, and in the vast majority of cases is performed on a healthy woman with a healthy baby. *See* David Stout, "An Abortion Rights Advocate Says He Lied About Procedure," *The New York Times* (February 26, 1997).

Since *Roe*, the Supreme Court has recognized a right for women
to have abortions until birth for health purposes. This has always
been said to be in regard to the health of the mother. And yet
abortion doctors have used this as grounds for terminating any
baby with a handicap. So the "health" right has somehow
morphed into a right to kill our unhealthy children. Mom is not
the focus here; the baby is. We don't like the handicap, and we
want our handicapped child to disappear.

Ginsburg's footnote 3 is controversial because she is saying in
public what people are doing in private. Why is Justice Ginsburg
talking about handicaps? It's not mentioned by the majority
opinion, but the baby whose killing is described in *Carhart II* had
Down's syndrome.[670] Perhaps that's why Justice Ginsburg, out of
the blue, is talking about "anomalies." She's attempting to justify
the killing of a baby outside the birth canal, and she thinks that
identifying the victim's handicap does so.

Two years after writing this footnote, Justice Ginsburg would
make a notorious gaffe in a *New York Times* interview. "Frankly
I had thought at the time *Roe* was decided, there was concern
about population growth and particularly growth in populations
that we don't want to have too many of."[671] We don't actually
know what "populations" Ginsburg has in mind. Is she talking
about racial minorities? The poor? Her comment is like a dog
whistle. If you know the people she's talking about, you're just
as bad as she is.

Yet her footnote in *Carhart II* might inform our speculations. Is
Justice Ginsburg talking about the handicapped?

---

[670] *Supra* note 626 and text.
[671] *Supra* note 8.

Yes, *Roe v. Wade* is about the autonomy of women, and the right of a woman to control her body. But in order to have this right to abort a pregnancy, the Supreme Court had to define the unborn as sub-human. The baby's humanity had to be denied. And this was done until birth. And we can abort pregnancies for "health" reasons until birth. And so a handicapped child might be killed in the ninth month.

Justice Ginsburg apparently likes the word "anomalies." She uses it twice in her footnote. "(N)early all women carrying fetuses with the most serious central nervous system anomalies chose to abort their pregnancies."[672] Like much of the Supreme Court's social science, this is wrong. In the USA the termination rate for babies with Down's is about 67%, while the termination rate for healthy babies is close to 40%.[673] So that's a sizable increase, but it's not as though there's no pro-life resistance to this agenda.

On November 13, 2011 the *New York Post* ran a rather odd article called "The End of Down Syndrome."[674] The article claims "a new, simple way to detect Down syndrome in a fetus means the condition will be virtually extinct." So have we found a cure for Down's syndrome? No, apparently the idea is that we will abort these children out of existence.

It's rather disquieting to think about making all the handicapped people disappear from our society. After all, the handicapped were the first people the Nazis tried to remove, before the Jews, before the gays, before the gypsies. Are we improving the world by removing the blind, the deaf, the people with Down's or cerebral palsy? Is that our wish, to make these people disappear?

---

[672] *Supra* note 96.

[673] Jamie Natoli, et al, "Prenatal Diagnosis of Down Syndrome: A Systematic Review of Termination Rates (1995-2011) *Prenatal Diagnosis* (February 2012).

[674] Mayrav Saar, "The End of Down Syndrome," *New York Post* (November 13, 2011).

Is abortion our cure?

The Supreme Court doesn't actually like to talk about abortion. It would much rather talk about choice. And our "choice" is more like a wish. I wish I wasn't pregnant. I wish I didn't have a handicapped child. I wish I had a little girl with blonde hair and blue eyes. Apparently the Supreme Court is in the wish-fulfillment business. Yes, we can make your pregnancy disappear. Yes, we can make your handicapped child go away. Yes, you are entitled to the child you want to have.

As long as we don't see the unborn, that makes it okay. If we don't see them, they don't exist. If they don't exist, we're not making anybody disappear.

It's a violation of federal law to discriminate against the handicapped.[675] Are we discriminating against the handicapped when we abort them?

And what do we make of sex-selection? Parents can choose if they want a boy or a girl, and abort the other. Is the creation of a child a miracle of life, or are we shopping at the mall? Christians worry about the commercialization of Christmas. Well, should we buy a prostitute, rent a uterus, abort an unwanted girl and sell her body parts to medical researchers?

Needless to say, defining the unborn as commodities might have unintended consequences.

At least four states have outlawed sex-selection abortions, and North Dakota has outlawed the aborting of babies with Down's

---

[675] The Americans With Disabilities Act of 1990 forbids discrimination in employment, public services, public accommodations, and telecommunications. *See also* "Hate Crimes Against Individuals With Disabilities," www.civilrights.org.

syndrome.[676] Of course, the Supreme Court wants to avoid the ugly ramifications of its own work. But as science keeps advancing forward, the Court will have to get more and more specific about a woman's "right to choose."

And what do feminists say about women who make their daughters disappear?

In her book *Unnatural Selection*, Mara Hvistendahl reports that there are 160 million "missing" women in the world.[677] Most of them have disappeared in Asia, in China and India. And of course it's abortion that has made all these baby girls vanish.

"You can beat it out! You can make it fall out! You can abort it! But you cannot give birth to it!" Those are signs put up by Communist officials in Chinese villages in an attempt to enforce the horrific one-child policy.[678] Girls are aborted across China.[679] Hvistendahl describes the skewed sex ratios throughout Asia, and all the problems that go along with having our two genders out of balance.

Hvistendahl herself is pro-choice, and is rather outraged that pro-life people keep citing her book in arguments against abortion. "I make very clear in my book that the victim is women--women who in the 1960's and 1970's were used as pawns in a Western drive to reduce birth rates in Asia, women who later aborted female fetuses against the backdrop of patriarchy, and women who, now that they are scarce, find themselves at greater risk of

---

[676] *See* Melissa Steffan, "First State Bans Abortions Based on Down Syndrome, Gender," *Christianity Today* (March 27, 2013).
[677] Mara Hvistendahl, *Unnatural Selection* (2011).
[678] *Id*.
[679] *Id*.

being trafficked, kidnapped, or sold by their parents to men desperate to find wives."[680]

Yet, as Ross Douthat points out, Hvistendahl's book does seem rather outraged by the callous disregard of human life that abortion seems to create.[681] For instance, Hvistendahl describes a scene in a New Delhi hospital. A medical student is upset because there is a stray cat that is feeding on an aborted baby.

"Why hadn't the fetus been disposed of more carefully?"

"Because it was a girl," the nurse replied.

No doubt Hvistendahl included that scene in her book to illustrate the sexism of allowing dead girls to become cat food. But you can't criticize the sexism unless you recognize the humanity of the dead girl.

One of the basic problems with abortion, from the very beginning, is that it stinks of the master plan. Socialists who want to control human reproduction exported abortion to Asia, in order to limit those populations. Is that racism? In Asia the women abort girls, for cultural or political reasons. Is that sexism?[682]

Yet the problem of abortion is more basic than racism or sexism. We have dehumanized the unborn. Legally they do not exist. They do not count. Hvistendahl's book counts them (160 million girls missing!) but she doesn't count them, too. They're girls but they're not girls. They're missing but they never existed.

---

[680] Mara Hvistendahl, "Blaming Abortion For Disappearing Girls," *Salon* (June 30, 2011).

[681] Ross Douthat, "160 Million and Counting," *The New York Times* (June 26, 2011).

[682] And not just in Asia. The United Kingdom is starting to see skewed sex ratios, too. *See* Nico Hines, "How Widespread is Sex-Selective Abortion?" *The Daily Beast* (January 16, 2014).

Hvistendahl's book is an interesting bit of social science. We are using abortion to make unwanted babies disappear. And, because of sexism and racism, we are seeing sex ratios completely out of whack in much of Asia. And yet this focus on numbers, on statistics, reduces a human being to just another number.

Unnatural Selection is an interesting statistical argument. The sex ratios are out of balance, and this is leading to atrocities against women. Hvistendahl suggests there is a greater risk of women "being trafficked, kidnapped or sold by their parents" because of abortion.

Yet, if skewed gender numbers are our only problem, the socialist minds behind the one child policy can simply dictate a new regime of aborting boys for several years until the numbers come out right. Would that satisfy Ms. Hvistendahl?

A focus on statistics can distract us from the horror of what we are talking about. For instance, whenever we talk about some abortion atrocity, you can always count on somebody to say it is a "small percentage."[683]

There have been approximately 56 million abortions in the 40 years following ***Roe v. Wade***. The Supreme Court has to be right on all of them. Not most of them, or almost all of them, or 99% of them. If one baby has been killed, ***Roe v. Wade*** is a baby-killing opinion. The Supreme Court actually describes the killing of a baby in the second ***Carhart*** opinion.[684]

In the context of intentional homicides, statistical arguments can actually be outrageous. It's a kind of dehumanization all by itself, minimizing the atrocity by reducing a human being to a number.

---

[683] ***See*** note 554
[684] ***Supra*** note 208.

343

Jack the Ripper killed a very small percentage of prostitutes in the world. Is it appropriate to talk that way?

The numbers distract us, confuse us, and upset us. If pro-lifers are 99% wrong, then ***Roe v. Wade*** is still a mass-murdering opinion. You're not Mao, you're more like Pol Pot. And if our error rate is a tiny and insignificant one percent of one percent, then we only murdered 5,000 babies. In terms of government atrocities, that's tiny. Although it's still a thousand times worse than Jack the Ripper.

Chapter 19

One of the appellate briefs in the *Carhart* litigation describes a market where baby parts are sold to pharmaceutical companies and university research labs.[685] Of course the abortion industry itself is a highly profitable billion-dollar industry. But selling baby parts is a lucrative side business that has developed in the years after *Roe v. Wade*. And one of the suspicions surrounding this business model is that abortion doctors need to get the baby out of the womb first in order to provide "high quality" fetal parts.

In other words, there is a financial motivation for killing babies outside the birth canal. If you do a D&E abortion, which involves decapitating and dismembering the baby inside the uterus, you could be destroying a valuable resource--the baby parts that could be sold for profit.

But of course a major problem with partial-birth abortion is that we are now killing babies outside the birth canal. It implicates murder in a very primal for many of us. We see the homicide and we are upset. And there is the additional problem that once you induce birth, you might have a live newborn on your hands, a newborn whom you want to kill.

Indeed, an appellate brief in the *Carhart* litigation describes the murder of a newborn.[686] This brief, filed by attorneys working for the United States Justice Foundation, contained transcripts of reports done by investigators for *20/20* and *Life Dynamics*. The latter is a pro-life group that is doing an interview with "Kelly," a woman who obtains fetal tissue for scientific research organizations.

---

[685] *Supra* note 565.
[686] *Id*.

Q: Why don't you start by telling us how long did you work for the abortion clinic?

A: Well, for one, I did not work for an abortion clinic as an employee. I worked for an outside source, hired with a team, to go in and dissect and procure fetal tissue, basically to dissect tissue for high-quality sales.

Q: Okay. So you were actually working for an outside company that was gathering fetal tissue, but you were doing this inside the clinics?

A: Right. But we were never employees of the abortion clinic. What we did was we would have a contract with an abortion clinic that would allow a certain number of us to go in there on certain days, and we would procure fetal tissue for research. We would get a generated list each day to tell us what tissue researchers, pharmaceutical companies, universities were looking for. Then we would go and look at the patient charts. We had to screen out all the ones we didn't want. What I mean by that is that we would not use anything that had STD's or fetal anomalies. These had to be the most perfect specimens we could give the researchers for the best value that we could sell for.

Q: What gestational ages were you talking about for these babies?

A: We would look starting at seven weeks all the way up to 30-plus.

Q: All the way to over 30 weeks gestation, you were harvesting parts from aborted babies?

A: That's correct. That's correct. And we--we were looking anywhere from eyes, livers, brains, thymuses, and especially cardiac blood, cord blood, the blood from the liver, even blood from the limbs that we would get from the veins.

Q: Now, just a minute ago you said that you had to screen out all the babies with abnormalities.

A: Right.

Q: But when you're talking about babies at 30 weeks gestation, wouldn't the majority of these abortions be for abnormalities?

A: No. I mean there was only probably like 10 percent that had abnormalities. The rest were very healthy donors. And how we knew that they were healthy was, one, we would check to see, if they--the mother had any prenatal care that suggested she had birth defects, if that was the reason why she was there to have the abortion. But 95 percent of the time, no, it was just that she was there to get rid of the baby.

Q: So how many of the later terms, the ones that are around 30 weeks or so, would you see in a week?

A: Probably an estimate of 30 or 40 a week.

Q: Of the late terms?

A: Of the late terms.

Q: Of the late terms.

A: That's anywhere from 22 weeks all
the way up to 30 weeks-plus.

Later in the brief, the anonymous woman "Kelly" talks about the
day she decided to quit her job:

Q: How is it that you came to be
talking to Life Dynamics? I mean you're
working in this abortion clinic,
gathering fetal parts. It seems like
we'd be the last people you'd want to
talk to.

A: Well, when I was working, there
was an incident that came my way, and
my staff's way, that there was a set of
twins, at 24 weeks gestation, brought
back to us. These twins were both in
pan and they were both alive. Meaning
that there was maybe just a couple of
nicks from the tongs that had pulled
them out. But these fetuses, were
moving and gasping for air. And the
doctor came back and basically looked
at us and said, got you some good
specimens, twins. And I looked at him
and said, there's something wrong
here. They are moving. I don't do this.
This is not in my contract.

Q: So they just brought you these
babies and said, here, do whatever you
want with them?

A: That's correct. And I told him I
would not be any part of extinguishing

their lives. So he basically got a bottle
of sterile water and poured it in the
pans until the fluid ran up to their
mouths and nose and basically let them
drown themselves, which didn't take
very long. And I did not stay in the
room to watch that. I left the room,
because I would not watch those
fetuses moving.

Q: So he basically--I mean not
basically--what he did do was kill those
babies outside the mother's womb?

A: That's correct.

Q: After they'd been born?

A: That's correct. And then we, staff,
did procure fetal tissue from those,
under protest.

Q: Do you know how long it took those
babies to die?

A: No, because we left the room. I
would not watch. And that's basically
when I decided that it was wrong.
Basically, I--I did not want to be there
when that happened.

The Supreme Court was put on notice by this brief. If you find a right to "partial-birth abortion," if you say it's legal and right to kill babies outside the birth canal, you are opening the door to murder. Of course there will be murders. It's like night follows day. And this is infanticide in the classical sense. It's the murder of a newborn child.[687]

---

[687] The drowning of the two babies described in this appellate brief is illegal in all 50 states. Indeed, an abortion doctor was convicted of murder in 1983 for doing something almost identical to the behavior described in this brief. *See*

A decade after **Carhart**, Dr. Kermit Gosnell was convicted of several counts of murder for killing newborns in his abortion clinic. This was a shocking, momentous event. An abortion doctor is finally going to jail for killing a baby.[688] And yet none of us should be shocked that Dr. Gosnell was killing newborns. We all know from **Stenberg v. Carhart** that abortion doctors had gotten into the habit of inducing birth. **Carhart** describes a specific procedure where the doctor is killing the baby in the middle of birth. The doctor avoids a murder prosecution by keeping part of the baby within the birth canal, thus keeping the baby within the legal status of property.

But to induce birth you first have to give the pregnant mother a pill. It's called Cytotec.[689] And Cytotec is unpredictable in regards to when the mother gives birth. The child might be born anytime during a 24-hour period after the mother swallows these pills. And what this means is that the doctor is often not in the room when the child is born.

---

note 688. And yet **Roe v. Wade** has confused many people on this issue, including famous people. *See* notes 691-692 and text.

[688] It's not the first time, however. In 1979, Dr. Raymond Showery dropped a premature baby girl into a bucket of water. Several employees would later testify that bubbles rose to the surface. Dr. Showery then put the baby in a plastic bag and tied it shut. The bag moved as if the baby was trying to breathe, and then it stopped moving. One nurse testified that Dr. Showery said, "If you see any movement or anything, you don't see anything, you don't know anything." He also instructed his nurses to look the other way. The baby was kept in a freezer along with all the other aborted infants. Police were unable to determine which of the dead babies was the murder victim. In 1983, Showery was convicted of murder and sentenced to 15 years in prison. While he was out on bail pending his appeal, Dr. Showery continued doing abortions until he sliced into a woman's uterus and killed her, too. *See* note 252.

[689] According to **Carhart II**, only a minority of abortion doctors who perform partial-birth abortion use drugs to induce birth. Many of them simply pull the baby outside the birth canal with forceps.

In other words, the doctor will miss his opportunity to do a partial-birth abortion. And he will have a live newborn on his hands.

Dr. William Waddill strangled a newborn that he had tried to abort. He killed a baby in a roomful of witnesses, and was shocked when he was prosecuted for murder. But the childbirth that happened in the Waddill case was highly unusual. Saline amniocentesis is supposed to kill inside the womb.

In the Jennie McCormack case, she caused her own abortion by swallowing Mifeprex and Cytotec. Mifeprex (a.k.a. RU-486) works by killing the child inside the uterus. Mifeprex can be dangerous to the mother, particularly later in pregnancy, as it can cause massive blood loss.[690] This is why this abortion pill is only indicated for use very early in the pregnancy.

Cytotec is safer than these other forms of abortion because Cytotec does not involve killing the baby. The mother is not swallowing a pill designed to abort a child. She's swallowing a pill that simply induces birth. If an abortion doctor is using Cytotec, it is likely that he will have babies who are born alive in his abortion practice.

Why are you inducing birth, and where is that newborn child?

Maybe the use of Cytotec should be regulated. Once the abortion industry started inducing birth, it was just a matter of time before an abortion doctor would be arrested and prosecuted for murder for killing a newborn.

After the **Carhart** opinion said that partial-birth abortion was a constitutional right, many states had the urge to re-affirm that a newborn infant is a citizen, and it's murder to kill a baby. In

---

[690] *See* notes 537-538 and text.

Illinois, for instance, there was a push to pass a Born Alive Infant Protection Act. Barack Obama, when he was a state senator, voted against this bill four times.[691]

It's a fair criticism of the Born Alive Infant Protection Act that we don't actually need it. Was Dr. Kermit Gosnell prosecuted for violating a "Born Alive Infant Protection Act"? No. He was prosecuted for murder, good old-fashioned murder. He was charged with murder for killing a human baby. A Born Alive Infant Protection Act is irrelevant and unnecessary as a matter of criminal law. Yes? It's symbolic. It's a plea from pro-life people to pro-choice people, asking for reassurance. We're not killing newborns, right? And Obama refuses to give that reassurance. Apparently it would undermine *Roe v. Wade* to recognize the humanity of a newborn infant.

These votes would be politically inconvenient when Barack Obama decided to run for President. In 2008, Obama argued that he had always recognized a newborn baby's right to life. "I hate to say that people are lying, but here's a situation where folks are lying. I have said repeatedly that I would have been completely in, fully in support of the federal bill that everybody supported--which was to say--that you should provide assistance to any infant that was born--even if it was as a consequence of an induced abortion. That was not the bill that was presented at the state level. What that bill also was doing was trying to undermine *Roe v. Wade*."[692]

---

[691] In particular Obama objected to this line: "A live child born as a result of an abortion shall be fully recognized as a human person and accorded immediate protection under the law." This line was removed, and still Obama voted against the bill.

[692] David Brody, "Obama Gets Heated on Born Alive Infant Protection Act," *Christian Broadcasting Network* (August 16, 2008).

The fact checker for *The Washington Post* writes that "Obama misrepresented the facts during this interview."[693] *Politifact* agreed, saying that Obama had voted against a born-alive bill that was "virtually identical to the federal law."[694] *FactCheck.org* also agreed: "Obama's claim is wrong."[695]

Why did Barack Obama oppose the Born Alive Infant Protection Act? He was worried about *Roe v. Wade*. It will somehow "undermine" *Roe v. Wade* to protect newborn infants.

In his *Carhart* concurrence, Justice Stevens says that it's "irrational" to object to killing a baby outside the birth canal, since we are already decapitating and dismembering babies of the same age inside the uterus. "(T)he notion that either of these two equally gruesome procedures performed at this late stage of gestation is more akin to infanticide than the other, or that the State furthers any legitimate interest by banning one but not the other, is simply irrational."[696]

Of course pro-lifers have been making this argument since 1973! If a newborn has a right to life, than a partially-born infant has a right to life, and an unborn child has a right to life, too. Pro-lifers would resolve the irrationality by recognizing the humanity of the unborn. *Roe v. Wade* is based on an irrational prejudice we have against babies we cannot see.

Stevens and Ginsburg would resolve this prejudice by dehumanizing babies outside the birth canal, too. But this is

[693] Josh Hicks, "Did Obama Vote to Deny Rights to Infant Abortion Survivors?" *The Washington Post* (September 10, 2012). Hicks said he "could have awarded Four Pinocchios to the former Illinois senator," but "that interview is several years old now."
[694] The National Right to Life Committee said it, Politifact confirmed it. Angie Drobnic Holan, "2003 Legislation Had Neutrality Clause," *Politifact* (October 9, 2008).
[695] "Obama and 'Infanticide,'" *FactCheck.org* (August 25, 2008).
[696] *Supra* note 495.

actually forbidden by our Constitution. As a legal matter, birth is quite important. Birth is when people become citizens. And the 14th Amendment specifically says that newborns are citizens. ("All persons born...are citizens of the United States.") Our legal authorities are explicitly forbidden from killing born infants.

In other words, if our discrimination in favor of born infants is irrational, and it is, we can only fix this problem by recognizing the humanity of the unborn. The Supreme Court can do this. Congress can do this. It's simply a matter of enforcing the equal protection clause, which goes beyond protecting citizens to protect all people.

Congress has explicit 14th Amendment authority to enforce the 14th Amendment.[697] And Congress has an additional authority to naturalize people and make them citizens. While birth in our country is sufficient for citizenship, it is not necessary. ("All persons born or naturalized...are citizens of the United States.") What this means is that Congress can naturalize unborn children, and make them citizens, too.

Yet the Supreme Court tried to go the other way, and start dehumanizing babies outside the birth canal. This was a disastrous move for the Supreme Court, and for *Roe v. Wade*, as Justice Kennedy immediately grasped. Kennedy knows all-too-well how describing these brutal and gruesome medical procedures would make his beloved Supreme Court look.

---

[697] Section 5 reads, "The Congress shall have power to enforce, by appropriate legislation, the provisions of this article." What this means is that Congress can overrule *Roe v. Wade* by statute. They can pass a federal law recognizing the humanity of the unborn and enforcing their right to the equal protection of the laws. It is, of course, up to the states to define when people die. But Congress (or the Supreme Court) can make sure these laws are applied to all the people in the state in the same way.

Instinctively many Americans recoil at partial-birth abortion. Even the words upset people, which is why the abortion industry feels the obligation to use initials as a euphemism (D&X). It was a momentous step for the abortion industry to start killing babies in the middle of birth. It opened the door to murder. And in Dr. Gosnell's case, he went right through it.

Like many abortion doctors, Kermit Gosnell was having difficulties with the D&E. Performing that medical procedure in 2000 on a 19-year-old girl, Dr. Gosnell accidentally cut her cervix and sliced into her uterus.[698] The girl, Semika Shaw, would die from infection and sepsis two days after the surgery.

Margo Davidson, her cousin, is a state senator in Pennsylvania. "I believe that I am the only member of this house that was directly touched by the tragedy at the Gosnell clinic."[699] After the death of her cousin at the hands of Dr. Gosnell, Davidson would vote for new health regulations to protect women from the abortion industry.

Unbelievably, until the day federal authorities raided Dr. Gosnell's abortion clinic in 2010, health inspectors had not set foot inside his clinic since 1993.[700] There was simply no oversight from state authorities. But there was still one available mechanism for controlling abortion doctors in Pennsylvania--fear of lawsuits.

After the death of Semika Shaw, Dr. Gosnell would be sued by her survivors for his negligence. His insurance company paid $400,000 to the girl's family.[701] And so Kermit Gosnell adopted this new abortion practice of inducing birth. Why? Birth is safer than D&E abortion, and he was less likely to be sued in the future.

---

[698] *Supra* note 211.
[699] Dave Andursko, "Meet Semika Shaw," *Life News* (April 26, 2013).
[700] *Supra* note 211.
[701] *Id*.

This does not excuse the lack of oversight by health authorities in Pennsylvania. To allow an abortion clinic to operate for 17 years without a health inspection is negligent, to put it mildly. It shows a remarkable disregard for the safety of newborn infants and pregnant women. Dr. Gosnell is using Cytotec on his pregnant patients and inducing birth. And yet no live babies are coming out of his clinic?

The grand jury indictment against Gosnell is kept on-line by the district attorney's office.[702] The indictment is unusual in that it includes an attack on the medical and legal authorities in the state of Pennsylvania. Over the years many women were injured, and even killed, inside Dr. Gosnell's abortion clinic. Many reports were filed with health authorities. And yet these authorities never bothered to visit Dr. Gosnell's clinic, or take a look inside. This disregard for health, for safety, for our laws, led to what the British tabloids refer to as a "House of Horrors" in Philadelphia.[703]

State health officials had no idea what was going on inside Gosnell's abortion clinic. Very likely none of us would know, if federal authorities had not raided the clinic in 2010. The FBI and DEA had a warrant to investigate Dr. Gosnell for drug trafficking, specifically for selling illegal prescriptions on the black market for the drug Oxycontin.[704] In the course of their investigation for illegal narcotics, the federal authorities discovered that unlicensed non-doctors were doing abortions in the clinic, and that a woman named Karnamaya Mongar had died under suspicious circumstances a few months before.

---

[702] *Id*. Seth Williams is the first African-American district attorney in Philadelphia. He was adopted as a child.
[703] *See* Lydia Warren, "House of Horrors Abortion Clinic Worker Was Handed a Screaming Newborn With No Eyes or Mouth and Asked To Deal With It," *The Daily Mail* (April 9. 2013).
[704] *Supra* note 211.

The federal officers invited state officials to participate in the raid. Armed with a warrant, the authorities invaded Dr. Gosnell's abortion clinic on February 18, 2010.

From the grand jury report:

> There was blood on the floor. A stench of urine filled the air. A flea-infested cat was wandering through the facility, and there were cat feces on the stairs. Semi-conscious women scheduled for abortions were moaning in the waiting room or the recovery room, where they sat on dirty recliners covered with bloodstained blankets.
>
> All the women had been sedated by unlicensed staff--long before Gosnell arrived at the clinic--and staff members could not accurately state what medications or dosages they had administered to the waiting patients. Many of the medications in inventory were past their expiration dates.
>
> Investigators found the clinic grossly unsuitable as a surgical facility. The two surgical procedure rooms were filthy and unsanitary--Agent Dougherty described them as resembling "a bad gas station restroom." Instruments were not sterile. Equipment was rusty and outdated. Oxygen equipment was covered with dust, and had not been inspected. The same corroded suction tubing used for abortions was the only tubing available for oral airways if assistance for breathing was needed. There was no functioning resuscitation or even monitoring equipment, except

> for a single blood pressure cuff in the recovery room.
>
> The search team discovered fetal remains haphazardly stored throughout the clinic--in bags, milk jugs, orange juice cartons, and even in cat-food containers. Some fetal remains were in a refrigerator, others were frozen. Gosnell admitted to Detective Wood that at least 10 to 20 percent of the fetuses were probably older than 24 weeks gestation...
>
> The investigators found a row of jars containing just the severed feet of fetuses. In the basement, they discovered medical waste piled high.[705]

After the arrest of Dr. Kermit Gosnell and his staff, one of his non-physician abortionists, Steve Massof, entered into a plea agreement with the state. Massof would plead guilty to multiple counts of murder in the third degree. He would serve as a witness against his boss, Dr. Gosnell, who was charged with multiple counts of murder for killing newborns, with performing illegal late-term abortions, and also for killing one of his pregnant patients through sheer disregard for her safety.

Massof testified that he saw over 100 babies born alive who had their necks snipped. During busy times, when several women were giving birth all at once, Massof told the jury that "it would rain fetuses. Fetuses and blood all over the place."[706] Steve Massof used that rather striking metaphor to describe a busy day when many women are giving birth at the same time.

---

[705] *Id*.
[706] Cheryl Sullenger, "Gosnell Employee: 'It Would Rain Fetuses and Blood' Everywhere." *Life News* (April 5, 2013).

It is disquieting how people will use the "fetus" word to describe newborns. The *New York Times*, for instance, routinely referred to any baby murdered in the Gosnell case as a "fetus."[707] Dr. Gosnell himself always referred to a newborn as a "fetus." All the people in his clinic would also say "fetus."

Massof himself killed at least 50 newborns.[708]

Dr. Gosnell (or one of his unlicensed staff) would give Cytotec to the pregnant mother to induce birth. But the actual time of birth would vary. What this meant was that often the doctor was not present when the mother went into labor. One of the abortion clinic employees, Latosha Lewis, testified at his indictment:

> A lot of times this happened when (Gosnell) wasn't there. If...a baby was about to come out, I would take the woman to the bathroom, they would sit on the toilet and basically the baby would fall out and it would be in the toilet and I would be rubbing her back and trying to calm her down for two, three, four hours until Dr. Gosnell comes.[709]

One or two babies fell out of patients each night, according to Lewis. They dropped out on lounge chairs, on the floor of the clinic, or sometimes in the bathroom. More than once a baby would be born into toilet water.

Kareema Cross, an uncertified medical assistant, also witnessed a baby born into a toilet.[710] Cross said the baby was 12-16 inches

---

[707] *See* Andrew Rosenthal, "Kermit Gosnell and Reproductive Care," *The New York Times* (April 15, 2013).
[708] Mary Chastain, "Employee Described Filthy Conditions and Babies Born Alive at Gosnell Clinic," *Breitbart* (April 19, 2013).
[709] *Supra* note 211.
[710] *Id*.

long and was struggling to swim and breathe. Cross testified on the stand that yet another unlicensed employee, Adrienne Moton, fished the baby out of the toilet and snipped the child's neck in front of the mother.

The documentary *3801 Lancaster* has a scene with one of the prosecutors, Ann Pontiera, discussing Dr. Gosnell's killing practices in an informational hearing with state senators.[711]

> There was one baby, that when it was born, one of the workers was playing with it for several minutes, before the worker did exactly what Dr. Gosnell did: snip the back of the neck. And when we use the word 'snip,' it is a scissors, taking a bony part of a vertebra and cutting it. This is a very, very painful thing.

Some of the slaughtered babies were so big, even clinic employees who were accustomed to the practice were shocked. One such child was born in July 2008 to a 17-year-old girl, Shaquana Abrams. The pregnant minor was accompanied to the clinic by her great aunt, who was paying for the abortion. After an ultrasound was performed on Abrams, Dr. Gosnell told the aunt that the girl's pregnancy was further along than she had originally told him. The procedure would cost more than the $1,500 that had been agreed upon; it would now cost $2,500.

The aunt paid Gosnell in cash.

The next morning, Abrams was given an ultrasound by Kareema Cross. Cross recorded the baby as having a gestational age of 29.4 weeks. She testified that the girl appeared to be seven or eight months pregnant.

---

[711] *3801 Lancaster*, www.youtube.com (January 14, 2013).

For the next 13 hours, Abrams was given a large amount of Cytotec to induce labor and delivery. She complained of pain and was heavily sedated by the unlicensed staff. According to Cross, Abrams was left to labor for hours and hours, often by herself. Eventually she gave birth to a large baby boy. Prosecutors would later refer to the child as "Baby Boy A." According to Cross, Dr. Gosnell joked, "This baby is big enough to walk me to the bus stop."[712] Cross estimated that the baby was 18 to 19 inches long. She said the baby was nearly the size of her own six pound, six ounce newborn daughter.

Cross testified that the baby was alive and breathing normally, although not for long. 10 to 20 seconds after the baby was born, while the mother was asleep, "the doctor just slit the neck," said Cross.[713]

A neonatologist viewed a photograph of Baby Boy A. Based on the baby's size, hairline, muscle mass, subcutaneous tissue, well-developed scrotum, and other characteristics, the doctor opined that the boy was at least 32 weeks, if not more, in gestational age when he was killed.[714]

Shortly before midnight, the doctor released Abrams to go home. Her aunt described her condition on the witness stand. "She was moaning. She was standing up, she was like holding her stomach, doubled over."[715]

She remained in pain for days and could barely eat. A few days after her abortion, Abrams was admitted to Crozier-Chester Hospital. Doctors there found that she had a severe infection and

---

[712] Jon Swaine, "Kermit Gosnell: US Abortion Doctor Could Be Put To Death Over Baby Charnel House," *The Telegraph* (April 12, 2013).
[713] *Supra* note 211.
[714] *Id.*
[715] *Id.*

blood clots that had travelled to her lungs. She would be hospitalized for ten days.

One of Dr. Gosnell's patients, "Makeda," talks about her many abortions in the movie, *3801 Lancaster*.[716]

> I asked them, I said, "Is it okay that I get another abortion?" "Fine. Fine." They even had this woman sit down with me, and she told me that women in Brazil have at least 21 abortions and they're still able to conceive. And that was it for me. I basically said, you know what? This has to be okay. It was the norm for me. After she had coached me into believing that that was the norm.
>
> (Over) the next fourteen years, I would have eight abortions. Eight. And I look back at it, and it's like, "God, what was I thinking?" I was 21 years old. And I can't sit here and say part of it was not my fault. It was. But I feel like I was led to believe that it was okay. Every time I came in there. It was okay. It was okay to treat it as a form of contraception.
>
> After I got older and I found the right person, we just could not conceive. And I went to the doctor. And I found out my body was so ravaged from abortion.
>
> It's all about money. It's all about greed. He wasn't helping anybody.

Terry Moran, who was once the co-anchor for *Nightline*, tweeted that "Kermit Gosnell is probably the most successful serial killer

---

[716] *Supra* note 711.

in the history of the world." This is quite possibly true, and yet it does not capture the entire truth of the matter. If Dr. Gosnell is such an infamous man, why didn't *ABC* report the news while it was happening?

ABC had a self-imposed blackout on the murder trial of Kermit Gosnell. As reported by the *Media Research Center*, "ABC News has permitted no coverage, discussion or mention of the case, not even a single utterance of Dr. Gosnell's name."[717] Kirsten Powers, in her *USA Today* column, writes, "A Lexis-Nexis search shows none of the news shows on the three major national television networks has mentioned the Gosnell trial in the last three months. The exception is when *Wall Street Journal* columnist Peggy Noonan hijacked a segment on *Meet the Press*."[718]

Apparently, Dr. Gosnell is such a powerful serial killer than he controls our media, too. He is the most successful, omnipotent serial killer in the history of the world. He's so powerful no one dares speak his name. Not *ABC*, not *NBC*, not *CBS*.

Are the people who run our networks not upset about the murder of newborns? Or do they believe that *Roe v. Wade* is so important that we must be silent as newborns are killed?

Is Kermit Gosnell a rogue abortionist who has utterly departed from the standards of the abortion industry when he started to kill newborns? That's the story now. But if that's the truth, what explains the startling lack of interest from our media? It's more like Peggy Noonan is a rogue journalist who has to "hijack" *Meet the Press*.

---

[717] Scott Whitlock, "Finally: 56 Days Later, ABC Ends Blackout and Covers Gosnell House of Horrors," www.mrc.org (May 13, 2013).
[718] *Supra* note 578.

All the pro-lifers were excused from the jury pool in the Gosnell case, and still he was convicted of murder. That's the reality of our society, how we feel about the murder of a baby. We like babies, and we don't like it when people kill them.

Our Supreme Court has been a little silent about discussing murder in its abortion opinions. Perhaps that's part of how we make abortion work for us. We skip over the details.

It is only a matter of time before we have a pro-lifer sitting on our Supreme Court. And what happens when one of these objectors puts on the black robes of a Supreme Court Justice? What happens when she says radical things like "a person is a live human being," or "a baby has a right to life"?

What happens when more and more journalists are pro-life? Can *Roe v. Wade* withstand all the photographs of aborted infants that are already on-line? Can it withstand a brutal pro-life documentary like *Hard Truth*? How long can we suppress the truth of abortion and hide it from our people, and what happens as tens of millions of Americans find out what is going on?[719]

And if *Roe v. Wade* can't stand up to this truth, should it stand?

---

[719] Justice Scalia and President Reagan are just two of the people who have analogized *Roe v. Wade* to *Dred Scott*, and abortion to slavery. In both cases, human beings are being defined as non-people. And yet, if this pro-life criticism of *Roe* is right, what does that mean for Justice Scalia's plan to overturn *Roe v. Wade* and send the issue back to the states? After all, federalism did not solve slavery. And an attempt at a compromise--the Missouri Compromise--was a disaster. No, the only acceptable solution is to recognize that a baby inside a uterus is a human being with a right to life. Many people assume that this means all abortions are murder. But that is not the case. Yes, *Roe v. Wade* should be overruled, and the states should be free to resolve the abortion controversy as best they can. But they cannot simply kill innocent babies. The Constitution is quite clear on that. And there is nothing wrong or bad in requiring states to follow their own laws in regard to when people die.

Taylor Carmichael is a former attorney and the author of *My Absolutely Insane Attempt To Rank All Cinema*. He resides in Charlotte.

www.ingramcontent.com/pod-product-compliance
Lightning Source LLC
Chambersburg PA
CBHW061616210326

41520CB00041B/7457